WEST ACADEMIC PUBLISHING'S EMERITUS ADVISORY BOARD

JESSE H. CHOPER
Professor of Law and Dean Emeritus
University of California, Berkeley

YALE KAMISAR
Professor of Law Emeritus, University of San Diego
Professor of Law Emeritus, University of Michigan

MARY KAY KANE
Professor of Law, Chancellor and Dean Emeritus
University of California, Hastings College of the Law

LARRY D. KRAMER
President, William and Flora Hewlett Foundation

JAMES J. WHITE
Robert A. Sullivan Emeritus Professor of Law
University of Michigan

WEST ACADEMIC PUBLISHING'S LAW SCHOOL ADVISORY BOARD

JOSHUA DRESSLER
Distinguished University Professor Emeritus
Michael E. Moritz College of Law, The Ohio State University

MEREDITH J. DUNCAN
Professor of Law
University of Houston Law Center

RENÉE McDONALD HUTCHINS
Dean and Joseph L. Rauh, Jr. Chair of Public Interest Law
University of the District of Columbia David A. Clarke School of Law

RENEE KNAKE JEFFERSON
Joanne and Larry Doherty Chair in Legal Ethics &
Professor of Law, University of Houston Law Center

ORIN S. KERR
Professor of Law
University of California, Berkeley

JONATHAN R. MACEY
Professor of Law,
Yale Law School

DEBORAH JONES MERRITT
Distinguished University Professor,
John Deaver Drinko/Baker & Hostetler Chair in Law
Michael E. Moritz College of Law, The Ohio State University

ARTHUR R. MILLER
University Professor, New York University
Formerly Bruce Bromley Professor of Law, Harvard University

GRANT S. NELSON
Professor of Law Emeritus, Pepperdine University
Professor of Law Emeritus, University of California, Los Angeles

A. BENJAMIN SPENCER
Dean & Chancellor Professor of Law
William & Mary Law School

CALIFORNIA COMMUNITY PROPERTY

GUIDE TO THE COURSE AND THE BAR EXAM

Second Edition

John E.B. Myers
Visiting Professor of Law
U.C. Hastings College of the Law

HORNBOOK SERIES®

The publisher is not engaged in rendering legal or other professional advice, and this publication is not a substitute for the advice of an attorney. If you require legal or other expert advice, you should seek the services of a competent attorney or other professional.

Hornbook Series is a trademark registered in the U.S. Patent and Trademark Office.

© 2018 LEG, Inc. d/b/a West Academic
© 2021 LEG, Inc. d/b/a West Academic
    444 Cedar Street, Suite 700
    St. Paul, MN 55101
    1-877-888-1330

West, West Academic Publishing, and West Academic are trademarks of West Publishing Corporation, used under license.

Printed in the United States of America

ISBN: 978-1-63659-124-7

Summary of Contents

	Page
CHAPTER 1. INTRODUCTION	1
CHAPTER 2. COHABITATION AGREEMENTS	17
CHAPTER 3. PREMARITAL AGREEMENTS	21
CHAPTER 4. INTRODUCTION TO MARITAL PROPERTY	43
CHAPTER 5. CHARACTERIZATION AND PRESUMPTIONS	53
CHAPTER 6. PENSIONS AND OTHER EMPLOYMENT-RELATED BENEFITS	93
CHAPTER 7. A POTPOURRI OF CHARACTERIZATION ISSUES	117
CHAPTER 8. TRANSMUTATIONS	139
CHAPTER 9. DEBTS	145
CHAPTER 10. MANAGEMENT AND CONTROL	163
CHAPTER 11. DIVISION OF PROPERTY ON DIVORCE	169
CHAPTER 12. ANNULMENT	185
CHAPTER 13. WHEN DEATH ENDS MARRIAGE	193
CHAPTER 14. COMMUNITY PROPERTY EXAM QUESTIONS	201

APPENDIX. CALIFORNIA FAMILY CODE 251

TABLE OF CASES 281

TABLE OF STATUTES 283

INDEX 287

Table of Contents

Page

CHAPTER 1. INTRODUCTION 1
§ 1.1   Marriage Contract 2
§ 1.2   Requirements for Valid Marriage 3
§ 1.3   Common Law Marriage 4
§ 1.4   Jurisdiction in Divorce Litigation 5
        § 1.4(a)   Jurisdiction to Grant Divorce 5
        § 1.4(b)   Jurisdiction over Financial Aspects of
                          Divorce 6
        § 1.4(c)   Jurisdiction over Child Custody 6
§ 1.5   Superior Court Authority in Divorce Cases 7
§ 1.6   California Family Law Is a Form-Driven Practice 7
§ 1.7   Steps in a Divorce 7
        § 1.7(a)   Start a Case—Petition and Summons 7
        § 1.7(b)   Serve Respondent 8
        § 1.7(c)   Preliminary and Final Declarations of
                          Disclosure 9
        § 1.7(d)   Four Paths to Divorce 9
§ 1.8   Child Custody 11
§ 1.9   Child Support 12
§ 1.10   Spousal Support 14
§ 1.11   *Res Judicata* in Family Law 16

CHAPTER 2. COHABITATION AGREEMENTS 17
§ 2.1   Contracts Between Unmarried Cohabitants 17
§ 2.2   Constructive and Resulting Trusts 18
§ 2.3   Questions 18
§ 2.4   Change on the Horizon? 20

CHAPTER 3. PREMARITAL AGREEMENTS 21
§ 3.1   Agreements in Family Law 22
§ 3.2   Premarital Agreement Defined 22

§ 3.3	Parties to Premarital Agreement Are Not in a Confidential Relationship	22
§ 3.4	Why a Prenup?	23
§ 3.5	California Uniform Premarital Agreement Act	24
§ 3.6	Premarital Agreements Must Be in Writing, However, Exceptions to Statute of Frauds Apply	28
§ 3.7	Premarital Agreement Cannot Adversely Affect Child Support	29
§ 3.8	Waiver of Spousal Support	29
§ 3.9	Premarital Agreement Must Be Voluntary	31
§ 3.10	How Much Time to Think About a Prenup?	32
§ 3.11	Is the Prenup Voluntary?	32
§ 3.12	Should a Prenup That Is Financially Unfair at the Outset of Marriage Be Enforceable?	33
§ 3.13	Should a Prenup That Is Fair at the Outset Be Enforceable at Divorce, Years Later, if Enforcement Is Unfair at Divorce?	35
§ 3.14	Problems on Premarital Agreements	36
§ 3.15	Professional Responsibility and Issues Regarding Premarital Agreements	41

CHAPTER 4. INTRODUCTION TO MARITAL PROPERTY ... 43

§ 4.1	When Property Issues Arise During Marriage	43
§ 4.2	Systems of Marital Property in the United States	44
§ 4.3	History of Equitable Distribution and Community Property	44
	§ 4.3(a) Equitable Distribution	44
	§ 4.3(b) Community Property	48
§ 4.4	Marital Property Law in Other States	49
§ 4.5	All Property States	50
§ 4.6	Mortgage, Deed of Trust, and Encumbrance	51

CHAPTER 5. CHARACTERIZATION AND PRESUMPTIONS ... 53

§ 5.1	Characterization of Property in California	54
§ 5.2	Presumptions Characterize Property as Community or Separate	54
§ 5.3	Presumptions in California Law	56
	§ 5.3(a) Presumption and Inference Explained	57

§ 5.3(b)	Burden of Producing Evidence and Burden of Proof	58
§ 5.3(c)	Presumption Affecting Burden of Producing Evidence	59
§ 5.3(d)	Presumption Affecting Burden of Proof	59
§ 5.4	Basics of Characterization—Family Code §§ 760 and 770	60
§ 5.5	Separate Property	61
§ 5.6	Quasi-Community Property	62
§ 5.7	Exercises on Characterization	63
§ 5.8	Long Marriage Presumption	65
§ 5.9	Tracing	66
§ 5.10	Pro Rata Apportionment	68
§ 5.11	Source of Funds and Inception of Title	69
§ 5.12	Beginning and End of the Community—Date of Separation	71
§ 5.13	Form of Title Presumptions	73
§ 5.14	Title in One Spouse's Name	74
§ 5.15	Concurrent Ownership	75
§ 5.16	Concurrent Ownership During Marriage	76
§ 5.17	Concurrent Ownership When Marriage Ends in Divorce—Family Code § 2581	77
§ 5.18	When Marriage Ends in Divorce: Reimbursement of Separate Property Contribution to Community Property—Family Code § 2640	80
§ 5.19	*Lucas* Gift Presumption—§ 2640 Is Not Retroactive	84
§ 5.20	Exercises with Family Code §§ 2581 and 2640	86
§ 5.21	Community Property Contributions to Separate Property: *Moore/Marsden* Apportionment	87
§ 5.22	Married Woman's Separate Property Presumption	90

CHAPTER 6. PENSIONS AND OTHER EMPLOYMENT-RELATED BENEFITS 93

§ 6.1	Pension as Community Property	94
§ 6.2	Government Retirement Systems	94
§ 6.3	Private Sector Retirement Systems	94
§ 6.4	Defined Benefit and Defined Contribution Plans	95
§ 6.5	Determining the Community Property Share of a Pension	97
§ 6.6	Lawyer's Responsibility Regarding Pensions	99

§ 6.7	Methods of Dividing Pensions 100
	§ 6.7(a) Dividing a Defined Contribution Pension 100
	§ 6.7(b) Dividing a Defined Benefit Pension: Cash out or Wait and See 100
§ 6.8	Qualified Domestic Relations Order (QDRO) to Divide ERISA Pension 103
§ 6.9	QDRO to Collect Child or Spousal Support 107
§ 6.10	Joining Pension Plan as a Party 107
§ 6.11	Military Retirement 107
§ 6.12	Social Security Retirement 108
§ 6.13	*Gillmore* Election 109
§ 6.14	Disability Benefits 109
§ 6.15	Military Disability 111
§ 6.16	Early Retirement 112
§ 6.17	Is Employment-Related Health Insurance Community Property? 113
§ 6.18	Severance Pay 113
§ 6.19	Accrued Vacation and Sick Days 113
§ 6.20	Stock Options 114
§ 6.21	Life Insurance 114

CHAPTER 7. A POTPOURRI OF CHARACTERIZATION ISSUES 117

§ 7.1	Business as Community or Separate Property 117
§ 7.2	Increased Value of Business 118
	§ 7.2(a) Increased Value of Separate Property Business—*Van Camp* or *Pereira* 119
	§ 7.2(b) Increased Value of Community Business After Separation 121
§ 7.3	Goodwill 121
§ 7.4	Educational Degrees 125
§ 7.5	Gambling Proceeds 125
§ 7.6	Intent of the Lender—a Tracing Method to Rebut the Community Property Presumption 126
§ 7.7	Commingled Bank Accounts 127
	§ 7.7(a) Direct Tracing 128
	§ 7.7(b) Indirect Tracing—Exhaustion Method 129
	§ 7.7(c) Simple Samples 130
§ 7.8	Improvements 131

	§ 7.8(a)	One Spouse Uses Her/His Separate Property to Improve the Other Spouse's Separate Property.. 133
	§ 7.8(b)	One Spouse Uses Community Property to Improve the Other Spouse's Separate Property.. 133
	§ 7.8(c)	One Spouse Uses Community Property to Improve Her/His Own Separate Property 133
	§ 7.8(d)	One Spouse Uses Her/His Separate Property to Improve Community Property..................... 134
	§ 7.8(e)	One Spouse Uses Her/His Separate Property to Improve Her/His Own Separate Property.. 134
§ 7.9	Personal Injury Damages 134	
	§ 7.9(a)	Personal Injury Award—Injured Spouse....... 134
	§ 7.9(b)	Personal Injury Debt—Injuring Spouse......... 135
§ 7.10	Are Pets Property? 135	
§ 7.11	Collectibles... 136	
§ 7.12	Wedding Gifts 136	
§ 7.13	Engagement Ring... 137	

CHAPTER 8. TRANSMUTATIONS 139
§ 8.1   Pre-1985 Transmutations... 139
§ 8.2   Writing Requirement for Post-1985 Transmutations... 140
§ 8.3   Transmutations and Fiduciary Duties 142
§ 8.4   Uniform Voidable Transactions Act............................... 142

CHAPTER 9. DEBTS 145
§ 9.1   Four Sets of Debt Rules 145
§ 9.2   Debts During Marriage... 146
         § 9.2(a)   During Marriage, Liability of Community Property.. 146
         § 9.2(b)   During Marriage, Liability of Separate Property.. 147
         § 9.2(c)   Questions on Debts During Marriage 147
§ 9.3   During Marriage, Priority of Payment of Tort Debts ... 148
§ 9.4   During Marriage, Protecting Paycheck from Spouse's Premarital Debts... 150
§ 9.5   Necessaries During Marriage... 151
§ 9.6   Support Debt from Previous Relationship..................... 154

§ 9.7	Characterization of Debts on Divorce 155
	§ 9.7(a) Premarital Debts Are Separate Debts—§ 2621 158
	§ 9.7(b) Debts Before Judgment Is Final Are Separate Debts—§ 2624 158
	§ 9.7(c) Debts Incurred After Separation and Prior to Judgment for Non-Necessaries Are Separate Debts—§ 2623(b) 158
	§ 9.7(d) Debts Incurred After Separation and Prior to Judgment for Necessaries—§ 2623(a) 159
	§ 9.7(e) Debts Incurred During Marriage and Prior to Separation Can Be Separate or Community 160
	§ 9.7(f) Timeline for Debts on Divorce 160
	§ 9.7(g) After the Family Court Divides Community Property, What Property Can a Creditor Take to Satisfy Debt?—Family Code § 916 161
§ 9.8	Exam Questions on Debts 161

CHAPTER 10. MANAGEMENT AND CONTROL 163

§ 10.1	Equal Management and Control 163
§ 10.2	Gifts of Community Property 164
§ 10.3	Gifts Between Spouses 164
§ 10.4	Furniture of the Home; Mobile Home 165
§ 10.5	Spouse Operating a Community Property Business 166
§ 10.6	Management and Control of Community Real Property 166
§ 10.7	Spouses Are in a Fiduciary Relationship Regarding Community Property 166
§ 10.8	Remedies for Breach of Fiduciary Duty 167
§ 10.9	Bank Account in One Spouse's Name 168

CHAPTER 11. DIVISION OF PROPERTY ON DIVORCE 169

§ 11.1	Marital Settlement Agreement (MSA) 169
§ 11.2	Division by the Court Following Trial 170
	§ 11.2(a) Exceptions to Equal Division 170
	§ 11.2(b) Court Divides Property at Time of Divorce 170
	§ 11.2(c) Methods to Achieve Equal Division 171
§ 11.3	Omitted Assets 173

§ 11.4	What Property Can Creditors Attach After the Divorce Court Divides Community Property? 174
§ 11.5	Property Division Is *Res Judicata* 174
§ 11.6	Out of State Community Property 175
§ 11.7	Authority Regarding Jointly Held Separate Property 175
§ 11.8	*Epstein* Credits and *Watts* Charges 175
§ 11.9	Reimbursement Summary 177
§ 11.10	Relationship Between Spousal Support and Property Division: The Problem of Double Dipping 178
§ 11.11	Property Problems 180

CHAPTER 12. ANNULMENT 185

§ 12.1	Why Annulment Instead of Divorce? 185
§ 12.2	Basis for Annulment 186
§ 12.3	Void Marriage 186
§ 12.4	Voidable Marriage 186
§ 12.5	Putative Spouse 188
§ 12.6	Relation-Back Doctrine 189
	Questions: Should Relation Back Apply? 190
§ 12.7	Questions on Annulment 191

CHAPTER 13. WHEN DEATH ENDS MARRIAGE 193

§ 13.1	Testate or Intestate 193
§ 13.2	Probate Code Definition of Community Property 193
§ 13.3	Probate Code Definition of Quasi-Community Property 195
§ 13.4	Problems on Characterization 196
§ 13.5	Debts When Marriage Ends in Death 198

CHAPTER 14. COMMUNITY PROPERTY EXAM QUESTIONS 201

§ 14.1	California Bar Exam Community Property Questions 201
§ 14.2	Law School Community Property Exams 223
§ 14.3	Analysis of Chapter Questions and Examples 234

APPENDIX. CALIFORNIA FAMILY CODE 251

Table of Cases 281

Table of Statutes 283

Index 287

CALIFORNIA COMMUNITY PROPERTY

GUIDE TO THE COURSE AND THE BAR EXAM

Second Edition

Chapter 1

INTRODUCTION

Analysis

§ 1.1   Marriage Contract
§ 1.2   Requirements for Valid Marriage
§ 1.3   Common Law Marriage
§ 1.4   Jurisdiction in Divorce Litigation
§ 1.5   Superior Court Authority in Divorce Cases
§ 1.6   California Family Law Is a Form-Driven Practice
§ 1.7   Steps in a Divorce
§ 1.8   Child Custody
§ 1.9   Child Support
§ 1.10 Spousal Support
§ 1.11 *Res Judicata* in Family Law

Welcome to community property! As you know, California is a community property state. The California Bar Examination tests community property. The fact that the Bar tests community property is probably the reason you are reading this book. Of course, it is possible you have had an interest in community property since you were a little kid, but I doubt it. More likely, you are enrolled in community property to pass the bar, and that's a perfectly good reason! Some readers are interested in practicing family law, and for them understanding community property is a must. Even if your only reason for taking the course is the bar, you will find knowledge of community property relevant to many areas of practice, not to mention *your* own life.

Most of the book is devoted to the details of California community property law. Understanding community property, however, requires an introduction to aspects of family law that are not directly related to property. Chapter 1 discusses a number of these non-property aspects of family law. Chapter 2 addresses contracts between unmarried cohabitants. Chapter 3 deals with premarital agreements. Chapter 12 covers annulment. The balance of the book focuses on community property.

Most statutes regarding community property are located in the Family Code. The Family Code is cited throughout the book. Other California codes and federal statutes are cited when appropriate. Sections of the Family Code and the Probate Code are found in the Appendix.

One more thing before we get started. Chapters 1 through 13 contain many questions. Section 14.3, in Chapter 14, contains analysis of the questions asked in Chapters 1 through 13. As well, Chapter 14 contains actual California bar exam questions, plus law school final exam questions, along with analysis of the bar and law school exams.

§ 1.1 Marriage Contract

The community property system applies to married persons. The moment a couple marries, community property law applies by operation of law unless the couple opts out of the community property system by agreement.

Under California law, marriage ends one of three ways: death, divorce, or annulment (Family Code § 310).

Marriage is a contract. Family Code § 300(a) provides, "Marriage is a personal relation arising out of a civil contract between two persons, to which the consent of the parties is necessary." Of course, marriage is no ordinary contract. In *Perez v. Sharp*, 32 Cal. 2d 711, 714, 198 P.2d 17 (1948), the Supreme Court observed, "Marriage is thus something more than a civil contract subject to regulation by the state; it is a fundamental right of free men."

How does a marriage contract differ from a commercial contract? Many ways. The parties to a typical commercial contract can rescind the contract by mutual agreement. Not so with marriage, which can be terminated only by a court or death. Marriage is deeply personal, and founded on love and trust. Commercial contracts are arms-length.

In 2015, the U.S. Supreme Court handed down the momentous decision in *Obergefell v. Hodges*, 576 U.S. 644, 135 S.Ct. 2584 (2015), guaranteeing same sex couples the right to marry. Prior to *Obergefell*, California same sex couples could not marry.[1] When same sex marriage was not available, the Legislature created a legal status called domestic partnership (§ 297 et seq.). The Family Code defines domestic partners as "two adults who have chosen to share one another's lives in an intimate and committed relationship of mutual caring." (§ 297(a)). A couple registers their partnership with the Secretary of State. The community property system applies to registered domestic partners. Now that same sex marriage is legal, many couples marry rather than register as domestic partners. Today, opposite sex couples can register as domestic partners.

§ 1.2 Requirements for Valid Marriage

Legal requirements to marry vary in detail from state to state. In all states, consent of the parties is required. California Family Code § 300(a) provides that marriage requires the consent of the parties, capable of making a contract. The minimum age to marry is 18 (§ 301). A person under age 18 may marry with a judge's permission (§§ 302–323).

The law requires a marriage license. A couple obtains a license from a county clerk (§§ 306, 350–360). The license is good for 90 days (§ 356).

A marriage must be solemnized (§§ 306, 400–402). A marriage may be solemnized by a religious leader or a secular official such as a judge or clerk. "No particular form for the ceremony of marriage is required for solemnization of the marriage, but the parties shall declare, in the physical presence of the person solemnizing the marriage and necessary witnesses, that they take each other as spouses." (§ 420(a)). A member of the Armed Forces who is deployed can be married without being physically present (§ 420(b)). The person solemnizing the marriage signs the marriage license and returns it to the county clerk within 10 days of the wedding. (§§ 422–423). When the license is returned to the clerk, it becomes a marriage certificate (§ 300(b)). A marriage that conforms to the

---

[1] There was a brief period prior to *Obergefell* during which same sex marriage was legal in California.

requirements of the Family Code is not invalid because it does not conform to the requirements of a religion (§ 420(c)).

California recognizes the validity of marriages from other states and countries. Family Code § 308 provides, "A marriage contracted outside this state that would be valid by the laws of the state of the jurisdiction in which the marriage was contracted is valid in California."

§ 1.3 Common Law Marriage

A "common law" marriage occurs when a couple considers themselves married and acts accordingly, but the couple does not meet the requirements of a license and marriage ceremony. In *People v. Lucero*, 747 P.2d 660, 663 (Colo. 1987), the Colorado Supreme Court wrote, "A common law marriage is established by the mutual consent or agreement of the parties to be husband and wife, followed by a mutual and open assumption of a marital relationship."

The requirements for common marriage are: (1) Agreement between the parties to be married at that time; (2) The parties are competent to marry; (3) The parties cohabit as a married couple; (4) The parties hold themselves out to the world as married; and (5) The parties have a reputation as a married couple.[2]

Common law marriage is available in Colorado, Iowa, Kansas, Montana, Rhode Island, Texas, and Washington, D.C. Common law marriage does not exist in California, although California recognizes a common law marriage from another state (§ 308).

Consider Mary and John. They live in Texas, a state that allows common law marriage. Nine years ago, Mary and John began dating. John got a job in Atlanta, Georgia. Eight years ago, Mary moved to Atlanta to live with John. Seven years ago, they separated and Mary moved back to Texas. Two weeks after returning to Texas, Mary discovered she was pregnant. After learning Mary was pregnant, John moved back to Texas. The couple's daughter was born six years ago. Mary and John purchased a home together in Texas, six years ago. They got a Veterans Administration loan for

---

[2] *See* Zharkova v. Gaudreau, 45 A.3d 1282 (R.I. 2012) for a good description of the elements of common law marriage.

the home, and the loan papers list them as husband a wife. Four years ago, John began working in Kuwait. When John returned to the U.S. on vacation, he stayed with Mary and their child. While working in Kuwait, John had medical insurance, and Mary and the child were insured on John's policy, with Mary listed as his spouse. During the relevant time, Mary and John had separate bank accounts, and filed their taxes as single persons. After finishing his work in Kuwait, John returned to live with Mary. After learning that Mary had been unfaithful, John filed for divorce in Texas. Does a common law marriage exist between Mary and John?

§ 1.4   Jurisdiction in Divorce Litigation

A divorce case is a lawsuit and like all lawsuits, the court must have jurisdiction. In analyzing jurisdiction, it is helpful to divide a divorce into three parts: (1) The divorce itself, (2) Child custody, and (3) The financial aspects of divorce—child support, spousal support, property division, and attorney fees.

As you recall from civil procedure, in the typical civil case, the court must have subject matter jurisdiction *and* personal jurisdiction. In divorce litigation, subject matter jurisdiction is always necessary. Personal jurisdiction is not always required.

§ 1.4(a)   Jurisdiction to Grant Divorce

A court has subject matter jurisdiction to grant divorce if at least one spouse is domiciled in the state. In *Williams v. North Carolina,* 317 U.S. 287, 63 S. Ct. 207 (1942), the Supreme Court held that subject matter to grant divorce is based on domicile of one or both parties. Personal jurisdiction over an absent spouse is not required to grant divorce, although the Due Process Clause requires notice of the divorce proceeding.

All states have a residency requirement for divorce. California's residence requirement for divorce is Family Code § 2320(a), which provides, "A judgment of dissolution of marriage may not be entered unless one of the parties to the marriage has been a resident of this state for six months and of the county in which the proceeding is filed for three months next preceding the filing of the petition."[3]

If a couple that is born and raised in California gets married in California and later divorces in California, no jurisdictional issues are likely to arise. The California court clearly has subject matter jurisdiction *and* personal jurisdiction over the parties. Similarly, if a couple married in Iowa, but moved to California years ago, jurisdictional issues are unlikely to arise. But what of the following situation? A married couple has always lived in Virginia. One of them moves to California and meets the California residency requirement. The other spouse has never set foot in California. Can the spouse living in California get divorced in California? California has no personal jurisdiction over the spouse in Virginia. The answer is yes. The spouse now domiciled in California, who meets the residency requirement, can get divorced in California.

§ 1.4(b) Jurisdiction over Financial Aspects of Divorce

A court must have subject matter jurisdiction *and* personal jurisdiction over both parties to adjudicate the financial aspects of divorce, including property division, child support, spousal support, and attorney fees. *Kulko v. Superior Court*, 436 U.S. 84, 98 S. Ct. 1690 (1978).

§ 1.4(c) Jurisdiction over Child Custody

Subject matter jurisdiction regarding custody of children is governed by the Uniform Child Custody Jurisdiction and Enforcement Act (Family Code §§ 3400 et seq.), and the federal Parental Kidnapping Prevention Act (28 U.S.C. § 1738A). Personal jurisdiction over both parents is *not* required to adjudicate child custody.

---

[3] Cal. Family Code § 2320. If a person has not lived in California long enough to file for divorce, the person can file for legal separation, which does not have a residence requirement. After the person has lived long enough in California to get a divorce, the Petition for legal separation is amended to seek a divorce. *See* Family Code § 2321.

§ 1.5 Superior Court Authority in Divorce Cases

The California Superior Court, sitting as a family court, has plenary authority over divorce, legal separation, and annulment. Family Code § 2010 provides, "The court has jurisdiction to inquire into and render any judgment and orders that are appropriate concerning the following: (a) The status of the marriage . . . . (b) The custody of minor children of the marriage. (c) The support of children . . . . (d) The support of either party. (e) The settlement of the property rights of the parties. (f) The award of attorney's fees and costs."

§ 1.6 California Family Law Is a Form-Driven Practice

Practice of family law in California relies heavily on forms published by the Judicial Council of California. There are some 300 family law forms! Many Judicial Council forms are mandatory, that is, practitioners must use the prescribed forms. Many California family law attorneys subscribe to software that includes the forms. A popular program is from The Rutter Group,™ owned by Thomson Reuters. The Rutter Group updates the Judicial Council forms and sends updated versions to subscribers. In addition to proprietary services, you can Google "California Family Law Forms," and be directed to the Judicial Council website where all the forms are available free. It should be added that the Judicial Council website contains hundreds of non-family law forms. For example, the website contains form subpoenas.

§ 1.7 Steps in a Divorce

Getting divorced in California is complex and time consuming, and that's when everything goes smoothly! When disagreement occurs over children, support, or property, the process takes many months, even years. It is useful for students new to family law to have an introduction to the steps in the divorce process. Each step is complicated.

§ 1.7(a) Start a Case—Petition and Summons

A divorce is started by filing a Petition and a Summons in court (§ 2330). The Petition is Family Law form 100, or FL-100. The

Summons is FL-110. The Summons contains a Standard Family Law Restraining Order (RO). The RO applies *automatically* to the Petitioner the moment the Petition is filed. The RO applies *automatically* to the Respondent the moment the Respondent is served with the Petition and Summons.[4]

The RO restrains a parent from removing a child from California without permission. The RO limits the ability of spouses to engage in major financial transactions without the consent of the other spouse or court order. It will not surprise you to learn that the RO limits the ability of spouses to sell or encumber community property during the divorce process. It will surprise you to learn that the RO places similar limits on a spouse's ability to deal with their separate property! Why the limit on separate property? Because, until the parties or the court make a definitive finding, what one spouse believes is their separate property may, in the eyes of the other spouse, be community property. The RO calls a halt to *all* major financial transactions until the property is characterized and divided by agreement or court order.

§ 1.7(b) Serve Respondent

You know from civil procedure that the respondent/defendant in a law suit must be served with the petition/complaint and the summons. The same is true in divorce (§ 2331). There are three ways to personally serve the Respondent with the Petition, the Summons, and a blank Response (FL-120). First, the sheriff can serve the respondent. If the respondent is incarcerated, the warden or sheriff serves the papers. Second, a professional process server can serve the papers. Third, any adult *other* than the Petitioner can serve the papers.

If the sheriff serves the respondent, the sheriff files a sheriff's proof of service of summons with the court. If a process server serves the papers, the process server files a Proof of Service of Summons (FL-115). If an adult serves the papers, the adult files the Proof of Service of Summons (FL-115). Without proof of service, the case cannot progress.

---

[4] *See* Marriage of Desouza, 54 Cal. App. 5th 25, 266 Cal. Rptr. 3d 890 (2020).

In some cases, the Petitioner has no idea how to find the Respondent, making personal service impossible. In such circumstances, a judge can approve substituted service by publication in a newspaper or by posting. Publication in a paper is expensive. Posting is not. For a judge to grant service by posting, the Petitioner files a Judicial Council form outlining the steps taken to find the Respondent (FL-980). If the judge is persuaded a diligent search was made, the judge signs an order that the Summons be posted in a place where the Respondent might see it—typically the courthouse (FL-982). After the required posting time expires, the Petitioner files a form for proof of service of summons by posting (FL-985).

§ 1.7(c) Preliminary and Final Declarations of Disclosure

Once a divorce is underway, the Petitioner has 60 days to complete Preliminary Declarations of Disclosure (PDDs), and mail the PDDs to the other spouse. The PDDs are Judicial Council forms that require detailed disclosure of financial information. The PDD's are not filed with the court, except a form indicating the PDDs were sent to the spouse. If the Respondent files a Response (FL-120), the Respondent completes PPDs, and sends them to Petitioner. If the Respondent does not file a Response, the case can go to judgment by default without PDDs from Respondent.

If a Response is filed, both spouses file Final Declarations of Disclosure (FDDs) toward the end of the case. FDDs can be waived in a marital settlement agreement. PDDs can't be waived.

§ 1.7(d) Four Paths to Divorce

In California, there are four paths to divorce. First, default judgment with no marital settlement agreement (MSA) (True Default). Second, default with an MSA (Default with Agreement). Third, Respondent files a Response and the parties have an MSA (Uncontested Case). Fourth, Respondent files a Response and the parties cannot agree. The case is resolved at trial (Contested Case.)

True Default. A Respondent who is served with a Petition and Summons has 30 days to file a Response (FL-120). If Respondent does not respond, Petitioner can file the forms required for a True

Default. The forms are: (1) FL-115—Proof of Service of Summons; (2) FL-165—Request to Enter Default, along with a stamped envelope addressed to Respondent; (3) FL-141—Declaration Regarding Service of Declaration of Disclosure; (4) FL-170—Declaration for Default or Uncontested Dissolution or Legal Separation; (5) FL-180—Judgment (5 copies); (6) FL-190—Notice of Entry of Judgment; and (7) two stamped envelopes addressed to Petitioner and Respondent, so the court can send the Judgment and the Notice of Entry of Judgment to the parties.

If you are wondering to yourself, "How do I remember all the forms!?" Take heart. There is a cheat sheet that tells you the forms you need for each path to divorce. The cheat sheet is itself a Judicial Council form—FL-182.

Default with Agreement. If spouses agree on all issues, the quickest and least expensive way to divorce is Default with Agreement. The Agreement is an MSA. Expenses are saved because no Response is filed, saving the filing fee. As well, litigation costs are avoided.

As with True Default, Default with Agreement requires many forms. Refer to your cheat sheet, FL-182.

Uncontested Case. In many cases, it is not clear at the outset if spouses will reach agreement. Litigation may be needed. Settlement often takes months. When early agreement is not obvious, a Response is filed to prevent Petitioner from filing for default. With the Response in place, there is time to negotiate toward agreement, draft an MSA, and proceed to judgment without trial.

It comes as a surprise to many people that with the first three paths to judgment, the parties typically never see a judge! Everything is handled on paper. Eventually, a judge signs the Judgment (FL-180), but the judge does so in chambers, without taking testimony from the parties. One day, the Judgment of Divorce simply arrives in the mail!

Contested Case. A contested case goes to trial on one or more issues. Counties have local rules on settlement conferences, trial readiness conferences, discovery and motion deadlines, trial briefs, marking exhibits, witness lists, assignment of judges for trial, and a host of related matters.

Trials of family law matters are bench trials. Every judge has her own approach to trial. Some judges are sticklers for the rules of evidence. Other judges, realizing there is no jury, apply the rules more flexibly than they would in a criminal trial.

§ 1.8 Child Custody

Child custody is the most sensitive issue in family law. Let's begin with a few terms. Legal custody is the right to make decisions about a child's medical care, where the child lives and goes to school, and innumerable day-to-day issues (§ 3006). It is common for parents to share joint legal custody. If one parent is unfit or disinterested, sole legal custody is appropriate.

Physical custody is the right to have the child live with the custodial parent all or part of the time. Sole physical custody means the child lives full time with the custodial parent. Joint physical custody means the child lives part of the time with each parent (§§ 3003–3007, 3085).

The law's preference in custody matters is to maximize involvement of both parents in the child's life. The California Legislature stated, "It is the public policy of this state to assure that children have frequent and continuing contact with both parents after the parents have separated or dissolved their marriage" (§ 3020(b)).

When a parent does not have physical custody, the parent typically has rights of visitation, or as it is often called today, "parenting time." Visitation can be denied when needed for a child's safety (§ 3100).

Parental rights and responsibilities are the same whether or not parents marry.

Most parents agree on custody, and the judge approves their agreement (*See* §§ 3011(e)(2); 3022)). When parents cannot agree on custody, the judge employs the best interests of the child standard. The question is: What custody arrangement is best for the child? In conducting a best interest analysis, the judge considers all evidence shedding light on a child's short- and long-term interests—the totality of the circumstances. The judge has broad discretion.

Family Code § 3011 lists factors the court considers in finding a child's best interest:

1. The child's health, safety, and welfare. This factor invites the court to consider all evidence that is relevant to the child's best interests.

2. When a court finds that a parent seeking custody has perpetrated domestic violence against the other parent or the child during the past five years, there is a rebuttable presumption that it is not in the child's best interest for the abuser to have sole or joint legal or physical custody (§ 3044(a)). The presumption against custody to an abuser is not rebutted by the law's normal preference for frequent and continuing contact with both parents (§ 3044(b)(1)). An abusive parent must convince the court he has changed.

3. The existing relationship between the child and each parent.

4. Habitual use of illegal drugs or abuse of alcohol or prescription drugs. The court may order testing for drugs or alcohol for any person seeking custody (§ 3041.5).

5. The court considers "which parent is more likely to allow the child frequent and continuing contact with the noncustodial parent" (§ 3040(a)(1)).

§ 1.9 Child Support

Parents have a moral and legal responsibility to support their children. Family Code § 4053(a) states, "A parent's first and principle obligation is to support his or her minor children according to the parent's circumstances and station in life."

The duty of support continues until a child is 18, or, if the child is still in high school, until the child graduates or turns 19, whichever occurs first (§ 3901(a)). The duty of child support applies whether or not parents marry. Family Code § 3910(a) provides that parents have a duty to support an incapacitated adult child regardless of the child's age.

A parent can bring an action for child support in the appropriate court, and failure to pay court-ordered support is punishable by sanctions and, in extreme cases, contempt. Chronic failure to support one's children is a crime.

Subject matter jurisdiction regarding child support exists when the child is in California. Personal jurisdiction over both parties is required. When personal jurisdiction cannot be obtained over an out-of-state obligor parent, the Uniform Interstate Family Support Act is available (§§ 5700.101 et seq.).

Grandparents do not have a legal obligation to support grandchildren (§ 3930). An adult child is obliged to support a parent who is in need and unable to provide the necessities (§ 4400).

A parent's discharge in bankruptcy does not end the responsibility for past or future child support (11 U.S.C. § 523(a)(5)).

California uses a state-wide mathematical formula to determine child support (§ 4055). The formula considers how much time the children spend with each parent (time share) and parental income. Income is broadly defined as "income from whatever source derived" (§ 4058(a)), and includes "commissions, salaries, royalties, wages, bonuses, rents, dividends, pensions, interest, trust income, annuities, workers' compensation benefits, unemployment insurance benefits, disability insurance benefits, social security benefits, and spousal support actually received" (§ 4058(a)(1)). The support figure produced by the formula is considered presumptively correct (§ 4057(a)).

In some circumstances, judges impute income to a parent that the parent doesn't actually have. Family Code § 4058(b) states, "The court may, in its discretion, consider the earning capacity of a parent in lieu of the parent's income, consistent with the best interests of the children."

The child support formula allows the following deductions from income (§ 4059): taxes, mandatory union dues, mandatory payments to retirement, cost of health insurance, child or spousal support actually paid for the benefit of a person in a different relationship, and job related expenses (§ 4059(e)). In some cases, an obligor spouse can claim an extreme financial hardship deduction (§§ 4059(g); 4070–4073).

In addition to child support, the court orders parents to provide health insurance for the child (§ 3753).

Child support orders are made in family court proceedings. In addition, California has a system of child support commissioners whose judicial work focuses on support (§ 4250). The Commissioner is assisted by an attorney from the office of Child Support Services.

§ 1.10 Spousal Support

Historically, alimony was permanent, that is, for life. Today, if divorcing spouses are young and able to work, the judge may award no spousal support. If support is awarded, it may be limited to a number of years, with the idea that the supported spouse should become financially self-sufficient. In relatively short marriages (less than 10 years), when support is awarded, it is common to see an award for half the length of the marriage, with a "hard" end date, after which the court's jurisdiction over support terminates. Permanent spousal support usually is reserved for long marriages, especially marriages in which the supported spouse has not worked in decades or at all.

Section 4330(a) authorizes courts to order spousal support. When spousal support is requested, Family Code § 4320 provides:

> In ordering spousal support . . . , the court shall consider all of the following circumstances:
>
> (a) The extent to which the earning capacity of each party is sufficient to maintain the standard of living established during the marriage, taking into account all of the following:
>
>> (1) The marketable skills of the supported party; the job market for those skills; and the time and expenses required for the supported party to acquire the appropriate education or training to develop those skills; and the possible need for retraining or education to acquire other, more marketable skills or employment.
>>
>> (2) The extent to which the supported party's present or future earning capacity is impaired by periods of unemployment that were incurred during the marriage to permit the supported spouse to devote time to domestic duties.

(b) The extent to which the supported party contributed to the attainment of an education, training, a career position, or a license by the supporting party.

(c) The ability of the supporting party to pay spousal support, taking into account the supporting party's earning capacity, earned and unearned income, assets, and standard of living.

(d) The needs of each party based on the standard of living established during the marriage.

(e) The obligations and assets, including the separate property, of each party.

(f) The duration of the marriage.

(g) The ability of the supported party to engage in gainful employment without unduly interfering with the interests of dependent children in the custody of the party.

(h) The age and health of the parties.

(i) Documented evidence of any history of domestic violence . . . between the parties, including, but not limited to, consideration of emotional distress resulting from domestic violence perpetrated against the supported party by the supporting party, and consideration of any history of violence against the supporting party by the supported party.

(j) The immediate and specific tax consequences to each party.

(k) The balance of hardships to each party.

(*l*) The goal that the supported party shall be self-supporting within a reasonable period of time. Except in the case of a marriage of long duration [10 years], a "reasonable period of time" for purposes of this section shall be one-half the length of the marriage. However, nothing in this section is intended to limit the court's discretion to order support for a greater or lesser length of time, based on any of the other factors listed in this section . . . and the circumstances of the parties.

(m) The criminal conviction of an abusive spouse shall be considered in making a reduction or elimination of a spousal support award [to an abusive spouse].

(n) Any other factors the court determines are just and equitable.

The trial judge has broad discretion to award appropriate spousal support. The overarching questions are: Does one spouse need support, and can the other spouse afford to pay? The court also considers the standard of living during marriage. The more affluent the standard of living, and the lower the capacity of the supported spouse to maintain that standard, the greater the need for support.

§ 1.11 *Res Judicata* in Family Law

The Latin *res judicata* translates to "a thing decided." A final family law judgment is res judicata. A party unhappy with the judge's decision can appeal or seek reconsideration. A motion for reconsider must be filed within 10 days of the judge's decision (Code of Civil Procedure § 1008). A party cannot seek reconsideration simply because the party disagrees with the judge's decision. The party seeking reconsideration must allege new facts or circumstances that were not know prior to the judge's decision.

Of greatest relevance to this book, the portion of a divorce judgement dividing property is *res judicata*, and cannot be modified. By contrast, court orders regarding custody of children are subject to modification if circumstances change in the future. As well, orders regarding child support are subject to modification. Orders concerning spousal support are complicated—some are subject to modification, others are not.

Chapter 2

COHABITATION AGREEMENTS

Analysis

§ 2.1   Contracts Between Unmarried Cohabitants
§ 2.2   Constructive and Resulting Trusts
§ 2.3   Questions
§ 2.4   Change on the Horizon?

Half a century ago, living together in an intimate relationship outside marriage was "living in sin." Today, it is common for lovers to live together. When a non-marital cohabiting relationship ends, former lovers do not owe each other support. The system of community property does not apply to unmarried cohabitants. When cohabitants have children, the rules for custody and child support are the same as for married parents.

§ 2.1   Contracts Between Unmarried Cohabitants

Unmarried cohabitants can contract with each other regarding property and support. The leading case is *Marvin v. Marvin*, 18 Cal. 3d 660, 557 P.2d 106, 134 Cal. Rptr. 815 (1976). In *Marvin,* the Supreme Court wrote:

> We conclude: (1) The provisions of the Family Law Act do not govern the distribution of property acquired during a nonmarital relationship; such a relationship remains subject solely to judicial decision. (2) The courts should enforce express contracts between nonmarital partners except to the extent that the contract is explicitly founded on the consideration of meretricious sexual services. (3) In the absence of an express contract, the courts should inquire into the conduct of the parties to determine

whether that conduct demonstrates an implied contract, agreement of partnership or joint venture, or some other tacit understanding between the parties. The courts may also employ the doctrine of quantum meruit, or equitable remedies such as constructive or resulting trusts, when warranted by the facts of the case.

In a *Marvin* agreement, a couple can contract regarding how property is owned. The contract may detail whether earnings are considered property of the earner or the couple. The couple may craft a "pooling agreement" if they like. A contract can specify that support obligations are or are not created. The parties can agree that one will perform services, paid for by the other.

To bring a *Marvin*-style action, there must be evidence of a stable and significant relationship arising out of cohabitation (*Bergen v. Wood,* 14 Cal. App. 4th 854, 18 Cal. Rptr. 2d 75 (1993)). The fact that the couple had or planned to have children does not render the relationship illicit (*Della Zoppa v. Della Zoppa,* 86 Cal. App. 4th 1144, 103 Cal. Rptr. 2d 901 (2001)).

§ 2.2 Constructive and Resulting Trusts

In *Marvin,* the Supreme Court referred to resulting and constructive trusts as possible remedies. A constructive trust is an involuntary "trust" imposed by a court on someone who has misappropriated property. The purpose of the trust is to prevent unjust enrichment. The wrongdoer is compelled to transfer property to the rightful owner. A constructive trust is not based on the intention of the parties. It is imposed to remedy a wrong. (*See* Civil Code § 2224).

A resulting trust arises by operation of law when property is transferred to a person who is operating in good faith but who is not the intended owner. Unlike a constructive trust, which is a remedy for intentional wrongdoing, a resulting trust carries out the intent of the parties and restores property to the true owner.

§ 2.3 Questions

1. Judy and Wesley were lovers and lived together 15 years. They never married. Before Judy and Wesley met, Wesley had been married and had three children, all of whom were adults by the time

Judy and Wesley started living together. Judy worked full time at Wal-Mart. Wesley owned and worked a farm. The couple lived on the farm. In addition to income from the farm, Wesley ran a hay bailing and hauling business that netted about $30,000 a year. During the relationship, Wesley purchased several pieces of farm land, putting title in his name alone. Judy and Wesley had a joint bank account into which they deposited their incomes. All bills were paid from the joint account. Wesley withdrew funds from the account to pay the mortgages on his various properties. During his relationship with Judy, Wesley used money from the joint account to make monthly contributions to a 401(k) retirement account in his name. Wesley developed cancer and died. When he died, the joint bank account contained $40,000. The 401(k) contained $750,000. In probate, Wesley's daughter is appointed personal representative. Does Judy have a claim against the estate for an interest in any of the property in Wesley's name? Would the results be different if Judy and Wesley had married? *Johnson v. Estate of McFarlin,* 334 S.W.3d 469 (Mo. Ct. App. 2010).

2. Abe was married when he started a sexual relationship with Beth. Abe never divorced his wife. Beth remained Abe's mistress until Abe died. During their ten year relationship, Abe did not live with Beth. Abe would visit Beth at her home a couple of times a week, but he did not stay the night. Upon Abe's death, Beth seeks to enforce an oral agreement she says Abe made to support Beth for the rest of her life. The executor of Abe's estate refuses to make any payments to Beth. How will Beth prove the agreement existed? If Beth can prove the agreement, is it enforceable? *Cochran v. Cochran,* 89 Cal. App. 4th 283, 106 Cal. Rptr. 2d 899 (2001); *Bergen v. Wood,* 14 Cal. App. 4th 854, 18 Cal. Rptr. 2d 75 (1993); *Taylor v. Fields,* 178 Cal. App. 3d 653, 224 Cal. Rptr. 186 (1986).

3. Should the law require *Marvin* agreements to be in writing? In 2010, the New Jersey Legislature amended the Statute of Frauds to require "palimony agreements" to be in writing and signed by the parties. The New Jersey Statute provides: "No action shall be brought upon any of the following agreements or promises, unless the agreement or promise, upon which such action shall be brought or some memorandum thereof, shall be in writing, and signed by the party to be charged therewith . . . : A promise by one party to a non-marital personal relationship to provide support or

other consideration for the other party, either during the course of such relationship or after its termination. For the purposes of this subsection, no such written promise is binding unless it was made with the independent advice of counsel for both parties."[1] Do you favor requiring a writing? Won't such a requirement occasionally lead to injustice?

§ 2.4 Change on the Horizon?

There is movement in the United States and abroad to give unmarried cohabitants in long-term relationships rights to property similar to the rights enjoyed by married persons. See John G. Culhane, Cohabitation, Registration, and Reliance: Creating a Comprehensive and Just Scheme for Protecting the Interests of Couples' Real Relationships, 58 *Family Court Review* 145 (2020).

---

[1] N.J. Stat. Ann. § 25:1–5(h).

Chapter 3

PREMARITAL AGREEMENTS

Analysis

§ 3.1	Agreements in Family Law
§ 3.2	Premarital Agreement Defined
§ 3.3	Parties to Premarital Agreement Are Not in a Confidential Relationship
§ 3.4	Why a Prenup?
§ 3.5	California Uniform Premarital Agreement Act
§ 3.6	Premarital Agreements Must Be in Writing, However, Exceptions to Statute of Frauds Apply
§ 3.7	Premarital Agreement Cannot Adversely Affect Child Support
§ 3.8	Waiver of Spousal Support
§ 3.9	Premarital Agreement Must Be Voluntary
§ 3.10	How Much Time to Think About a Prenup?
§ 3.11	Is the Prenup Voluntary?
§ 3.12	Should a Prenup That Is Financially Unfair at the Outset of Marriage Be Enforceable?
§ 3.13	Should a Prenup That Is Fair at the Outset Be Enforceable at Divorce, Years Later, if Enforcement Is Unfair at Divorce?
§ 3.14	Problems on Premarital Agreements
§ 3.15	Professional Responsibility and Issues Regarding Premarital Agreements

Individuals in intimate relationships—married and unmarried—may contract with each other regarding many aspects of their relationship. Regarding married couples, Family Code § 1500 provides, "The property rights of spouses prescribed by statute may be altered by a premarital agreement or other marital property agreement."

§ 3.1 Agreements in Family Law

Family law attorneys draft the following agreements: Contracts between unmarried cohabitants who are *not* planning to marry, often called *Marvin* agreements (Chapter 2). Contracts in contemplation of marriage, called premarital or ante-nuptial agreements (Chapter 3). Contracts during marriage that change ownership of property are transmutation agreements. (Chapter 8). Contracts between divorcing spouses, to settle their affairs are marital settlement agreements (MSA) (§ 11.1).

§ 3.2 Premarital Agreement Defined

Family Code § 1610(a) defines premarital agreement as "an agreement between prospective spouses made in contemplation of marriage and to be effective upon marriage." A premarital agreement is a contract, and "the rules applicable to the interpretation of contracts have been applied generally to premarital agreements."[1] Thus, the parties must have the capacity to contract. Normal contract defenses apply.

§ 3.3 Parties to Premarital Agreement Are Not in a Confidential Relationship

Married couples are in a confidential relationship and owe each other duties of honesty and fair dealing (Family Code §§ 721; 1100) (*See* Chapter 10). Is a couple planning to marry and thinking about a premarital agreement in a confidential relationship? In some states the answer is yes. In *Marriage of Hill and Dittmer*, 202 Cal. App. 4th 1046, 1053, 136 Cal. Rptr. 3d 700 (2011), however, the Court of Appeal wrote, "Parties negotiating a premarital agreement are not presumed to be in a confidential relationship that would give rise to fiduciary duties owed between spouses or to the presumption of undue influence when a transaction benefits one of the parties."[2]

---

[1] Marriage of Bonds, 24 Cal. 4th 1, 13, 5 P.3d 815, 99 Cal. Rptr. 2d 252 (2000).

[2] You will see in Chapter 10 that when a married couple enters into a transmutation agreement that favors one spouse economically over the other spouse, the law creates a presumption that the favored spouse exerted undue influence over the economically disadvantaged spouse.

§ 3.4 Why a Prenup?

Relatively few engaged couples have a prenuptial agreement. Prenups traditionally are used primarily by two groups: (1) Wealthy individuals seeking to protect wealth from claims by new partners, and (2) Older individuals with children from a previous marriage who desire to pass property to their children.

The most common reason for a premarital agreement is to opt out of California's community property system. (*See Marriage of Facter*, 212 Cal. App. 4th 967, 152 Cal. Rptr. 3d 79 (2013)). Under a properly worded premarital agreement, property that would be community property remains the separate property of the spouse who earned it. In *Marriage of Bonds*, 24 Cal. 4th 1, 13, 5 P.3d 815, 99 Cal. Rptr. 2d 252 (2000), the Supreme Court wrote, "From the inception of its statehood, California has retained the community property law that predated its admission to the Union .... At the same time, applicable statutes recognized the power of parties contemplating a marriage to reach an agreement containing terms at variance with community property law." In *Marriage of Hill and Dittmer*, 202 Cal. App. 4th 1046, 136 Cal. Rptr. 3d 700 (2011), the Court of Appeal put it this way, "Parties contemplating marriage may validly contract as to their property rights, both as to property then owned and as to property and earnings that may be acquired during the marriage."

A premarital agreement can opt entirely or partially out of the community property system. For example, Abe and Beth are planning to marry. Abe owns a business. Abe understands that once he is married, any increased value of his separate property business that is attributable to marital efforts will be partly community property (*See* § 7.2). Abe wants the business and any increased value to remain his separate property. Abe and Beth can execute a premarital agreement to accomplish that goal, while otherwise remaining in the community property system. Before marriage, Beth bought a home. She makes monthly mortgage payments with her paycheck. Once Beth and Abe marry, Beth's paycheck is community property, and if she makes mortgage payments with her income from work, the home will become part community property and part separate property (*See* § 5.17). Beth would like the home to remain entirely her separate property. This can be achieved in a prenup.

A premarital agreement can be used to plan for death as well as divorce. For example, couples who have children from previous relationships typically want to leave property to their kids as well as their new spouse. A prenup can accomplish this goal.

§ 3.5 California Uniform Premarital Agreement Act

In 1983, the National Conference of Commissioners on Uniform State Laws promulgated the Uniform Premarital Agreement Act (UPAA). The UPAA has been adopted by more than half the states. California's version of the UPAA follows.

§ 1600. Short title

This chapter may be cited as the Uniform Premarital Agreement Act.

§ 1601. Effective date of chapter

This chapter is effective on and after January 1, 1986, and applies to any premarital agreement executed on or after that date.[3]

§ 1610. Definitions

As used in this chapter:

(a) "Premarital agreement" means an agreement between prospective spouses made in contemplation of marriage and to be effective upon marriage.

(b) "Property" means an interest, present or future, legal or equitable, vested or contingent, in real or personal property, including income and earnings.

§ 1611. Form and execution of agreement; consideration

A premarital agreement shall be in writing and signed by both parties. It is enforceable without consideration.

---

[3] A premarital agreement executed prior to the effective date of the Uniform Act is governed by law in effect at the time of execution.

§ 1612. Subject matter of premarital agreements

(a) Parties to a premarital agreement may contract with respect to all of the following:

(1) The rights and obligations of each of the parties in any of the property of either or both of them whenever and wherever acquired or located.

(2) The right to buy, sell, use, transfer, exchange, abandon, lease, consume, expend, assign, create a security interest in, mortgage, encumber, dispose of, or otherwise manage and control property.[4]

(3) The disposition of property upon separation, marital dissolution, death, or the occurrence of any other event.

(4) The making of a will, trust, or other arrangement to carry out the provisions of the agreement.

(5) The ownership rights in and disposition of the death benefit from a life insurance policy.

(6) The choice of law governing the construction of the agreement.

(7) Any other matter, including their personal rights and obligations, not in violation of public policy or a statute imposing a criminal penalty.

(b) The right of a child to support may not be adversely affected by a premarital agreement.

(c) Any provision in a premarital agreement regarding spousal support, including, but not limited to, a waiver of it, is not enforceable if the party against whom enforcement of the spousal support provision is sought was not represented by independent counsel at the time the agreement containing the provision was signed, or if the provision regarding spousal support is unconscionable at the time of enforcement. An otherwise unenforceable provision in a premarital agreement regarding spousal support may not be enforceable solely because the party

---

[4] The law regarding management and control of community property is addressed in Chapter 10. A premarital agreement can change the rules governing management and control.

against whom enforcement is sought was represented by independent counsel.

§ 1613. Effective date of agreements

A premarital agreement becomes effective upon marriage.

§ 1614. Amendment or revocation of agreements

After marriage, a premarital agreement may be amended or revoked only by a written agreement signed by the parties. The amendment or the revocation is enforceable without consideration.

§ 1615. Unenforceable agreements; unconscionability; voluntariness

(a) A premarital agreement is not enforceable if the party against whom enforcement is sought proves either of the following:

(1) That party did not execute the agreement voluntarily.

(2) The agreement was unconscionable when it was executed and, before execution of the agreement, all of the following applied to that party:

(A) That party was not provided a fair, reasonable, and full disclosure of the property or financial obligations of the other party.

(B) That party did not voluntarily and expressly waive, in writing, any right to disclosure of the property or financial obligations of the other party beyond the disclosure provided.

(C) That party did not have, or reasonably could not have had, an adequate knowledge of the property or financial obligations of the other party.

(b) An issue of unconscionability of a premarital agreement shall be decided by the court as a matter of law.

(c) For the purposes of subdivision (a), it shall be deemed that a premarital agreement was not executed voluntarily unless the court finds in writing or on the record all of the following:

(1) The party against whom enforcement is sought was represented by independent legal counsel at the time of the signing of the agreement or, after being advised to seek

independent legal counsel, expressly waived, in a separate writing, representation by independent legal counsel. The advisement to seek legal counsel shall be made at least seven calendar days before the final agreement is signed.

(2) One of the following:

(A) For an agreement executed between January 1, 2002, and January 1, 2020, the party against whom enforcement is sought had not less than seven calendar days between the time that party was first presented with the final agreement and advised to seek independent legal counsel and the time the agreement was signed. This requirement does not apply to nonsubstantive amendments that do not change the terms of the agreement.

(B) For an agreement executed on or after January 1, 2020, the party against whom enforcement is sought had not less than seven calendar days between the time the party was first presented with the final agreement and the time the agreement was signed, regardless of whether the party is represented by legal counsel. This requirement does not apply to nonsubstantive amendments that do not change the terms of the agreement.

(3) The party against whom enforcement is sought, if unrepresented by legal counsel, was fully informed of the terms and basic effect of the agreement as well as the rights and obligations the party was giving up by signing the agreement, and was proficient in the language in which the explanation of the party's rights was conducted and in which the agreement was written. The explanation of the rights and obligations relinquished shall be memorialized in writing and delivered to the party prior to signing the agreement. The unrepresented party shall, on or before the signing of the premarital agreement, execute a document declaring that the party received the information required by this paragraph and indicating who provided the information.

(4) The agreement and the writings executed pursuant to paragraphs (1) and (3) were not executed under duress, fraud,

or undue influence, and the parties did not lack capacity to enter into the agreement.

(5) Any other factors the court deems relevant.

§ 1616. Void marriage, effect on agreement

If a marriage is determined to be void, an agreement that would otherwise have been a premarital agreement is enforceable only to the extent necessary to avoid an inequitable result.[5]

§ 1617. Limitation of actions; equitable defenses including laches and estoppel

Any statute of limitations applicable to an action asserting a claim for relief under a premarital agreement is tolled during the marriage of the parties to the agreement. However, equitable defenses limiting the time for enforcement, including laches and estoppel, are available to either party.

§ 3.6 Premarital Agreements Must Be in Writing, However, Exceptions to Statute of Frauds Apply

A premarital agreement must be in writing (Family Code § 1611). An oral premarital agreement is not enforceable. However, California courts apply well known exceptions to the statute of frauds when justice requires.[6] Thus, if one party to an oral premarital agreement performs her side of the agreement, a court will enforce the agreement.[7] As well, when one spouse relies to his detriment on an oral agreement, a court may estop the other spouse from raising the writing requirement.[8] Marriage itself is not a sufficient basis to enforce an oral premarital agreement.

---

[5] In California, and other states, some defective marriages are void, others are voidable. This subject is discussed in Chapter 12. In California, a marriage that is incestuous or bigamous is void.

[6] *See* Hall v. Hall, 222 Cal. App. 3d 578, 271 Cal. Rptr. 773 (1990).

[7] *See* Marriage of Garrity & Bishton, 181 Cal. App. 3d 675, 226 Cal. Rptr. 485 (1986).

[8] Estate of Sheldon, 75 Cal. App. 3d 364, 142 Cal. Rptr. 119 (1977).

§ 3.7 Premarital Agreement Cannot Adversely Affect Child Support

A parent's first duty is to protect, nurture, and support the parent's children. A premarital agreement—or any other agreement—cannot adversely affect a child's right to support.[9] On the other hand, a person signing a premarital agreement can *assume* a child support duty that would not otherwise apply, and courts enforce such agreements. For example, the duty to support ends when a child turns 18, unless the child is still in high school, in which case, the duty continues to age 19.[10] A couple signing a premarital agreement could contract to support adult children. The duty to support step-children ends when marriage ends. A prospective step-parent can assume an enforceable obligation to support step-children.

§ 3.8 Waiver of Spousal Support

One of the most controversial issues related to premarital agreements is enforceability of agreements to waive spousal support in the event of divorce. For decades, California courts held such waivers to be against public policy.[11] The leading case breaking with the past is *Marriage of Pendelton and Fireman,* 24 Cal. 4th 39, 99, 5 P.3d 839, 99 Cal. Rptr. 2d 278 (2000), in which the Supreme Court wrote, "When entered into voluntarily by parties who are aware of the effect of the agreement, a premarital waiver of spousal support does not offend contemporary public policy. Such agreements are, therefore, permitted . . . ." Today, a prospective spouse may waive spousal support provided the spouse was represented by independent counsel (Family Code § 1612(c)).

Even if a prospective spouse had an attorney, a California court will refuse to enforce a spousal support waiver if enforcement is unconscionable *at the time of divorce*—often years into the

---

[9] *See* Marriage of Facter, 212 Cal. App. 4th 967, 152 Cal. Rptr. 3d 79 (2013).
[10] Family Code § 3901(a). *See also,* Family Code § 3587 (court may approve an agreement between parents to support a child beyond age 18); § 3901(b) (parents can agree to pay additional support).
[11] *See* Marriage of Melissa, 212 Cal. App. 4th 598, 151 Cal. Rptr. 3d 608 (2013).

marriage.[12] For example, Tina and Ike marry during the first year of medical school. Before they marry, Tina and Ike sign a prenup containing mutual waivers of spousal support in the event of divorce. Fifteen years pass and Tina is a successful surgeon making over a million dollars a year. Ike recently was disabled in a ski accident and can no longer practice medicine. Tina and Ike are getting divorced and Tina seeks to enforce the waiver of spousal support. Tina is wealthy. Assuming Ike cannot work and needs support, a family court judge will likely refuse to enforce the spousal support waiver because doing so would be unconscionable.

Family Code § 1612(c) provides that waiver of spousal support is enforceable only if the waiving spouse was represented by counsel. The requirement of counsel was added by the Legislature in 2002. In *Marriage of Howell*, 195 Cal. App. 4th 1062, 126 Cal. Rptr. 3d 539 (2011), the Court of Appeal considered a premarital agreement entered into prior to enactment of § 1612(c), at a time when representation by counsel was not absolutely required for a valid spousal support waiver. When the Howell's agreement was signed, it complied with then-existing California law. In *Howell*, the divorcing spouse who challenged the spousal support waiver was not represented by an attorney when she signed the prenup. The issue was whether Section 1612(c)—mandating counsel—should be applied retroactively. If so, the spousal support waiver was invalid. The Court of Appeal concluded the Legislature did not intend Section 1612(c) to apply retroactively to premarital agreements entered before 2002. It is true that Family Code § 4(c) provides that amendments to the Family Code are, generally, retroactive. However, the Court concluded Section 4(c) did not govern. The Court ruled Section 1612(c) is not retroactive. As you proceed with your study of community property, you will encounter the issue of retroactivity and Section 4(c).[13]

---

[12] *See* Marriage of Facter, 212 Cal. App. 4th 967, 984, 152 Cal. Rptr. 3d 79 (2013) (lengthy marriage; husband was a very successful attorney; wife was a high school graduate who was a stay at home parent. "[W]e have little difficulty in concluding that the Agreement's spousal support waiver is presently unconscionable.").

[13] An amendment to the Family Code cannot be applied retroactively when doing so would deprive a person of a vested property right.

§ 3.9 Premarital Agreement Must Be Voluntary

A premarital agreement must be voluntarily. California's UPAA does not define voluntary.[14] In *Marriage of Bonds*, 24 Cal. 4th 1, 17, 5 P.3d 815, 99 Cal. Rptr. 2d 252 (2000) the Supreme Court wrote, "Courts frequently consult dictionaries to determine the usual meaning of words. *Black's Law Dictionary* defines 'voluntarily' as 'Done by design . . . . Intentionally and without coercion.'"[15] The *Bonds* court outlined factors shedding light on voluntariness: (1) Presence or absence of coercion, fraud, duress, or undue influence, (2) Did the party understand the agreement and, in particular, understand the rights being waived? (3) Was there full disclosure of property and debts?[16] (4) Did the party have adequate time to study the agreement? (5) Was the party represented by independent counsel?[17] (6) Was the party sufficiently mature and intellectually capable of understanding the agreement? (7) Were the parties of equal or unequal bargaining power and sophistication? The *Bonds* court concluded, "The question of voluntariness must be examined in the unique context of the marital relationship."[18]

The *Bonds* factors regarding voluntariness overlap the criteria specified in Family Code § 1615(c). Section 1615(c) provides that a prenuptual agreement is voluntary only if *all* of the following are satisfied: (1) The party against whom enforcement is sought was represented by independent counsel, or waived in writing the right to counsel;[19] (2) If the person did not have an attorney, the person

---

[14] *See* Marriage of Bonds, 24 Cal. 4th 1, 17, 5 P.3d 815, 99 Cal. Rptr. 2d 252 (2000) ("The commissioners, however, did not supply a definition of the term 'voluntarily,' nor was there much discussion of the term.").

[15] 24 Cal. 4th at 16.

[16] *See* James O. Pearson, Jr., Failure to Disclose Extent or Value of Property Owned as Ground for Avoiding Premarital Contract, 3 A.L.R. 5th 394 (1992).

[17] *See* Marriage of Bonds, 24 Cal. 4th 1, 23, 5 P.3d 815, 99 Cal. Rptr. 2d 252 (2000) (the court discussed at length whether the fact that a person was not represented by independent counsel rendered a premarital agreement involuntary. The court concluded that legal advice is an important factor in the voluntariness inquiry, but that a premarital agreement can be voluntarily entered into without legal advice. "It seems evident that the commissioners who enacted the Uniform Act intended that the presence of independent counsel (or a reasonable opportunity to consult counsel) should be merely one factor among several that a court should consider in examining a challenge to the voluntariness of a premarital agreement.").

[18] Marriage of Bonds, 24 Cal. 4th 1, 26, 5 P.3d 815, 99 Cal. Rptr. 2d 252 (2000).

[19] Regarding waiver of spousal support, counsel can't be waived.

was fully informed of the terms of the agreement and its effects; (3) The person had at least seven days to consider the agreement, before signing; (4) There was no fraud, undue influence, or duress; (5) The parties had the mental capacity to enter the agreement; and (5) No other factors indicate involuntariness.

§ 3.10 How Much Time to Think About a Prenup?

How much time does a person need between the time they receive a prenup and the time they sign it? Family Code § 1615(c)(2)(B) requires at least seven days between the time the person is first presented with the final version of the prenup and the time the prenup is signed. In *Marriage of Clarke and Akel,* 19 Cal. App. 5th 914, 228 Cal. Rptr. 3d 483 (2018), the Court of Appeal ruled that when an unrepresented party to a premarital agreement has less than seven days to consider the agreement, a provision in the agreement stating the party did have the seven days is invalid.

§ 3.11 Is the Prenup Voluntary?

1. Tom and Wendy are getting married in less than a month. Wedding plans are well-advanced. Invitations have been mailed. The wedding site is reserved and paid for. The caterer is employed. The cake is ordered. The wedding dress is at the seamstress following the final fitting. Dresses for the bridesmaids are hanging in closets. Relatives and friends from far and wide have made airline and hotel reservations. Ten days before the wedding, in the midst of these happy but hectic preparations, Tom tells Wendy, "I think it would be a good idea for us to have a prenup. I asked my lawyer to draft one for us. Here it is. What do you think?" Should the advanced state of wedding preparations be a factor in deciding whether Wendy's signature on the prenup is voluntary?[20]

2. Deborah and Victor's wedding was just weeks away. Victor's attorney drafted a prenup and advised Deborah to review the prenup with an independent attorney. Victor's attorney

---

[20] *See* Edwards v. Edwards, 16 Neb. App. 297, 744 N.W.2d 243 (2008)(the fact that wife had made wedding plans did not mean she was coerced into signing prenuptial agreement); Barocas v. Barocas, 94 A.D.3d 551, 942 N.Y.S.2d 491 (2012) ("Defendant's claims that she believed that there would be no wedding if she did not sign the agreement, that the wedding was only two weeks away and that wedding plans had been made, is insufficient to demonstrate duress.").

recommended independent counsel, and Deborah consulted the attorney. The attorney advised Deborah that the prenup was "unfair." The attorney advised Deborah not to sign the prenup. Victor paid the fee charged by Deborah's attorney. Deborah understood the prenup and decided to sign it. A few years later, Deborah files for divorce and claims the prenup is invalid because Victor paid the fee of the attorney she consulted. Should the fact that Victor paid the attorney invalidate the prenup?

3. If you are the attorney for the party who wants the prenup, what procedures will you put in place regarding financial disclosure and signing of the prenup to make sure the agreement cannot be challenged successfully years later if the marriage ends in divorce?

§ 3.12 Should a Prenup That Is Financially Unfair at the Outset of Marriage Be Enforceable?

With some premarital agreements, one party is wealthy, and the other isn't.[21] If the agreement opts out of the community property system, all of the wealthy party's accumulations during marriage remain separate property. There will be no community property to divide equally if the marriage dissolves. As a result, at divorce, the rich party remains rich, and the poor party is out of luck. This strikes some as unfair. On the other hand, if the less well-off party signed a prenup with eyes wide open, is it unfair to expect the poorer party to live with the agreement? This scenario raises the question whether a prenuptual agreement that is financially unbalanced should be enforceable.

Family Code § 1615(a)(2) provides an "unconscionable" prenup is not enforceable unless it is voluntary and fully informed. The UPAA does not define unconscionable. The North Dakota Supreme Court grappled with the meaning of unconscionable in *Sailer v. Sailer,* 788 N.W.2d 604, 606 (N.D. 2010), where the court wrote, "Although the issue of whether a premarital agreement is unconscionable presents a question of law, the analysis turns on factual findings related to the relative property values, the parties'

---

[21] *See, e.g.,* Marriage of Facter, 212 Cal. App. 4th 967, 152 Cal. Rptr. 3d 79 (2013).

financial circumstances, and their ongoing need." The fundamental question usually is: How one-sided is the agreement?

Close reading of Section 1615(a)(2) reveals that some unconscionable/unfair agreements *are* enforceable![22] Section 1615(a)(2) states that an unconscionable agreement *is* enforceable if the disadvantaged party was given fair, reasonable, and full disclosure of the other party's property, or waived the right to disclosure, and if the disadvantaged party signed voluntarily.[23]

Is it good public policy to enforce an unconscionable/unfair premarital agreement that was signed voluntarily? On one hand, absent coercion or fraud, adults have the right to make bad deals. Contract law usually is not so paternalistic that it protects us from our folly. On the other hand, aren't there differences between signing a contract for a car and signing a premarital contract?[24] If you enter a one-sided contract with a car dealer, you have no one to blame but yourself. But should the result be the same if you sign a one-sided premarital agreement? Is it fair to allow one party— typically the party with the most to lose—to be bound by an *unconscionable/unfair* premarital agreement?[25] The American Law Institute's *Principles of the Law of Family Dissolution* analyze the differences between a marrying couple and a couple of merchants:

> While there are good reasons to respect contracts relating to the consequences of family dissolution, the family context requires some departure from the rules that govern the commercial arena. The relationship between contracting parties who are married, or about to marry, is different than the usual commercial relationship in ways that matter in the law's treatment of their agreements. Persons planning to marry usually assume that they share with their intended spouse a mutual and deep concern for

---

[22] *See* Marriage of Bonds, 24 Cal. 4th 1, 16, 5 P.3d 815, 99 Cal. Rptr. 2d 252 (2000).

[23] For analysis of fair and reasonable financial disclosure, *see* Friezo v. Friezo, 281 Conn. 166, 914 A.2d 533 (2007).

[24] *See* American Law Institute, *Principles of the Law of Family Dissolution: Analysis and Recommendations* § 7.02, p. 956, Comment (2002).

[25] The California Supreme Court discussed the differences between commercial contracts and premarital agreements in Marriage of Bonds, 24 Cal. 4th 1, 24–27, 5 P.3d 815, 99 Cal. Rptr. 2d 252 (2000).

one another's welfare. Business people negotiating a commercial agreement do not usually have such expectations of one another. The distinctive expectations that persons planning to marry usually have about one another can disarm their capacity for self-protective judgment, or their inclination to exercise it, as compared to parties negotiating commercial agreements.[26]

Iowa's version of the Uniform Premarital Agreement Act (IUPAA) allows judges to refuse to enforce unconscionable/unfair premarital agreements. The Iowa Supreme Court wrote in *Marriage of Shanks,* 758 N.W.2d 506, 514 (Iowa 2008), "In contrast to the UPAA [and the California] approach, unconscionability alone is sufficient to render a premarital agreement unenforceable under the IUPAA, notwithstanding fair and reasonable financial disclosure. . . . Under the IUPAA, courts may address unconscionability claims whether or not appropriate financial disclosures are made."

Which approach to you favor, Iowa or California? Do you favor upholding unconscionable premarital agreements that were signed voluntarily? Or do you prefer the more paternalistic approach that allows judges to set aside unconscionable/unfair prenups?

§ 3.13 Should a Prenup That Is Fair at the Outset Be Enforceable at Divorce, Years Later, if Enforcement Is Unfair at Divorce?

The American Law Institute's *Principles of the Law of Family Dissolution* grapple with the enforceability of premarital agreements that turn out to be unfair when they are sought to be enforced years after they are signed. The *Principles* take the position that a premarital agreement should not be enforced if enforcement would "work a substantial injustice."[27] The *Principles* conclude, "When many years have passed since the agreement was executed, when the parties first have children in common after execution, or when the circumstances of the parties have

---

[26] American Law Institute, *Principles of the Law of Family Dissolution: Analysis and Recommendations* § 7.02, p. 956 (2002).

[27] American Law Institute, *Principles of the Law of Family Dissolution: Analysis and Recommendations* § 7.05, p. 982 (2002).

unforeseeably changed, courts must examine the agreement before enforcing it to ensure . . . that such enforcement will not work a 'substantial injustice.' "[28]

What is a "substantial injustice"? Does the "substantial injustice" language create a potential escape hatch from virtually any prenup? Should parties be entitled to rely on their prenup in the event of divorce? Put differently, if you voluntarily sign a prenup, should you be stuck with it?

§ 3.14 Problems on Premarital Agreements

1. Bill was a wealthy seventy-seven-year-old businessman when he married Rabha, who was much younger. Rabha was born and grew up in Morocco. Rabha met Bill when she travelled to the United States to visit her brother. Within two months, Bill and Rabha were engaged. Bill had his attorney draft a premarital agreement. The agreement provided that in the event of divorce, each party waived their interest in the other party's property and their rights to equitable distribution of property, spousal support, retirement, life insurance, and attorney's fees. The agreement provided that each party gave up the right to inherit from the other. The only asset Rabha was entitled to under the agreement was $100,000 if she and Bill were still married and living together when Bill died. The agreement did not disclose Bill's assets. Rabha's native language is Arabic, and when she signed the premarital agreement, she spoke little English. She relied on translators for oral and written communication in English. The parties were married 15 years. Now, they are divorcing. Rabha testifies that she thought she was signing a "paper for marriage, like a license or something. I signed it without reading it." Rabha was not given a copy of the agreement to review before signing. Rabha was not advised on the agreement by an attorney. Is the agreement

---

[28] American Law Institute, *Principles of the Law of Family Dissolution: Analysis and Recommendations* § 7.02, p. 955 (2002). Elsewhere, the Comment to Section 7.05 states, "In sum, nearly all premarital agreements involve special difficulties arising from unrealistic optimism about marital success, the human tendency to treat low probabilities as zero probabilities, the excessive discounting of future benefits, and the inclination to overweigh the importance of the immediate and certain consequences of agreement—the marriage—as against its contingent and future consequences." p. 987.

enforceable? *Chaplain v. Chaplain*, 54 Va. App. 762, 682 S.E.2d 108 (2009).

    2. Randall is an attorney in private practice. Teresa has a bachelor's degree in business. Teresa has worked in the marketing department of a casino, as a secretary, and as a bookkeeper and office manager. Randall and Teresa were married in Jamaica. At the time of the marriage, Randall owned valuable commercial properties. Teresa had no assets to speak of. Randall has a large income. It is the second marriage for both, and each has children from their first marriage. While contemplating marriage, Randall and Teresa discussed Randall's desire for a premarital agreement. Randall said he wanted to preserve his assets for his children in the event the marriage failed. Randall said he would not marry again without a premarital agreement protecting his property "for my kids." Teresa agreed, stating that she was not marrying Randall for his money. Randall drafted a premarital agreement and presented it to Teresa ten days before the wedding. The agreement stated that each party would maintain separate ownership of their assets acquired before and during marriage, and that they did not intend to hold jointly-owned property except the marital home and a joint bank account. The agreement contained a mutual waiver of alimony. The agreement disclosed Randall's assets. Randall encouraged Teresa to consult an attorney, which she did. The attorney explained the agreement to Teresa. Randall and Teresa signed the agreement the day before leaving for Jamaica. Prior to and during the six year marriage, Teresa worked in Randall's office as a bookkeeper and secretary. In the divorce, Teresa argues that the premarital agreement was not signed voluntarily and that the agreement was unconscionable. Teresa seeks division of marital property and spousal support. Teresa acknowledges that she is employable, but points out that the jobs she is qualified for will require her to live at a standard much lower than she enjoyed while married to Randall. Is the premarital agreement enforceable? Does the fact that Randall said he would not marry again without a premarital agreement render the agreement unenforceable? Do the facts that Randall is an attorney and that Teresa worked for him render the agreement unenforceable? Does the fact that enforcement of the agreement means Teresa will have to lower her

standard of living render the agreement unenforceable? *Marriage of Shanks,* 758 N.W.2d 506 (Iowa 2008).

3. Debra and Dave have been married 10 years. They have one child, who is nine. Four days before their wedding, the parties signed a premarital agreement. At the time, Dave was represented by counsel; Debra was not. The premarital agreement, which was drafted by Dave's attorney, stated that both parties had "fully disclosed his or her present approximate net worth," that "each party had full opportunity to review the agreement," and that "both parties acknowledge their understanding of the effect and content of the agreement." The agreement listed Dave's separate property as six parcels of real property. The agreement did not list the values of the properties. Debra had no assets at the time of marriage. The agreement provided that neither party would acquire any interest in the property of the other, whether that property was acquired prior to or during marriage. During the marriage, Dave's income was derived entirely from buying and selling real property, all of which was titled in his name alone. Over the course of the marriage, Dave bought and sold 75 parcels of real estate. Debra was a full time homemaker. Recently, Debra filed for divorce. In the divorce, Debra challenges the premarital agreement, arguing that she did not enter into the agreement voluntarily and that the agreement is unconscionable. Debra asks the judge to declare the premarital agreement invalid and to characterize all of the property owned by Dave before marriage, during marriage, and at divorce as marital property. Dave argues the premarital agreement is valid and should be enforced, meaning that all of the real property owned by Dave in his business, including the property he owns at the time of divorce, is his separate property. What should be the outcome? *Marsocci v. Marsocci,* 911 A.2d 690 (R.I. 2006).

4. When Joyce and Robert married, she was 44, he was 52. It was the second marriage for each. Joyce is a teacher. Robert owns and works a large farm. Robert owned the farm before marrying Joyce. During the marriage, Robert paid the monthly mortgage on the farm with income from farming. During the marriage, Robert purchased five additional pieces of farm land, paying for the land with income from his farming operation, putting title in his name alone. Joyce helped with the farm, including doing the books for the operation.

Two days before their wedding, Joyce and Robert entered into a prenuptual agreement prepared by Joyce's attorney. The agreement follows:

This antenuptual contract is entered into this [two days prior to the wedding], between Robert Jones, hereinafter for convenience referred to as Husband, and Joyce King, hereinafter for convenience referred to as Wife, Witnesseth:

I. Husband and Wife intend to marry each other soon, and it is agreed that after such marriage, all of the properties of any name or nature, real, personal or mixed, wherever they may be found, belonging to Husband before marriage shall be and remain forever his personal estate, and that this shall include all interest, rents, and profits which may in time accrue or result in any manner from increase in value, or be collected for the use of the same in any way.

II. All properties of any name or nature, real, personal or mixed, wherever the same shall be found which belong to Wife before marriage shall be and remain forever her personal estate, and this shall include all interest, rents, and profits which may in time accrue or result in any manner from increase in value, or be collected for the use of the same in any way.

III. Each party agrees to sign with the other, all title paper, deeds or other papers necessary to transfer property when sold to a purchaser, in any event, it is necessary that such title papers be executed by a man and wife, either in this state or any other state, and this courtesy shall be prompt at any time and in any place.

IV. Husband agrees to, from his own personal estate, assume necessary expense of support and maintenance of Wife.

V. Nothing herein shall be construed to be a bar to either party to this agreement, giving any property of which they may be possessed to the other party by will or otherwise. Each party to this agreement shall control their personal estate as described herein, and do with the properties thereof whatsoever they wish and will, by his or her orders or directions or by will, the same as either could or would do if no marriage existed between them. That upon the demise of each party, their personal estates shall pass by their individual Wills, or by law to their individual heirs, and each party waives any claim of participation they may otherwise be entitled to by law in the estate of the other.

The agreement did not list what property Joyce or Robert owned prior to the marriage. After 25 years of marriage, Joyce filed for divorce. In the divorce action, Joyce argues the premarital agreement is invalid for two reasons. First, the agreement did not specify what property Robert owned at the time of the marriage. Second, the agreement did not mention divorce or separation. It mentioned only property rights during marriage and at death. Because the agreement did not mention property rights at divorce, the agreement should not apply at divorce. Robert admits that the premarital agreement did not disclose the nature and extent of his property. He claims, however, that the agreement should be enforced because during their 14 month courtship, Joyce learned the extent of Robert's property. As for the argument that the agreement did not mention divorce, Robert argues that "common sense" indicates the agreement should be applied in the event of divorce. How should the judge rule on these two issues? How would you draft the agreement differently to avoid such issues? *Smetana v. Smetana,* 726 N.W.2d 887 (S.D. 2007).

5. Husband is seeking a divorce. Husband argues that a premarital agreement regarding property division and spousal support is enforceable. Wife argues the premarital agreement is not enforceable. Wife met Husband while she was working as a nurse. Husband is a doctor. They began living together in Wife's home. After the parties became engaged, Husband purchased a larger home. Wife rented her home. They did not set a wedding date, but at midnight on December 28, Husband asked Wife if she wanted to get married at the courthouse later that day! Wife agreed. Wife did not learn that Husband expected her to sign a premarital agreement until they were on the way to the courthouse to be married. Husband told Wife they had to stop at his attorney's office to sign "the

marriage papers," and it was not until Wife was at Husband's attorney's office that she realized Husband wanted her to sign a prenuptual agreement. Wife was shocked at the request and began crying. Husband's attorney discussed the agreement with her, and she understood that in the event the parties divorced, Husband "would reserve control over certain things that he had," including the marital residence. Wife understood that she would not have a claim to Husband's IRA, pension plans, and stocks that he owned before the marriage. Wife understood that she was waiving any claim to spousal support. Husband's attorney sent Wife and Husband to another attorney, "his good friend," so Wife could review the agreement with a separate attorney. Husband was approximately 10 feet away, outside an open door, when Wife discussed the agreement with her "independent" counsel. The attorney only skimmed through the agreement. Wife was crying, and was trying to whisper to the attorney because Husband looked mad. Wife refused to sign the agreement, so she and Husband returned home. Husband told Wife that he would not have the nerve to get married if she did not sign the agreement. They returned to the attorney's office, and Wife signed the agreement. They made it to the courthouse in time to marry. Is the agreement enforceable? *Hood v. Hood,* 72 So. 3d 666 (Ala. Ct. App. 2011).

§ 3.15 Professional Responsibility and Issues Regarding Premarital Agreements

Can one attorney represent both parties to a premarital agreement? The West Virginia Supreme Court of Appeals addressed this question in *Ware v. Ware,* 224 W. Va. 599, 687 S.E.2d 382, 390 (2009), where the court wrote:

> This Court has previously recognized that, in certain instances, dual representation is never appropriate, even if both parties are willing to consent. It is improper for a lawyer to represent both the husband and the wife at any stage of the separation and divorce proceeding, even with full disclosure and informed consent. The likelihood of prejudice is so great with dual representation so as to make adequate representation of both spouses impossible, even where the separation is "friendly" and the divorce uncontested.

Like divorce actions, the nature of prenuptial agreements is such that the parties interests are fundamentally antagonistic to one another. Indeed, the purpose of a prenuptial agreement is to preserve the property of one spouse, thereby preventing the other from obtaining that to which he or she might otherwise be legally entitled. . . . Accordingly, the Court holds that one attorney may not represent, nor purport to counsel, both parties to a prenuptial agreement.

It is never a good idea to represent both parties. Some family law attorneys caution against even meeting the unrepresented party.

Chapter 4

INTRODUCTION TO MARITAL PROPERTY

Analysis

§ 4.1   When Property Issues Arise During Marriage
§ 4.2   Systems of Marital Property in the United States
§ 4.3   History of Equitable Distribution and Community Property
§ 4.4   Marital Property Law in Other States
§ 4.5   All Property States
§ 4.6   Mortgage, Deed of Trust, and Encumbrance

California's community property system applies to married couples and registered domestic partners. Because domestic partnerships are uncommon, the remainder of the book refers to married couples. You saw in Chapter 3 that it is possible to contract out of the community property system with a premarital agreement. Absent such a contract, the community property system applies automatically—by operation of law—the moment a couple marries.

§ 4.1   When Property Issues Arise During Marriage

Over the course of a marriage, property issues can arise at three times: (1) During marriage. (2) When death ends marriage. When death ends marriage, distribution of property is governed by the law of wills, trusts, intestate succession, probate, and related topics. Chapter 13 addresses property issues at death. (3) Community property issues arise when a marriage ends in divorce, legal separation, or annulment.

§ 4.2 Systems of Marital Property in the United States

American states employ one of two systems of marital property: equitable distribution or community property. In equitable distribution states, "marital property" is divided equitably. In community property states, "community property" is divided equally or equitably, depending on the state. The two systems of marital property are increasingly similar. At this writing, 2021, the nine community property states are Arizona, California, Idaho, Louisiana, Nevada, New Mexico, Texas, Washington, and Wisconsin.

§ 4.3 History of Equitable Distribution and Community Property

This section offers a brief historical introduction to the two systems of marital property: equitable distribution and community property.

§ 4.3(a) Equitable Distribution

To understand today's equitable distribution system of marital property, it is useful to examine marital property law at the Nation's birth. After the Revolutionary War, the states continued their adherence to much of the English law of domestic relations. In particular, states perpetuated English law relegating married women to an inferior status vis à vie husbands. Describing the English subordination of married women, William Blackstone (1723–1780) wrote in his *Commentaries on the Laws of England*:

> By marriage, the husband and wife are one person in law: that is, the very being or legal existence of the woman is suspended during the marriage, or at least is incorporated and consolidated into that of the husband: under whose wing, protection, and cover, she performs everything; and is therefore called in our law—French a feme-covert; is said to be covert-baron, or under the protection and influence of her husband, her baron, or lord; and her condition during marriage is called her coverture . . . . Upon this principle, of an union of person in husband

and wife, depend almost all the legal rights, duties, and disabilities, that either of them acquire by the marriage.

When a woman married, ownership of her personal property passed to her husband. The husband could sell the property and his creditors could reach *her* property to satisfy *his* debts. A married woman's real property fell under the husband's control as well, although he could not sell her real property without her consent. In many states, a married woman could not enter into binding contracts. A married woman could not make a will. For many legal purposes, women were placed in the same category as children and "idiots."[1]

Over the years, mechanisms emerged to ameliorate somewhat a wife's subordinate position regarding property. Thus, some states allowed a married couple to agree that the wife would retain control of her property. Sometimes, a woman's parents created a trust for their daughter, placing property in trust in order to remove the property from the control of the daughter's husband. In some states, married women who wished to go into business were authorized to transact business and enter contacts.

From early days, reformers agitated against inequitable treatment of married women.[2] Calls for reform gathered steam and reached a crescendo in 1839, when Mississippi passed the first married women's property act. The act provided: "That any married woman may become seized or possessed of any property, real or personal, by direct bequest, demise, gift, purchase, or distribution, in her own name, and as of her own property . . . ." Although the Mississippi law was a step forward, it by no means bestowed equality on women. Amanda Sims writes, "The 1839 [married women's property act] did nothing more than legally pass title to property to a married woman, while reserving all the privileges of ownership to her husband and providing her some recourse in retaining her separate property from his creditors, but she benefited only in the continued possession of the property, not necessarily in

---

[1] In early English law, the term idiot referred to persons who, today, we call developmentally delayed, or, to use an increasingly out-of-favor term, mentally retarded. The term lunatic was employed to describe a person with mental illness.

[2] *See* Tracy A. Thomas, *Elizabeth Cady Stanton and the Feminist Foundations of Family Law* (2016).

the enjoyment of the usual benefits of property ownership."[3] Following Mississippi's lead, other states adopted married women's property acts.[4]

Divorce was uncommon during the nineteenth century. When a divorce action was commenced, legal rules derived from England (only partially alleviated by married women's property acts) combined with then-common forms of property ownership to form a double disadvantage for women. Recall that by the old law, a married woman's property was controlled by her husband. Thus, a wife's property rested in the hands of the man she was divorcing. Add that it was common for title to property to be in the husband's name alone. Thus, the family home or farm typically stood in the husband's name. As well, some courts held that the husband was presumed to be the owner of all personal property.

Throughout the nineteenth century and into the twentieth, divorce courts in non-community property states typically assigned property based on title or ownership. The American Law Institute's *Principles of the Law of Family Dissolution* observe, "Under the traditional common-law system there was no concept of marital property. Even after a long marriage the divorce court had no general authority to allocate to one spouse property whose title was held by the other spouse or which was acquired with the other spouse's earnings."[5] Under the "title theory" of marital property, the

---

[3] Amanda Sims, *Patriarchy and Property: The Nineteenth-Century Mississippi Married Women's Property Acts*. Thesis submitted to the faculty of Brigham Young University, Department of History, August, 2007, p. 8.

[4] *See* Stall v. Fulton, 30 N.J.L. 430 (N.J. 1863)(the court quotes the married women's property act of 1852: "that it shall be lawful for any married female to receive, by gift, grant, devise, or bequest, and hold to her sole and separate use, as if she were a single female, real and personal property, and the rents, issues, and profits thereof; and the same shall not be subject to the disposal of her husband, nor be liable for his debts."); Ellen Dannin, *Marriage and Law Reform: Lessons from the Nineteenth-Century Michigan Married Women's Property Acts*, 20 Texas Journal of Women and the Law 1 (2010).

[5] American Law Institute, *Principles of the Law of Family Dissolution: Analysis and Recommendations*, p. 648 (2000) ("Equitable doctrines such as constructive trust were occasionally employed to justify departure from these legal rules, but in many common-law states their use was closely constrained. The traditional homemaker thus could leave a 40-year marriage with essentially no property, even though her husband had created a valuable business during the marriage, relying in part on her assistance." *Id.*).

judge's job was simple: determine who held title or ownership and assign property accordingly.

Consider the hypothetical couple Willodene and Henry, who married in 1920. They lived in a non-community property, "title theory" state. Henry worked full time. Willodene stayed home and raised the children. They purchased a home and put title in Henry's name. All mortgage payments were from Henry's income from work. In 1930, Henry purchased a farm, putting title in his name. Mortgage payments on the farm were from Henry's earnings at work. They bought a car, a truck, and a tractor, putting title in Henry's name. Their bank account was in Henry's name. Under the title theory of marital property, when Willodene and Henry divorce in 1935, Henry owns everything! If Willodene wanted an interest in titled property, she should have taken concurrent title with Henry. Deprived of any interest in "Henry's property," Willodene's only remedy was alimony or, if it existed in her state, the ancient remedy of dower.

Another example of the harsh impact of the title theory comes from the 1971 divorce of Jane and Edward Wirth, in New York.[6] Jane and Edward were married 22 years. Both worked outside the home. Fifteen years before they divorced, Edward started a "crash savings program" with his paycheck, telling Jane he was saving "for the two of us for our latter days." From then on, family expenses were paid mostly with Jane's income, while Edward invested his paycheck in his own name. That is, Jane used her paycheck to support the family, while Edward invested his paycheck. On divorce, Jane argued that some of Edward's investments should be awarded to her. Under the title theory then in force in New York, however, Edward was the "owner" of his investments, and Jane was out of luck.

Chinks in the title theory developed in the first half of the twentieth century. Brett Turner writes, "Legislatures began passing statutes permitting the court to award the wife a share of the property to which she had directly contributed. These statutes were passed not all at once, but rather gradually over a period of years.... None of these enactments were equitable distribution

---

[6] Wirth v. Wirth, 38 A.D.2d 611, 326 N.Y.S.2d 308 (1971).

statutes in the modern sense."[7] Turner continues, "By the mid-1960s, the American law of divorce in general was well out of line with popular notions of sex roles and marriage."[8]

In 1970, the National Conference of Commissioners on Uniform State Laws took a major step forward with promulgation of the *Uniform Marriage and Divorce Act* (UMDA). Although the UMDA is most famous for introducing no-fault divorce, the UMDA also recommended abandonment of the title theory of property, and adoption of equitable distribution. Turner writes, "The property division of the UMDA can fairly be called the first equitable distribution statute."[9] By the 1980s, all non-community property states had adopted some form of equitable distribution.

The UMDA recommended a dual classification system in which property is either marital or separate. Marital property is property acquired during marriage through the effort of either spouse. Separate property is property acquired before marriage and property acquired during marriage by bequest, devise, or gift. Upon divorce, separate property belongs to the owner, while marital property is divided equitably. Today, equitable distribution states recognize the distinction between separate and marital property. Most equitable distribution states begin with a presumption that marital property should be divided equally.

§ 4.3(b) Community Property

Switching from equitable distribution to community property, the history is easier to tell. Today's community property system derives not from England, where husband and wife were one, and husband was "the one," but from continental Europe. Louisiana's community property system devolved from France. Other community property states inherited their systems from Spain. France and Spain found inspiration in early German and Roman law.

California's community property system comes to us via Mexico. You recall from your high school class on California history

---

[7] Brett R. Turner, *Equitable Distribution of Property*, § 1:3, pp. 8–9 (3d ed. 2005).

[8] *Id.* at 12.

[9] *Id.* at 16.

that prior to the Mexican-American war (1846–1848), California was part of Mexico. It is not surprising that when California separated from Mexico in 1848, the Mexican system of community property—already firmly ensconced—was in large measure retained.

Gold was discovered in 1849, and along with thousands of miners, lawyers crossed the Sierra Nevada. Lawyers from eastern states cut their legal teeth on Blackstone's *Commentaries* describing English law, not on Mexican community property law. When California became a state in 1850, the first community property laws blended principles of Mexican community property law and English marital property law.

The hallmark of the community property system is that marriage is a partnership and that property acquired through the effort or skill of either "partner" belongs to the community. Property that is not community is separate. Like the definition of separate property in equitable distribution states, community property jurisdictions define separate property as property acquired before marriage and acquisitions during marriage by gift, descent, or devise.

§ 4.4 Marital Property Law in Other States

Across the United States, marital/community property is generally defined as any property, real or personal, acquired during marriage through the time, effort, energy, or skill of a married person. As explained by the New York Court of Appeals, "Marital property is broadly defined as all property acquired by either or both spouses during the marriage."[10] The Texas Court of Appeal wrote, "Under Texas law, property possessed by either spouse during or on dissolution of the marriage is presumed to be community . . . ."[11] Marriage is an economic partnership, and property generated by either partner belongs to both. Thus, a spouse's paycheck is marital/community property. As well, pension benefits that are derived from

---

[10] Price v. Price, 69 N.Y.2d 8, 12, 503 N.E.2d 684 (1986).
[11] Sink v. Sink, 364 S.W.3d 340, 344 (Tex. Ct. App. 2012). The court went on to say, "[A] party who seeks to assert the separate character of property must prove that character by clear and convincing evidence."

employment are marital/community property to the extent acquired during marriage.

Alaska has an interesting law regarding marital property. In *McLaren v. McLaren*, 268 P.3d 323 (Alaska 2012), the Alaska Supreme Court stated, "Property acquired by a couple prior to marriage may be considered marital if the property was acquired during premarital cohabitation. The general rule is that courts divide property acquired only during marriage. But so long as the parties do marry, the trial court is free to consider the parties' entire relationship, including any period(s) of premarital cohabitation...."

Outside California, separate property is defined as property acquired before marriage as well as property acquired during marriage by gift, bequest, devise, or descent. On divorce, separate property belongs, in most states, to the owner, and is not divided.

§ 4.5 All Property States

In approximately 15 states, judges have authority to divide all property, including separate property. In Massachusetts, for example, "the court may assign to either husband or wife all or any part of the estate of the other...."[12] Connecticut is an "all-property" state.[13] A Connecticut family court "may assign to either the husband or wife all or any part of the estate of the other."[14] Indiana law states, "In an action for dissolution of marriage, the court shall divide the property of the parties, whether: (1) owned by either spouse before marriage; (2) acquired by either spouse in his or her own right: (A) after the marriage; and (B) before final separation of the parties; or (3) acquired by their joint efforts."[15] In his book titled *Equitable Distribution of Property*, Brett Turner writes:

> The all-property system reaches fairer results in practice than one might at first suspect. Because the court can divide any asset owned by either party, it is possible in theory that the court might divide assets which have no connection with the marital partnership. In practice,

---

[12] Mass. Gen. Laws. Ann. Ch. 208, § 34. *See* Williams v. Massa, 431 Mass. 619, 728 N.E.2d 932 (2000).

[13] Krafick v. Krafick, 234 Conn. 783, 663 A.2d 365, 370 (1995).

[14] Conn. Gen. Stat. Ann. § 46b–81(a).

[15] Ind. Code Ann. § 31–15–7–4(a).

however, this is rarely done. Every all-property system includes contributions to acquisition as an equitable distribution factor, and under this factor property acquired from a nonmarital source is frequently divided unequally. When a substantial award of such property is made, the award is frequently justified by such valid equitable reasons as financial need. As a whole, therefore, decisions under the all-property system are generally consistent with the marital partnership theory and modern notions of fair division.

The major weaknesses of the all-property system are predictability and consistency.[16]

§ 4.6 Mortgage, Deed of Trust, and Encumbrance

Ubiquitous in the discussion of community property are mortgages, deeds of trust, and encumbrances. This section briefly introduces these terms.

A mortgage is a lien on property to secure repayment of a debt (Civil Code § 2920). A mortgage must be in writing and signed by the mortgagor. The debt is evidenced by a promissory note. A mortgagor owns the mortgaged property, and may sell the property, subject to the mortgage lien. Sale does not relieve the mortgagor of liability for the debt unless the mortgagee releases the mortgagor from liability. If the mortgagor defaults on the loan, the mortgagee can foreclose the mortgage, sell the property, and satisfy the indebtedness out of the proceeds of the sale.

A deed of trust, like a mortgage, secures repayment of a debt, and is, in effect, a lien on property. With a deed of trust, property is conveyed in trust to secure repayment of a debt. The trustee has authority to sell the property if the debt is not paid.

An encumbrance is a charge, burden, obstacle, or impairment on property that can impede transfer. Examples include a covenant running with the land, building restrictions, a right of way, an easement, condemnation proceeding, and a deed of trust. Civil Code

---

[16] Brett R. Turner, *Equitable Distribution of Property*. Vol. 1, § 2:8 (3d ed. 2005).

§ 1114 states, "The term 'incumbrance' includes taxes, assessments, and all liens upon real property."

Chapter 5

CHARACTERIZATION AND PRESUMPTIONS

Analysis

§ 5.1	Characterization of Property in California
§ 5.2	Presumptions Characterize Property as Community or Separate
§ 5.3	Presumptions in California Law
§ 5.4	Basics of Characterization—Family Code §§ 760 and 770
§ 5.5	Separate Property
§ 5.6	Quasi-Community Property
§ 5.7	Exercises on Characterization
§ 5.8	Long Marriage Presumption
§ 5.9	Tracing
§ 5.10	Pro Rata Apportionment
§ 5.11	Source of Funds and Inception of Title
§ 5.12	Beginning and End of the Community—Date of Separation
§ 5.13	Form of Title Presumptions
§ 5.14	Title in One Spouse's Name
§ 5.15	Concurrent Ownership
§ 5.16	Concurrent Ownership During Marriage
§ 5.17	Concurrent Ownership When Marriage Ends in Divorce—Family Code § 2581
§ 5.18	When Marriage Ends in Divorce: Reimbursement of Separate Property Contribution to Community Property—Family Code § 2640
§ 5.19	*Lucas* Gift Presumption—§ 2640 Is Not Retroactive
§ 5.20	Exercises with Family Code §§ 2581 and 2640
§ 5.21	Community Property Contributions to Separate Property: *Moore/Marsden* Apportionment
§ 5.22	Married Woman's Separate Property Presumption

§ 5.1 Characterization of Property in California

In California family law there are two types of property: Community property and separate property. The daily task of family law judges and attorneys is deciding whether items of property are separate, community, or a blend of the two. This process is called "characterization." Much of what you learn in this book concerns characterization of assets and debts.

§ 5.2 Presumptions Characterize Property as Community or Separate —MEMORIZE!!!

California law employs presumptions to help characterize property as separate or community. Presumptions do not solve all characterization issues, but presumptions play a central role in the community property system.

With each presumption discussed in this chapter, understand three things: (1) When does the presumption apply? (2) What does the presumption do? And (3) How is the presumption rebutted? To help get started, here are brief descriptions of critical presumptions, each of which is developed later:

- **General Community Property Presumption.** Real or personal property acquired during marriage and before separation by a married person while domiciled in California is presumed to be community property. The source of the general community property presumption is Family Code § 760.[1] Rebuttal is by tracing to a separate property source.

- **Long Marriage Presumption.** The long marriage presumption is a corollary of the general community property presumption. When a long marriage—typically, ten years or more—ends in divorce, it sometimes happens that no one remembers *when* an item of property was acquired. When this occurs, the general community property presumption is *not* triggered because the general community property

---

[1] The general community property presumption was adopted by the Legislature in 1850. In re Brace, 9 Cal. 5th 903, 918, 470 P.3d 15, 266 Cal. Rptr 3d 298 (2020).

presumption requires proof of the time of acquisition. If the item of property was *possessed* during a long marriage, the item is presumed to have been *acquired* during marriage, thus triggering the general community property presumption.

- **Property in Joint Tenancy.** Property acquired during marriage and prior to separation in joint tenancy is presumed to be community property during marriage (§ 760). Rebuttal is by tracing. If the marriage ends in divorce, the presumption in § 2581 applies to characterize the property as community property. After January 1, 1984, rebuttal of the § 2581 presumption must be in writing (§ 2581(a) and (b)).

- **Married Woman's Separate Property Presumption.** Property acquired prior to January 1, 1975 by a married woman by an instrument in writing is presumed to be the woman's separate property. Rebuttal is by tracing plus the husband's testimony that he did not intend a gift of his interest to wife.

- *Lucas* **Gift Presumption.** The *Lucas* gift presumption derives from the Supreme Court's decision in *Marriage of Lucas*, 27 Cal. 3d 808, 614 P.2d 285, 166 Cal. Rptr. 853 (1980). The Supreme Court ruled that when a spouse contributed separate property to the acquisition of community property, the spouse contributing separate property intended to gift the separate property to the community, and the donor spouse could not seek reimbursement of the separate property. The *Lucas* gift presumption ended January 1, 1984 with the enactment of § 2640.

- **Joint Bank Account.** Deposits by married persons to a joint account are presumed to be community property (Probate Code § 5305(a)). The community property presumption established by Probate Code § 5305(a) can be rebutted by tracing to separate property unless the couple has a written agreement that the funds in the account are community property.[2]

- **Family Expense Presumption.** The family expense presumption is a court-created rule invoked with commingled bank accounts. (*See* § 7.7). The presumption holds that family expenses are presumed to be paid with available community property rather than separate property.

§ 5.3 Presumptions in California Law

The California Evidence Code (CEC) sets forth two types of presumptions: Conclusive and rebuttable (CEC § 601). Rebuttable presumptions are of two types: (1) rebuttable presumptions affecting the burden of producing evidence and (2) rebuttable presumptions affecting the burden of proof (CEC §§ 603–606).

A conclusive presumption is not really a presumption. A conclusive presumption is a rule of law. When lawyers think of presumptions, they generally have in mind rebuttable presumptions: A presumption that can be rebutted with evidence. A true conclusive presumption cannot be rebutted with any amount of proof—it is irrebuttable. True conclusive presumptions are rare, although one is created by Family Code § 803, discussed in § 5.18. At common law there was a conclusive presumption that a baby born to a woman cohabiting with her husband who was not impotent or sterile was conclusively presumed to be a child of the marriage. This is not really a presumption: It is a rule of law. If the basic facts—married, living together, not impotent—were established, then the presumed fact—parentage—was conclusively established. Evidence to rebut the presumed fact was not admissible. Today, with DNA paternity testing, this presumption has been softened—it is no longer conclusive.

---

[2] Although a joint bank account is held in joint ownership, do not apply Family Code § 2581 to joint bank accounts.

§ 5.3(a) Presumption and Inference Explained

To understand presumptions, you need to understand the difference between an inference and a presumption. CEC § 600 defines the terms:

CEC § 600. "Presumption" and "Inference" Defined.

(a) A presumption is an assumption of fact that the law *requires* to be made from another fact or group of facts [the basic facts] found or otherwise established in the action. A presumption is not evidence.

(b) An inference is a deduction of fact that *may* logically and reasonably be drawn from another fact or group of facts found or otherwise established in the action. (emphasis added).

An inference is simply a thought process by which a person reasons from one thing to another—from an item of evidence to a conclusion. You draw inferences all the time. Suppose, for example, that on your driveway this morning you found the local newspaper. It is reasonable to infer the paper was tossed there by the paper delivery person. You infer how the paper got on the driveway from your experience. You don't actually know how the paper got there because you were asleep when it arrived. Nevertheless, you feel comfortable concluding the delivery person tossed it. If the question of who delivered your paper should somehow find its way into litigation—unlikely—the jury would be permitted to draw the same inference you drew about the paper. The jury would not be required to draw the inference, but could draw it if it chose to.

An inference, then, is a thought process. A person reasons from one fact to another: You look outside and see someone raise an umbrella: you infer it is raining. You see your friend emerge from the student recreation center all sweaty: you infer she was exercising.

Now, contrast an inference with a presumption. Like an inference, a presumption is not evidence. A presumption, like an inference, is a thought process; a process of reasoning from an item of evidence to a conclusion. The conclusion is the "presumed fact." The evidence leading to the presumed fact is the "basic facts." With a presumption, if the trier of fact finds the basic facts true, it is *required* to find the presumed fact true.³

There is a presumption that a letter correctly addressed and properly mailed with the right postage was received in the ordinary course of the mail. (CEC § 641). The basic facts are that the letter was correctly addressed and properly mailed, with the right postage. If the basic facts are established, then the trier of fact, *must* find the existence of the presumed fact—the letter was received. Proof of the basic facts brings the presumption into the case. If the party who denies the letter arrived does nothing to rebut the presumption, the jury will be instructed that it must find the presumed fact of delivery. So, it behooves the party denying receipt of the letter to do something! What? Offer evidence to rebut the presumption. For example, a witness could testify the letter was not received. The witness's testimony is sufficient to rebut the presumption. The jury may conclude the letter was received on the basis of permissible inferences from the evidence, but no presumption is involved.

To summarize, a presumption *requires* the trier of fact to conclude that one fact (presumed fact) exists if other facts (basic facts) exist. In the case of the letter, the trier of fact must conclude the letter was received in the ordinary course of the mail because a presumption applies. With the newspaper on your driveway, by contrast, the trier of fact is not compelled to conclude the delivery person delivered the newspaper because there is no presumption a paper was delivered by a delivery person.

§ 5.3(b) Burden of Producing Evidence and Burden of Proof

As mentioned above, there are two kinds of rebuttable presumptions: presumptions affecting the burden of proof, and presumptions affecting the burden of producing evidence. To understand the difference, you need to understand (1) the burden of producing evidence, or, as it is commonly called, the burden of going forward with evidence, and (2) the burden of persuasion, also known as the burden of proof.

---

[3] The trier of fact is required to find the presumed fact true unless the party against whom the presumption operates offers enough evidence to rebut the presumption.

The burden of producing evidence is the obligation of a party, at the proper point in a trial, to present evidence on an issue (CEC § 550). The evidence produced must be sufficient to permit the trier of fact to act on the evidence. In a negligence action, for example, plaintiff has the burden of producing evidence of defendant's negligence. The penalty for failing to produce evidence is that the judge rules against the party with the burden of production. If the plaintiff in the negligence suit fails to produce evidence of defendant's negligence, plaintiff is tossed out of court.

The burden of going forward with evidence (CEC § 550) must be distinguished from the burden of persuasion (burden of proof). The burden of proof is the burden of convincing the trier of fact that a fact is true. CEC § 500 states, "Except as otherwise provided by law, a party has the burden of proof as to each fact the existence or nonexistence of which is essential to the claim for relief or defense that he is asserting."

The presence in a civil case of a presumption can cause either or both of the burdens to shift from the party who started with the burden(s) to the other party! That is worth repeating. *A presumption can shift the burden of production and/or the burden of proof from one party to the other*. If your client has a burden of production or a burden of proof, and you invoke a presumption, you can shift one or both burdens to your opponent. You would like that, wouldn't you?

§ 5.3(c) Presumption Affecting Burden of Producing Evidence

A presumption affecting the burden of producing evidence arises when the party desiring the presumption proves the basic facts. The party against whom the presumption operates can rebut the presumption by offering evidence the judge believes is sufficient to prove the non-existence of the presumed fact. As soon as the rebuttal evidence is admitted, the presumption disappears from the case.

§ 5.3(d) Presumption Affecting Burden of Proof

In California community property law, the presumptions that are relevant to characterization of property are presumptions affecting the burden of proof. A presumption affecting the burden of proof shifts the burden of proof on an issue from the party who started with the burden to the other party. For example, under the general community property presumption, the spouse seeking to invoke the presumption has the burden of proving the basic facts—the property was acquired during marriage while domiciled in California. Proof of the basic facts raises the community property presumption. The burden of proof then shifts to the spouse seeking to prove the property is separate property—the separatizer—to rebut the presumption. If the separatizer fails to carry the burden of proof, the presumption stands and the property is characterized as community property.

§ 5.4 Basics of Characterization—Family Code §§ 760 and 770

This section introduces basic principles of characterization of assets. Characterization of debts is discussed in Chapter 9. When you confront a characterization problem, a good starting place is the general community property presumption. The general community property presumption is derived from Family Code § 760. Section 760 is the bedrock of California community property law:

> Except as otherwise provided by statute, all property, real or personal, wherever situated, acquired by a married person during marriage [and prior to separation] while domiciled in this state is community property.

The bracketed words [and prior to separation] are added to § 760 to clarify that property earned after a couple separates is generally separate property. The meaning of separation is addressed in § 5.12.

According to the general community property presumption, anything produced by the time, effort, energy, or skill of a married person is presumptively community property.[4] Thus, a married

---

[4] *See* Trenk v. Soheili, 58 Cal. App. 5th 1033, 273 Cal. Rptr. 3d 184 (2020) ("Under the plain language of Family Code section 760, the presumption that particular property belongs to the community applies whenever the property is acquired by a married person while domiciled in this state. The statute does not contain any requirement that the source of funds used to purchase the property must be proved before the presumption arises. To the contrary: The law is clear that the presumptions may be rebutted with proof that separate funds were used to purchase the property as issue.").

person's paycheck is community property, as is the person's employment-related pension. When a married person writes a book, royalties are community property. A copyright interest can be community property. If a married attorney takes a case on a continent fee and earns the fee during marriage, the fee is community property even if the fee is paid after the attorney separates from her spouse. The important point is not when the contingent fee is received, but when the fee was earned.

Suppose one spouse steals someone else's property or makes money selling illegal drugs. Are the profits of crime community property? The answer appears to be "yes."

Spouses have equal interests in community property. Family Code § 751, states, "The respective interests of each spouse in community property during continuance of the marriage relation are present, existing, and equal interests."

§ 5.5 Separate Property

Once you understand the general community property presumption created by § 760, turn your attention to separate property, defined in Family Code § 770:

> (a) Separate property of a married person includes all of the following: (1) All property owned by the person before marriage. (2) All property acquired by the person [during marriage and prior to separation] by gift, bequest, devise, or descent. (3) The rents, issues, and profits of the property described in this section.
>
> (b) A married person may, without the consent of the person's spouse, convey the person's separate property.

Family Code § 752 provides, "Neither spouse has any interest in the separate property of the other." A non-owner spouse has no legal right to control the separate property of the owner spouse. The owner of separate property can do whatever the owner likes with separate property.

One limit on unfettered authority over separate property can occur if an investment opportunity arises and a spouse decides to take advantage of the opportunity by investing separate property at a time when community property is available for the investment. If the investing spouse did not discuss the issue with the other spouse, a conflict of interest may occur. Another limitation on discretion to deal with separate property arises when a petition for divorce is filed and served on the respondent. When this occurs, an automatic restraining order restricts both spouses from undertaking major financial transactions with community property *or* separate property until the spouses agree to a particular transaction or a judge authorizes a transaction.

§ 5.6   Quasi-Community Property

Earlier you read, "In California family law, there are two types of property: Community property and separate property." We need to tweak this statement by adding quasi-community property. Family Code § 125 defines quasi-community property:

> "Quasi-community property" means all real or personal property, wherever situated, acquired . . . in any of the following ways:
>
> (a) By either spouse while domiciled elsewhere which would have been community property if the spouse had been in this state at the time of its acquisition.
>
> (b) In exchange for real or personal property, wherever situated, which would have been community if the spouse who acquired the property so exchanged had been domiciled in this state at the time of its acquisition.

Community property and quasi-community property are treated the same when a marriage ends. Nevertheless, you should put the correct label on property—community or quasi-community—for tests and the bar.

Under the Family Code, the labels community or quasi-community depend on *where* the acquiring spouse lived when the property was acquired. If the spouse lived in California, § 760 applies and the property is community property. If the spouse lived outside California, § 125 applies and the property is quasi-community property. Consider an example: Sue and Bill are married and live in Pasadena, California. They purchase a Picasso painting for cash. Section 760 applies and the Picasso is presumptively community property. Change the facts. When Sue and Bill buy the Picasso they live in Pasadena, Florida. (Yes, there is a Pasadena, Florida). After they buy the Picasso they move to Pasadena, California, and Bill starts divorce proceedings in California. Does § 760 apply? No, because they lived in Florida when they acquired the painting. In a California divorce, the Picasso is quasi-community property pursuant to § 125.

A California family court judge can characterize property as quasi-community property if both spouses move to California and the divorce proceeds in California. If only one spouse moves to California and the other spouse continues living elsewhere, a California judge cannot characterize property as quasi-community property.[5] But what if a non-California spouse makes a general appearance in California, or asks the California judge to apply California law? It appears a California judge can characterize property as quasi-community property when a spouse who has not moved to California makes a general appearance or consents to the court's application of California law.

Quasi-community property should not be confused with quasi-marital property. The latter term applies in annulment cases to describe property when a spouse believed in good faith that the marriage was valid (§ 2251(a)(1)). *See* § 12.5.

§ 5.7 Exercises on Characterization

With the basic definitions of community property, quasi-community property, and separate property in mind, answer the following questions. In each case, a couple is getting divorced in California. Characterize the property. For purposes of these questions, ignore the source of money used to acquire the property. Apply §§ 125, 760, and 770.

1. Wife and Husband, residing in San Jose, California, purchase Blackacre, located in San Jose. Characterize Blackacre. CP

---

[5] When a California judge characterizes property as quasi-community property, the judge effectively changes the ownership of the property as ownership was defined by the law of the state where the couple lived when the property was acquired. In Estate of Thornton, 1 Cal. 2d 1, 33 P.2d 1 (1934), the Supreme Court ruled it is constitutional to do so when both spouses move to California and seek legal redress in our courts. However, when only one spouse moves to California, it violates the constitutional rights of the out-of-state spouse for a California judge to change ownership of property.

Your first question is, "What does the title to Blackacre say?" That's the right question. For these introductory exercises, however, ignore the title and characterize the property by applying §§ 125, 760, and 770. The importance of title is addressed later.

2. Wife and Husband live in Davis, California. They purchase Greenacre in Billings, Montana. Characterize Greenacre. CP

3. Wife and Husband live in Billings, Montana. They purchase a vacation home on the California side of Lake Tahoe. Years later, they move to Sacramento, California, and divorce in Sacramento. Characterize the vacation home. QP

4. Husband and wife, live in Irvine, California. Husband buys a new car at a dealership in Irvine. Characterize the car. CP Again, you want to know whose name is on the title to the car, but for this question you don't know. Apply Sections 125, 760, and 770.

5. Alice and Ron have always lived in California. Before marrying Ron, Alice purchased a race horse named "Rocket." "Rocket" produced a foal named "Rocket Booster." Characterize Booster. SP Suppose Ron owned a stallion named "Fuel," and Rocket Booster is the result of a love affair between Rocket and Fuel? GP

6. During her marriage to Ruth, Sally spent three years completing a screen play in their home in Beverly Hills, California. In 2020, Ruth and Sally separated. In 2022, the screen play was purchased for $1,000,000. Characterize the million. CP

7. Gretchen and Juan are married and live in Big Sur, California. During marriage, Juan purchased a surfboard costing $400. Juan paid half the cost with cash from his work. He paid the other half with cash given to him for his birthday by his mom. Characterize the surfboard. CP(½), SP(½)

8. When Esmeralda was single, she inherited a portfolio of stocks from her father. The portfolio was valued at $3,000,000. The portfolio is managed by a stock broker. Esmeralda takes no part in managing the portfolio. She simply enjoys the checks she receives four times a year from profits on the investments. Esmeralda marries Tim. During their ten year marriage, the portfolio doubled in value to $6,000,000. The increase is due to the investment skill of the stock broker and growth in the stock market. Esmeralda and Tim are divorcing. Characterize the original $3,000,000 portfolio. SP

Tim claims that the increase in value of the portfolio—$3,000,000—is community property because it was acquired during marriage. Is Tim right? Change the facts. Rather than leave the management of the portfolio to her stock broker, Esmeralda took an active role in managing her investments. She met weekly with the stock broker and participated in decision making about buying and selling stocks. Does Esmeralda's involvement in managing the portfolio change the characterization of the original $3,000,000? What about the increase in value during the marriage? No

9. Before marriage, Abe purchased a car dealership in Los Angeles. Then, Abe and Beth marry. Characterize the car dealership. SP Characterize Abe's paycheck for working at the dealership during marriage. Suppose, at the end of the 10 year marriage the car dealership has doubled in value. Is the increased value separate property or community property? CP

§ 5.8 Long Marriage Presumption

The long marriage presumption was created by the courts. It is not really a separate presumption. Rather, it is an aspect of the general community property presumption. The long marriage presumption applies when it is impossible to determine *when* an item of property was acquired. The general community property presumption of Section 760 applies to property acquired during marriage. However, there is no presumption regarding *when* property is acquired. Thus, if it not possible to prove the time of acquisition, the general community property presumption does not apply. The long marriage presumption solves the problem by presuming that property *possessed* during a long marriage was *acquired* during the marriage, thus triggering the general community property presumption.

How long is a long marriage? Ten years is often used as a benchmark. An attorney might persuade a judge to apply the presumption to a marriage shorter than a decade.

The long marriage presumption arises when three conditions are established. First, the marriage is sufficiently long. Second, the date of acquisition is unknown, often because the item was acquired so long ago no one remembers. Third, the item was *possessed* during marriage. Normally, it is easy to prove an item was possessed during marriage.

Consider the following example: Fran and Fred married in 1990. At some point during the marriage—no one can remember when, except it was a long time ago—Fran purchased a sculpture by Michelangelo. Yes, *that* Michelangelo! Today, Fran and Fred are divorcing. There is no paperwork evidencing the purchase; nothing to document the date of purchase. Fran claims the sculpture is her separate property. Fred argues it is community property. How should the sculpture be characterized?

§ 5.9 Tracing

Tracing plays a pivotal role in characterization. Most of the time, tracing involves discovering what money paid for an item of property. It gets more complicated, but that's the basic idea. In a typical divorce, a family law attorney is presented with items of property: a farm, a home, a car, a boat, a pension, etc. If an item meets the requirements of the general community property presumption (§ 760), the item is presumed to be community property. If this characterization suits the client, great. However, if the client claims the item is the client's separate property, the attorney has to rebut the general community property presumption. The general community property presumption is rebutted by tracing the funds used to buy the item to separate property. The party seeking to rebut the general community property presumption has the burden of proof by a preponderance of the evidence.[6]

Consider four examples. First, a divorcing couple cannot agree on how to characterize a valuable vase. Wife claims the vase is community property. Husband argues it is his separate property. Wife proves that the vase was acquired during marriage and falls under the general community property presumption. Rebuttal of the general community property presumption is by tracing. If husband can trace the money used to buy the vase to his separate property, he will rebut the community property presumption and the vase will be his separate property. Husband's burden of proof is a

---

[6] *See* Marriage of Valli, 58 Cal. 4th 1396, 1400, 324 P.3d 274, 171 Cal. Rptr. 3d 454 (2014) ("A spouse's claim that property acquired during marriage is separate property must be proven by a preponderance of the evidence.").

preponderance of the evidence. If husband fails to present sufficient evidence—fails to carry his burden of proof—his effort to trace fails and the community property presumption stands.

Second, divorcing spouses, Daenerys (Dany) Targaryen and Jon Snow, cannot agree on whether an antique sword is community or separate. Jon invokes the general community property presumption. The presumption applies because the sword was acquired during marriage. To rebut the presumption and claim the sword as her separate property, Dany must trace. As it turns out, two years ago the sword was traded for a baby dragon. Dany purchased the dragon during the marriage, so the little fire breather falls under the general community property presumption. All is not lost for Dany, however, if she can trace the money used to purchase the dragon to an inheritance she received from her father. Assuming Dany can prove the money for the dragon came from the inheritance, she will succeed in rebutting the community property presumption. This question teaches us three lessons. First, a change in form of property does not change its character.[7] Exchanging a dragon for a sword does not change the characterization of the property. Second, it is possible to trace back through multiple changes in form. Third, *Game of Thornes* is real, not some TV show.

Third, Husband and Wife purchased the family home in 2010, putting title in both their names as joint tenants. The down payment of $45,000 was from Wife's separate property. Monthly mortgage payments are paid with community property. The couple is divorcing. Wife believes the house is part community property and part her separate property because of her separate property down payment. Later, you will learn that when property is held as joint tenants, on divorce the property is presumed to be entirely community property (Family Code § 2581. *See* § 5.17). If the presumption holds, the house is 100% community property. If Wife can trace the down payment to separate property, she is entitled to be reimbursed the $45,000 down payment (Family Code § 2640. *See* § 5.18). If the Section 2581 presumption is rebutted, then wife can

---

[7] *See* Marriage of Bonvino, 241 Cal. App. 4th 1411, 1423, 194 Cal. Rptr. 3d 754 (2015) ("Separate property does not change character simply because the owner is married, or the property is used in the marital relationship, or the property changes form or identity.")

press her argument that the house is part separate property and party community property (*See* § 5.10).

Fourth, Wife and Husband have a joint bank account into which they deposit their paychecks from work (community property). Into the same account they also deposit separate property each receives from income producing properties owned prior to marriage. The bank account contains community property and separate property and is referred to as a commingled account. If the couple divorces, one or both may want to characterize the money still in the account, or to characterize property purchased with money from the account. To characterize money in or withdrawn from a commingled account, it is necessary to trace the funds deposited and withdrawn to separate or community sources. California uses two tracing techniques to follow the money, discussed in § 7.7.

§ 5.10 Pro Rata Apportionment

When separate and community funds contribute to the acquisition of property, the property is normally part community and part separate. Ownership is based on the relative contributions to the property of community and separate property. This is called pro rata or pro tanto apportionment.

Consider a simple example. Hillary and Bill are married and live in Carmel-by-the-Sea, California, just south of Monterey. Both are avid surfers. Hillary buys a surfboard for $1,000, paying $500 of community property and $500 of her separate property. If Hillary and Bill divorce and can't agree about the surfboard, how will it be characterized? A surfboard has no title. In this situation, California looks to the source of funds used to purchase the property. As a result, the surfboard is half separate and half community. Characterization of the surfboard is tied to the relative contributions of separate and community property to the purchase.

The surfboard is easy: half and half. But what about the following? Before Hillary married Bill five years ago, Hillary purchased a home on Scenic Road in Carmel-by-the-Sea. Scenic Road is one of America's most expensive addresses. The home is 100 feet from the Pacific Ocean, with an unobstructed view of the beach and the water—a view worth its weight in gold. Hillary purchased the small, forty-year-old house for $7 million. She put $500,000 down and financed the balance with a loan from the bank, secured by a mortgage. Before marriage, monthly mortgage payments were obviously made with separate property. When Hillary and Bill married, mortgage payments were made with earnings from Hillary's employment—community property. If Hillary and Bill divorce, how should the Scenic Road home be characterized? Title is in Hillary's name alone since she was single when she acquired the property.[8] At the time of divorce, the home is worth $10 million. Should the home be treated like the surfboard?—pro rata apportionment based on the relative contributions of community and separate property? The answer is, yes. Under the source of funds rule, California courts use a formula to determine the separate and community shares. The formula is described in § 5.21.

Consider a final example. Jennifer and Chase marry in 2015, and shortly thereafter purchase a home, taking title as joint tenants with right of survivorship. The down payment on the home is from an inheritance Jennifer received from her parents (separate property). Monthly mortgage payments are made with funds from Jennifer and Chase's employment (community property). The two are divorcing. Section 2581 of the Family Code applies. (*See* § 5.17). Under § 2581, the property is 100% community property. Tracing to separate property will *not* rebut the § 2581 presumption. Because of § 2581, there is no pro rata apportionment. Jennifer may be entitled to reimbursement of her separate property contribution, but the property is *entirely* community property.

§ 5.11 Source of Funds and Inception of Title

When separate funds and community funds contribute to a purchase, community property states utilize the source of funds approach *or* the inception of title approach to characterize the property. In *Harper v. Harper*, 294 Md. 54, 448 A.2d 916 (1982), the Maryland Court of Appeal explained:

---

[8] During marriage, a spouse who holds title to property in their name alone can convey the property to the couple by an interspousal transfer deed, a quitclaim deed, or a warranty deed. The grantee spouse must accept the deed for the conveyance to be effective. The transaction is a transmutation. *See* Marriage of Wozniak, 59 Cal. App. 5th 120, 273 Cal. Rptr. 3d 421 (2020).

Courts in the majority of community property states in which the question has been considered have held that real property paid for in part before marriage and in part during marriage remains the separate property of the spouse who made the payments before marriage. The rationale underlying this rule is the inception of title theory.... The status of property as separate or community property is fixed as of the time when it is acquired. The word "acquired" contemplates the inception of title....

Courts in at least one community property state, California, have rejected the inception of title theory. In California, when real property is paid for in part before marriage from a spouse's separate funds and in part during marriage from community funds..., such property ... [is] characterized as part separate and part community. Under the California rule, the spouse contributing separate funds is entitled to a pro tanto separate property interest in such property ... in the ratio of the separate investment to the total separate and community investment in the property. Similarly, the community is entitled to a pro tanto community property interest in such property ... in the ratio of the community investment to the total separate and community investment in the property.

For most situations, California courts use the source of funds rule to characterize property: The court asks, What money paid for property? However, a California judge uses the inception of title theory when it makes sense to do so. For example, in *Marriage of Joaquin*, 193 Cal. App. 3d 1529, 239 Cal. Rptr. 175 (1987), prior to marrying Janiece, Steven executed a five year lease of his father's walnut orchard. The lease had an option to renew for an additional five years. During marriage, Steven operated the orchard and exercised the option to renew the lease. On divorce, Janiece claimed the renewed leasehold was community property because the renewal was "acquired" during marriage. Steven argued the leasehold was separate property because he acquired the option to renew prior to marriage. The Court of Appeal sided with Steven.

The court applied the inception of title theory to rule that Steven acquired the option before marriage.

§ 5.12 Beginning and End of the Community—Date of Separation

The community property system begins the moment the official presiding at the wedding says, "I now pronounce you married." Couples who do not want the community property system to apply to them can opt out with a premarital agreement (*See* Chapter 3).

The community property system ends when a couple separates. Family Code § 771(a) provides: "The earnings and accumulations of a spouse . . . after the date of separation of the spouses are the separate property of the spouse." Thus, a married person's paycheck for the two weeks prior to separation is community property. The person's paycheck for the two weeks following separation is separate property. Contributions to the person's retirement pension for the period prior to separation are community property. Contributions for the period following separation are separate property.

For community property purposes, a couple separates when at least one spouse decides the marriage is over *and* a spouse takes steps indicating an end of the economic community. In 2015, in *Marriage of Davis,* 61 Cal. 4th 846, 352 P.3d 401, 189 Cal. Rptr. 3d 835 (2015) the Supreme Court ruled that in nearly all cases, a couple must live separately to be "separated." The Legislature abrogated *Davis* in 2017 with Family Code § 70, which provides:

> (a) "Date of separation" means the date that a complete and final break in the marital relationship has occurred, as evidenced by both of the following:
>
>> (1) The spouse has expressed to the other spouse his or her intent to end the marriage.
>>
>> (2) The conduct of the spouse is consistent with his or her intent to end the marriage.
>
> (b) In determining the date of separation, the court shall take into consideration all relevant evidence.

Under § 70, it is possible, albeit difficult, to be separated while living under the same roof. The court considers the totality of circumstances to determine the date of separation.

For many couples, the date of separation is not important. For some couples, however, the date of separation has major financial implications, and such couples may litigate the separation date. Consider an example: Dell and Denise married in 2005. When they married, Dell was finishing a Ph.D. in history. Denise had her masters in computer science, and she took a job as a software engineer at a Silicon Valley startup. Now, the couple is divorcing. Dell teaches history at West Valley Community College in Saratoga, California. He makes a decent, albeit modest, income. Denise's company started small, but beginning in 2019, the company hit the big time. In 2020, Denise's salary increased from $150,000 a year to $2,000,000 a year, plus generous stock options that will be worth millions. In the divorce, Denise claims the parties separated in 2017 when Dell moved out of their condo and into his own apartment. For his part, Dell argues separation did not occur until the Petition for Divorce was filed, in 2021. If Denise is right, the community ended in 2017, and her vastly increased income starting in 2020, and the stock options, are her separate property. If Dell is right, all of Denise's income and stock options, up to filing the petition are community property.

Another situation in which the date of separation has important financial implications involves pensions. As you know, during marriage and prior to separation, employment-related pension contributions are community property. Consider Juanita and Juan. Juanita works for the State, and has a CalPERS pension. Juan owns his own business, and does not have a pension. Juanita and Juan married in 2013. Juan moved out after an argument in 2018. In 2022, Juan filed for divorce. What is the date of separation? If the date is 2018, then all of Juanita's post-2018 contributions to her pension are her separate property, and more of her pension belongs to her. But if the date of separation is 2022, more of the pension is community property belonging half to Juan.

What is the proper date of separation in the following case? Barbara and Richard married in 2005. They are now divorcing. They have two kids, aged 8 and 10. Barbara is a stay-at-home-parent.

Richard is an ophthalmologist, making a handsome income as an eye surgeon. In 2019, Richard left the family home and took up residence on his boat. He soon moved his young receptionist/girlfriend onto the boat with him. Although Richard never returned to live at home, he often ate dinner there with Barbara and the kids. Richard continued to receive his non-business mail at the family home. Two or three times a year, Richard, Barbara, and the children went on "family" vacations. Richard and Barbara often went, as a couple, to parties at friends' homes and to professional meetings of doctors. Richard regularly sent Barbara gifts for her birthday and their anniversary. The kids' school records list the parents as married. Barbara and Richard filed joint tax returns. Richard paid all the household expenses and the mortgage. Richard provided financial support for Barbara and the children. Richard regularly brought his laundry home and Barbara washed and ironed his clothes. Richard and Barbara did not have sex after Richard left in 2019. Barbara knew about the girlfriend, but hoped Richard would eventually return. Richard did not tell Barbara he never intended to reunify. In the divorce, Richard argues the date of separation was 2019, when he moved to the boat. Barbara argues the date of separation should be the date the Petition for divorce is filed in 2023. If Richard is right, all of his income after 2019 is his separate property. If Barbara is right, all that income is community property. What is the proper date of separation? (*Marriage of Baragry*, 73 Cal. App. 3d 444, 140 Cal. Rptr. 779 (1977)).

§ 5.13 Form of Title Presumptions

Some property has a title. Other property does not have a title. Estates in land have a title evidenced by the deed creating the estate. Cars and trucks have title documents issued by DMV. Airplanes and many boats have title documents. Stock certificates are a form of title ownership. Many items of personal property lack formal title. Your $40,000 Rolex watch lacks a title, as does your cell phone and your energy drink. For property with a title, California community property law establishes certain presumptions based on the way title is held—form of title presumptions.

Evidence Code § 662 creates a form of title presumption that "the owner of the legal title to property is presumed to be the owner of the full beneficial title." Family Code § 760 provides that property acquired during marriage is presumptively community property. Suppose wife purchases a car and puts title in her name alone. Does Evidence Code § 662 make the car presumptively wife's separate property? Or does Family Code § 760 control to presume the car is community property because it was acquired during marriage? In *In re Brace,* 9 Cal. 5th 903, 938, 470 P.3d 15, 266 Cal.Rptr.3d 298 (2020), the Supreme Court ruled, "Evidence Code section 662 does not apply to property acquired during marriage when it conflicts with Family Code section 760."[9]

§ 5.14 Title in One Spouse's Name

With the exception of the married woman's separate property presumption, described in § 5.22, placing title one spouse's name alone does not characterize the property as separate property. When property is acquired by a married person in that spouse's name alone, the presumption that applies is the general community property presumption of § 760.[10]

A question asked frequently of family law attorneys is: "My husband told me that because title to the truck is in his name, the truck is his. All the monthly truck payments come from our pay from work. Is he right? Is the truck his?" The answer is, the truck is not husband's separate property simply because his name is on the title. The fact that title is in his name makes no difference. What is important is what money paid for the truck. Unless wife signed a document giving husband her interest in the truck—a transmutation—the truck is community property. (For discussion of transmutations, *see* Chapter 8). The fact that DMV documents list husband as the owner does not change the characterization.

---

[9] In re Brace, 9 Cal. 5th 903, 912, 470 P.3d 15, 266 Cal. Rptr 3d 298 (2020) ("we hold that Evidence Code section 662 does not apply when it conflicts with the Family Code section 760 community property presumption. Further, we hold that when a married couple uses community funds to acquire property with joint tenancy title on or after January 1, 1975, the property is presumptively community property under Family Code section 760 in a dispute between the couple and a bankruptcy trustee.").

See also, Trenk v. Soheili, 58 Cal. App. 5th 1033, 273 Cal. Rptr. 3d 184 (2020) (post-Brace decision).

[10] *See* In re Brace, 9 Cal. 5th 903, 938, 470 P.3d 15, 266 Cal. Rptr 3d 298 (2020) ("It is true that Family Code section 760 also applies to situations where community property is titled in one spouse's name.")

§ 5.15 Concurrent Ownership

Under property law, unmarried people can own property concurrently as tenants in common or joint tenants. Married persons too can own property as tenants in common or joint tenants. In addition, married persons can own property concurrently as community property and as community property with right of survivorship. Community property with right of survivorship became available to married couples on July 1, 2001, and the right of survivorship operates identically to the right of survivorship in joint tenancy.

With joint tenancy, two or more people own undivided interests in property. Each owns the whole property.[11] Joint tenancy requires the four unities of time, title, interest, and right to possession. The hallmark of joint tenancy is the right of survivorship.[12] When one joint tenant dies, the remaining joint tenant owns the whole by operation of law. The deceased joint tenant cannot devise her interest in the property because it belongs to the survivor. For the same reason, no interest in the property passes by intestate succession. A joint tenancy can be severed (*See* Civil Code § 683.2), in which case the property becomes tenancy in common. Severance occurs when a joint tenant executes, delivers, and records a deed conveying the tenant's interest in the property. Severance can be accomplished by filing a document with the county recorder of deeds indicating intent to sever the joint tenancy.

Tenancy in common lacks the right of survivorship. A tenant in common can devise the tenant's interest in property to whomever the tenant wishes, and the interest passes by intestacy. Tenants in common can own unequal fractional interests in property.[13]

---

[11] *See* In re Brace, 9 Cal. 5th 903, 470 P.3d 15, 266 Cal. Rptr. 3d 298 (2020) ("a joint tenancy is one estate in which the rights of the spouses are identical and coextensive.").

[12] In In re Brace, 9 Cal. 5th 903, 916, 470 P.3d 15, 266 Cal. Rptr 3d 298 (2020) ("Joint tenancy creates a right of survivorship, whereby title passes to the surviving spouse without going through probate.").

[13] *See* In re Brace, 9 Cal. 5th 903, 920 470 P.3d 15, 266 Cal. Rptr. 3d 298 (2020) (with tenancy in common, "spouses can have unequal interests.").

Tenancy by the entirety does not exist in California,[14] but is available in some states. Tenancy by the entirety is a form of concurrent ownership between spouses and is similar to joint tenancy with right of survivorship.[15]

§ 5.16 Concurrent Ownership During Marriage

It is common in California for married couples to own property—most frequently the family home—as joint tenants with right of survivorship. Title is held in joint tenancy so that when the marriage ends in death, the right of survivorship applies to avoid probate. Although married couples can own property as tenants in common, this form of concurrent ownership is uncommon between California spouses.

During marriage, the community property presumption of § 760 applies to characterize property acquired in concurrent form during marriage as community property. The community property presumption can be rebutted by tracing to separate property. If the presumption is rebutted, the couple owns the property concurrently as separate property.

In *In re Brace*, 9 Cal. 5th 903, 470 P.3d 15, 266 Cal. Rptr. 3d 298 (2020), the Supreme Court analyzed the complex California history of concurrent ownership by married persons. Clifford and Ahn Brace married in 1972. They owned two properties as joint tenants. In 2011, Clifford—but not Ahn—filed for Chapter 7 bankruptcy. Under federal bankruptcy law, all community property becomes part of the bankruptcy estate subject to claims of creditors. The bankruptcy trustee claimed the Brace's two properties were community property and part of the bankruptcy estate. The trustee relied on Family Code § 760, the general community property presumption. Clifford and Ahn argued they owned their interests in the properties as separate property, relying of the presumption established by Evidence Code § 662. If Ahn's interest in the properties was her separate property, her half interest was not part

---

[14] Family Code § 750 provides, "Spouses may hold property as joint tenancy or tenants in common, or as community property, or as community property with right of survivorship." Tenancy by the entirety is absent from the list.

[15] If a couple purchases property in tenancy by the entirety while living in a state that has that form of title and then moves to California and divorces here, § 2581 applies.

of the bankruptcy estate subject to Clifford's creditors. (Family Code § 913. *See* Ch. 9). The federal bankruptcy court asked the California Supreme Court to determine which presumption applied—Evidence Code § 662 or Family Code § 760. The Supreme Court ruled, "Evidence Code section 662 does not apply when it conflicts with the Family Code section 760 presumption. Further, we hold that when a married couple uses community funds to acquire property with joint tenancy title on or after January 1, 1975, the property is presumptively community property under Family Code section 760 in a dispute between the couple and a bankruptcy trustee." (9 Cal. 5th at 912).

After *Brace*, it is clear that property acquired in concurrent ownership during marriage by a married couple domiciled in California falls under the general community property presumption of Family Code § 760. The community property presumption can be rebutted by tracing to separate property. The Supreme Court wrote, "[N]othing in our decision today precludes spouses from holding separate property as joint tenants or from transmuting community property held in joint tenancy as long as the applicable transmutation requirements are met. Nor does our opinion disturb the operation of the right of survivorship that typically accompanies joint tenancy title at death." (9 Cal. 5th at 912).

§ 5.17 Concurrent Ownership When Marriage Ends in Divorce—Family Code § 2581

When marriage ends in divorce, Family Code § 2581 is the starting place to characterize property held in concurrent ownership. Section 2581 provides:

> For the purpose of division of property on dissolution of marriage or legal separation of the parties, property acquired by the parties during marriage in joint form, including property held in tenancy in common, joint tenancy, or tenancy by the entirety, or as community property, is presumed to be community property. This presumption is a presumption affecting the burden of proof and may be rebutted by either of the following:
>
> (a) A clear statement in the deed or other documentary evidence of title by which the property is

acquired that the property is separate property and not community property.

(b) Proof that the parties have made a written agreement that the property is separate property.

A little history helps you understand § 2581. For generations, millions of California married couples took title to property—typically the family home—as joint tenants with right survivorship. California real estate agents encouraged married couples to put title in joint tenancy to avoid probate when one spouse died. But what if a marriage ended in divorce rather than death? At an earlier time, when a divorcing couple owned property as joint tenants, the judge often concluded their interests in the property were separate property rather than community property. The family court has no jurisdiction over separate property. The judge presiding over a divorce said to a divorcing couple, "Because you own your home as joint tenancy, your ownership interests are separate property. I have no authority to divide separate property, so I cannot do anything with your home. You will have to start a separate lawsuit to adjudicate your interests in your home." This made no sense. The judge conducting the divorce should be able to deal with the home, so the Legislature came up with a solution. When a divorcing couple owned a home as joint tenants, the law on divorce presumed the home was community property. The family court has authority over community property. If a marriage ended in death, the home was treated as a joint tenancy and the right of survivorship applied. Problem solved!

The earliest version § 2581 applied only to family homes and only when title was in joint tenancy. Over time, the Legislature expanded the community property presumption on divorce to all property held in joint tenancy—not just the family home—and expanded the forms of ownership to include tenancy in common.

The first paragraph of § 2581 creates a community property form of title presumption that applies on divorce. Apply the § 2581 community property presumption to property acquired after January 1, 1975 in concurrent ownership.

Subsections (a) and (b) of § 2581 specify how the § 2581 presumption is rebutted. Subsections (a) and (b) were enacted by the

Legislature effective January 1, 1984, and the two subjections are *not* retroactive. You cannot apply subsections (a) and (b) of § 2581 prior to January 1, 1984. Subsections (a) and (b) apply to any acquisition of property in joint form after January 1, 1984. After January 1, 1984, the § 2581 presumption of community property on divorce can only be rebutted in writing. Before January 1, 1984, the § 2581 presumption of community property could be rebutted in writing or with an oral agreement.

Suppose Wife and Husband acquired Blackacre in joint tenancy in 1980. They are divorcing today. Blackacre is presumptively 100% community property under § 2581. In the divorce, Wife argues that in 1980, she and Husband entered an oral agreement that in the event of divorce the property would *not* be community property. Subsections (a) and (b)—requiring a writing—don't apply because they are not retroactive. The result is that if Wife can prove the oral agreement by a preponderance of the evidence, she will prevail in her claim that the property does not fall within § 2581.

Subsections (a) and (b) of § 2581 specify that the § 2581 presumption can only be rebutted by a writing. Tracing to a separate property source of funds does *not* rebut the § 2581 presumption that on divorce, property is 100% community property. Rebuttal requires a writing *plus* tracing to separate funds. An example makes the point. In 2010, Wife and Husband purchased Blackacre in joint tenancy with right of survivorship. Wife made the $100,000 down payment with her separate property. Monthly mortgage payments are paid from community property. Today, the couple is divorcing. Does § 2581 apply? Yes. Wife would like to argue that Blackacre is part community property and part separate property because she used her separate property for the down payment. Assume Wife can trace her separate property into Blackacre. When Blackacre was acquired, no writing was executed that would satisfy subsections (a) or (b) to rebut the § 2581 presumption. Thus, Wife's ability to trace to the separate property down payment does not rebut the § 2581 presumption. Blackacre is 100% community property. Wife may be entitled to reimbursement of her down payment. Reimbursement is governed by Family Code § 2640, not § 2581. (*See* § 5.18).

What type of writing satisfies subsections (a) and (b) to rebut the community property presumption? A "clear statement in the deed" does the trick. Thus, a deed that states: "To Linda Carter and Michael Dazey, a married couple, in fee simple absolute, in joint tenancy with right of survivorship, and not as community property" should suffice. Alternatively, Linda and Mike could execute a side agreement in writing—*i.e.*, a writing apart from the deed—that contains language opting out of the § 2581 presumption.

Note that § 2581's community property presumption applies when property is "acquired by the parties during marriage in joint form." Consider Sue and Bob, who were not married when they purchased Greenacre together as joint tenants. Later they married. Still later, they are divorcing. Does § 2581 apply? No, because they did not acquire Greenacre "during marriage."

How about this scenario? Prior to marriage, Tiffany purchased Redacre. Obviously, Redacre was Tiffany's alone because she was single when she bought it. Only Tiffany's name is on the deed. Later, Tiffany married Belinda. During marriage, Tiffany executed a deed conveying Redacre to herself and Belinda as joint tenants, and Belinda accepted the deed. Does § 2581 apply in the event they divorce? Yes, because Tiffany and Belinda acquired their joint tenancy during marriage.

Finally, note that § 2581 applies to the "division of property on dissolution of marriage . . . ." Section 2581 applies in divorce proceedings. The section does *not* apply when a marriage ends in death. To repeat: Do not apply § 2581 if a marriage ends in death! When death ends a marriage, the right of survivorship aspect of joint tenancy operates in the normal fashion.

§ 5.18 When Marriage Ends in Divorce: Reimbursement of Separate Property Contribution to Community Property— Family Code § 2640

To understand Family Code § 2640, you need to be comfortable with two things: (1) Pro rata apportionment (§ 5.10), and (2) Family Code § 2581 (§ 5.17). Pro rata apportionment applies when separate property and community property pay for something. Recall the example of the surfboard from § 5.10, paid for half with community

§ 5.18   WHEN MARRIAGE ENDS IN DIVORCE   81

property and half with separate property. The surfboard is 50% community and 50% separate—pro rata apportionment.

On divorce, you apply pro rata apportionment unless a statute or an agreement between spouses precludes doing so. Family Code § 2581 *is* such a statute. Section 2581 precludes pro rata apportionment. Under § 2581, when title to property is taken in joint form, the property is presumed to be 100% community property. This is so even though the property was purchased with a combination of separate property and community property. Indeed, if § 2581 applies, the property is presumed to be 100% community property even if it is paid for *entirely* with separate property!

When you look at a set of facts and you see a combination of separate property and community property paying for something, your first thought is pro rata apportionment, and that is the correct thought. If § 2581 *doesn't* apply, you perform pro rata apportionment. However, if § 2581 *does* apply, you can't do pro rata apportionment because, pursuant to § 2581, the property is 100% community. Of course, if the § 2581 presumption is rebutted then you proceed with pro rata apportionment.

On divorce, Family Code § 2640 applies when § 2581 applies and property is 100% community property. Section 2640 allows the separate property contributor to be reimbursed the separate property contribution. The property remains 100% community property. Section 2640 is a reimbursement statute, not a pro rata apportionment statute. Section 2640 provides:

> (a) "Contributions to the acquisition of property" as used in this section, include downpayments, payments for improvements, and payments that reduce the principal of a loan used to finance the purchase or improvement of the property but do not include payments of interest on the loan or payments made for maintenance, insurance, or taxation of the property.
>
> (b) In the division of the community estate under this division, unless a party has made a written waiver of the right to reimbursement or has signed a writing that has the effect of a waiver, the party shall be reimbursed for the party's contributions to the acquisition of property of the

community property estate to the extent the party traces the contributions to a separate property source. The amount reimbursed shall be without interest or adjustment for change in monetary values and may not exceed the net value of the property at the time of the division.

A few words of explanation are useful about § 2640. Subsection (a) includes reimbursement for "improvements." Improvements are discussed in § 7.8.

Subdivision (b) refers to the "community estate." The community estate consists of community property and quasi-community property (Family Code § 63).

Subdivision (b) refers to "this division." The reference is to Division 7 of the Family Code, dealing with property.

Subdivision (b) provides that the right to reimbursement afforded by § 2640 can be waived in writing. A purported oral waiver is ineffective.

The amount reimbursed is "without interest." For example, if separate property contributed $20,000, the amount reimbursed under § 2640 is $20,000, *not* $20,000 plus interest.

Subdivision (b) states that the amount reimbursed "may not exceed the net value of the property at the time of the [divorce]." This phrase is directed to cases where the value of property goes down. For example, Wife and Husband purchase Blackacre for $300,000, taking title as joint tenants. Wife pays the down payment of $100,000 with her separate property. A year before the couple divorces, the building on Blackacre burns down, reducing the value of the property to $75,000. In the divorce, Wife will be reimbursed $75,000, but no more. In *Marriage of Walrath*, 17 Cal. 4th 907, 952 P.2d 1124, 72 Cal. Rptr. 2d 856 (1998), the Supreme Court wrote, "If there is insufficient equity at the time of the dissolution in the property to which the contribution was made to fully reimburse the contribution, the entire asset is awarded to the contributing spouse."

Section 2640 provides reimbursement of "payments that reduce the principal of a loan." With interest bearing loans, each installment payment combines (1) payment of interest on the loan, and (2) reduction of the loan itself—reduction of principal. During the early years of many loans (*e.g.*, car loans, home loans), the majority of each installment payment goes to interest, with relatively little to principal. Over time, this is reversed, with the majority of each payment for principal. Section 2640 allows reimbursement to the extent an installment payment reduced principal. Suppose, for example, that separate property paid the December mortgage payment of $3,000. That particular month, the interest paid was $1,500, and the principal paid was $1,500. If § 2640 applies, the amount reimbursed to the separate property contributor is $1,500. When separate property makes the initial down payment, the entire down payment is repaid pursuant to § 2640.

Family Code § 2581 provides that property held in joint form is presumptively 100% community property. When § 2581 applies and its community property presumption is not rebutted, then § 2640 applies to reimburse separate property contributions. When § 2640 applies, the separate property contribution is reimbursed prior to division of the community property.

If the community property presumption of § 2581 is rebutted, then § 2640 does *not* apply because the property is not 100% community property. When the § 2581 presumption is rebutted, pro rata apportionment tells us the property is part separate and part community. Section 2640 applies *only* when property is 100% community property. Another way of saying this is that the *only* time § 2640 applies is when § 2581 applies, *and* the § 2581 presumption is not rebutted. Still another way of thinking about § 2640 is that § 2640 never works alone. It always works in combination with § 2581—they are teammates. They sing duets, not solos.

Examples illustrate §§ 2581 and 2640 in action. Amber and Kennedy are married. They purchased a family home in January, 2017 in Fresno, taking title as joint tenants. The home cost $400,000. Each paid $20,000 in separate property toward the down payment. They obtained a bank loan for the balance of $360,000. Monthly mortgage payments in each year except 2019 were made with community property. All of the 2019 mortgage payments were made by Amber with her separate property. Now, Amber and

Kennedy are divorcing. Characterize the home. First, § 2581 applies because they own the home as joint tenants. There is no evidence of a writing to rebut the community property presumption of § 2581. Because § 2581 applies, the home is 100% community property. Neither spouse may use pro rata apportionment to seek a proportional ownership interest in the home. Since the home is 100% community property, § 2640 applies. There is no evidence either spouse waived the § 2640 right to reimbursement, so each spouse is reimbursed their separate property contribution. Kennedy is reimbursed $20,000, without interest for the down payment. Similarly, Amber is reimbursed $20,000 for the down payment. Amber will also be reimbursed the portion of each 2019 monthly mortgage payment that reduced the principal of the loan. After the § 2640 reimbursements are accounted for, the remaining value of the home is community property.

Bobby Sue and Billy Bob met at a rodeo. Billy Bob is a professional rodeo clown, keeping riders safe from bulls. Bobby Sue is a professional barrel racer. They married on horseback, and bought a home in Bakersfield for $300,000. The deed to the home is in joint tenancy. The deed states in part: "Joint tenants, with right of survivorship, and not as tenants in common, and not as community property." The down payment on the home was paid from Bobby Sue's separate property. Billy Bob and Bobby Sue put their rodeo income into a joint bank account, and each monthly mortgage payment is paid from this account. Bobby Sue and Billy Bob are divorcing. Characterize their home. The § 2581 presumption does not apply. The deed is sufficiently specific to rebut the § 2581 presumption. Because § 2581 does not apply, § 2640 cannot apply. Remember, §§ 2581 and 2640 work as a team. Section 2640 applies *only* when § 2581 applies, and the § 2581 presumption has not been rebutted. The Bakersfield home will be apportioned using pro rata apportionment.

§ 5.19 *Lucas* Gift Presumption—§ 2640 Is Not Retroactive

Family Code § 2640 went into effect January 1, 1984, and applies to transactions after that date. Section 2640 is not retroactive. It has no application to transactions prior to January 1,

1984. Family Code § 2581 applies to transactions before *and* after January 1, 1984.[16]

Suppose Wife and Husband purchased a home in Los Angeles in 1980, taking title as joint tenants. The down payment was with Husband's separate property. All mortgage payments were paid with community property. The mortgage was paid off in 2010. Wife and Husband are divorcing. Does § 2581 apply? Yes. The home is presumptively 100% community property. Assume there are no agreements to rebut the community property presumption. Will Husband be reimbursed his separate property down payment? Because the husband's down payment with separate property occurred before January 1, 1984, § 2640 does not apply—Section 2640 does not apply to transactions before January 1, 1984. In this scenario, the Supreme Court, in *Marriage of Lucas,* 27 Cal. 3d 808, 614 P.2d 285, 166 Cal. Rptr. 853 (1980), ruled that the spouse contributing separate property made a gift of the separate property to the community. This is called the *Lucas* gift presumption.

The *Lucas* gift presumption could be rebutted by evidence that the spouses had an agreement the spouse contributing separate property would be reimbursed. The reimbursement agreement could be written or oral.

The Legislature believed the *Lucas* gift presumption was bad policy. The Legislature concluded that when a marriage ends in divorce it is not realistic to presume that a spouse who contributed separate property to community property would be content with the idea of a gift to the community. Rather, the Legislature concluded the fair thing to do is reimburse the separate property contributor unless the contributor waived reimbursement. To achieve this result, the Legislature enacted § 2640 for the express purpose of abrogating the *Lucas* gift presumption. Indeed, § 2640 is sometimes called anti-*Lucas* legislation.[17] The Legislature intended § 2640 to

---

[16] Keep in mind that subsections (a) and (b) of § 2581, dealing with rebuttal of the 2581 presumption, are not retroactive.

[17] Marriage of Nicholson and Sparks, 104 Cal. App. 4th 289, 294, 127 Cal. Rptr. 2d 882 (2002)(Section 2640 "represents a specific legislative rejection of the general presumption that separate property used for community purposes is a gift, as it was applied in *In re Marriage of Lucas* . . . .").

be retroactive, but the California Supreme Court ruled it would be unconstitutional to apply § 2640 retroactively.

In the final analysis, § 2640 cannot be applied to transactions prior to January 1, 1984. For transactions prior to that date, § 2581 *can* apply to render property 100% community property. Section 2640, however, cannot apply. Rather, the *Lucas* gift presumption applies to separate property contributions to community property prior to January 1, 1984 unless there was an oral or written agreement that a gift was not intended.

§ 5.20 Exercises with Family Code §§ 2581 and 2640

This section provides an opportunity to work with Family Code §§ 2581 and 2640. answers pp. 231-238

1. In 1981, Fern and Guy married in Los Osos, California where they grew up. Not long after they married, they bought a home with a view of the ocean, taking title as joint tenants. The down payment was paid with a wedding gift to Guy from his parents, in the amount of $25,000. Monthly mortgage payments were paid with community property. Fern and Guy are divorcing. What are their rights to the home in Los Osos? CP

2. Gladys and Gilbert married in 2014, in California. They divorced seven years later. Prior to marriage, Gilbert owned a house in Lucerne, California. In 2018, Gilbert deeded the Lucerne house to Gladys and himself as joint tenants. There was a mortgage on the home. When Gilbert conveyed the home to Gladys and himself, the equity in the home was $246,000. In 2019, Gladys reduced the principal on the Lucerne home with $40,000 of her separate property. In 2020, the couple refinanced the Lucerne home, taking out $280,000 against their equity in the home. They used $100,000 of the money to pay off the mortgage on a Nevada property they purchased together. They used $100,000 to purchase a property in Utah. They used $80,000 to pay down the existing loan on the Lucerne property. Gladys and Gilbert agree that the Lucerne, Nevada, and Utah properties are community property. They do not agree on whether § 2640's entitlement to separate property reimbursement is limited to the original property (the Lucerne house), or whether, when the original property is refinanced and the

§ 5.21 COMMUNITY PROPERTY CONTRIBUTIONS TO SEPARATE PROPERTY

proceeds are used to purchase or pay down indebtedness on the original or other assets, the spouse who contributed separate property can trace the contribution to, and be reimbursed from those assets. What is the proper interpretation of § 2640? *See Marriage of Walrath,* 17 Cal. 4th 907, 952 P.2d 1124, 72 Cal. Rptr. 2d 856 (1998).

[doesn't apply b/c no reimb. agreemt.]

3. In 2017, Marley married Mary. In 2018, they purchased Greenacre in Napa, California, taking title as joint tenants. The down payment was paid by Mary from her separate property. Monthly deed of trust payments were paid from the joint bank account into which the couple deposited their paychecks. In 2022, Marley received an inheritance, and used it to pay off the remaining balance on the home. Mary and Marley are divorcing. Characterize Greenacre, and discuss reimbursement. [CP, neither 2581 nor 2640 apply]

What if Marley and Mary had put title in Marley's name alone. Would §§ 2581 and 2640 apply? How would Greenacre be characterized and divided? [no, presumption is CP if acquired during marriage]

§ 5.21 Community Property Contributions to Separate Property: *Moore/Marsden* Apportionment

It is common for newlyweds to come into marriage already owning property on which monthly mortgage payments are being made. Title is in the owner's name alone, and § 2581 does not apply unless the owner conveys the property to herself and her spouse during marriage in joint form. Assuming no such conveyance, if, during marriage, the owner spouse makes all mortgage payments with separate property, then the community acquires no interest in the property. However, if, during marriage, mortgage payments are made with community property, then the community acquires a proportional ownership interest in the property—pro rata apportionment.[18]

The leading case is *Marriage of Moore,* 28 Cal. 3d 366, 618 P.2d 208, 168 Cal. Rptr. 662 (1980). The Supreme Court described the formula to divide property into separate and community interests:

---

[18] *See* Marriage of Nevai, 59 Cal. App. 5th 108, 273 Cal. Rptr. 3d 288 (2020).

[margin note: formula to divide property into sep. & comm. interests]

The separate property percentage interest is determined by crediting the separate property with the down payment and the full amount of the loan less the amount by which the community property payments reduced the principal balance of the loan.[19] This sum is divided by the purchase price for the separate property percentage share. The community property percentage interest is found by dividing the amount by which community property payments reduced the principal by the purchase price.[20]

In *Marriage of Marsden*, 130 Cal. App. 3d 426, 181 Cal. Rptr. 910 (1982), the Court of Appeal clarified *Moore* by adding that the separate property percentage is credited with appreciation of the property before marriage. In practice, the calculation is called *Moore/Marsden* apportionment.

The California Judicial Council website describes *Moore/Marsden* as a formula:

$$CP = PPCP + (CP\% \times MApp)$$

CP: community property

PPCP: principle payments from community property

CP%: community property percentage – PPCP / purchase price

MApp: appreciation during marriage

$$SP = DP = PPSP + \text{Pre-MApp} + (SP\% \times MApp)$$

SP: separate property

DP: down payment

PPSP: principle payments from separate property

Pre-MApp: premarriage appreciation

SP%: separate property percentage = 100% – PPCP / purchase price

---

[19] The Court stated that the formula "has been commonly understood as excluding payments for interest and taxes." 28 Cal. 3d at 372.

[20] 28 Cal. 3d at 373–374.

§ 5.21 COMMUNITY PROPERTY CONTRIBUTIONS TO SEPARATE PROPERTY

The Judicial Council offers the following example of the calculation. The dates are changed:

Asma purchased a $300,000 home in 2005, before her marriage. She borrowed $240,000, made a down payment of $60,000, and paid $20,000 in principle [before marriage]. Asma married Manuel in 2010, when the house's fair market value was $400,000. During the marriage Asma and Manuel paid $30,000 principal on the loan from community property. When Asma and Manuel separate in 2020, the fair market value of the house was $700,000. The community and separate property interests are calculated as follows:

[handwritten note: house is SP]

Community and Separate Property Percentages

Community property percentage:

$30,000 / $300,000 = 10%

Asma's separate property percentage:

100% − 10% = 90%

Community Property Interest

	$30,000	CP payments
+	30,000	CP marriage appreciation (10% × $300,000)
	$60,000	

Asma's Separate Property Interest

	$60,000	down payment
+	20,000	SP principal payments
+	100,000	premarriage appreciation
+	270,000	SP marriage appreciation (90% × $ 300,000)
	$450,000	

Interests and Obligations on Dissolution of Marriage

Manuel's one-half of community interest:

$60,000 / 2 = $30,000

Asma's separate and community interests:

$450,000   SP interest
+ 30,000   one-half CP interest
─────────
$480,000

Asma is responsible for the balance due on the loan of $190,000.

If you are in law school because you are terrible at math, you are not alone. Fortunately, for those of us who are math impaired, we seldom have to "do the math" required by the *Moore/Marsden* formula. Software is available to do it for you. Many lawyers use the Propertizer™ program published the *California Family Law Report*. Propertizer does the math on most property problems. It also calculates child support. When *do* you need to check the math in *Moore/Marsden*? When you are casting a skeptical eye over your opponent's math!

§ 5.22 Married Woman's Separate Property Presumption

Before January 1, 1975, married women in California had no legal authority to make decisions about community property. Husbands had exclusive management and control of community property. Effective January 1, 1975, spouses have equal management and control of community property. Management and control is discussed in Chapter 10.

Because a married woman prior to January 1, 1975 lacked authority to make decisions regarding community property, the Legislature established a presumption to afford a modicum of economic protection for women. The presumption is codified in Family Code § 803, which provides:

> Notwithstanding any other provision of this part, whenever any real or personal property, or any interest therein or encumbrance thereon, was acquired before January 1, 1975, by a married woman by an instrument in writing, the following presumptions apply, and are conclusive in favor of any person dealing in good faith and for a valuable consideration with the married woman or her legal representative or successors in interest,

regardless of any change in her marital status after acquisition of the property:

(a) If acquired by the married woman, the presumption is that the property is the married woman's separate property.

(b) If acquired by the married woman and any other person, the presumption is that the married woman takes the part acquired by her as a tenant in common, unless a different intention is expressed in the instrument.

(c) If acquired by husband and wife by an instrument in which they are described as husband and wife, the presumption is that the property is the community property of the husband and wife, unless a different intention is expressed in the instrument.

When the Legislature enacted § 803 in the early Twentieth Century, the scenario the Legislature had in mind was a husband using community property to purchase property in his wife's name. The Legislature reasoned that when a husband used community property to buy property and put title in his wife's name he must have intended a gift to his wife of his half interest in the community property, thus making the entire property her separate property. The gift idea applied even when a husband used his separate property to make the purchase and put title in his wife's name. The property was presumptively wife's separate property.

The separate property presumption established by § 803 cannot be rebutted by tracing. That is, a husband cannot rebut the presumption by tracing the purchase money to community property or his separate property. Rebuttal requires tracing plus testimony from husband that he did not intend to give his interest to his wife.

Section 803 does not apply to acquisitions of property after January 1, 1975.

Section 803 refers to an "encumbrance." An encumbrance is defined in § 4.6. Common examples include a mortgage or deed of trust on real property.

Section 803 provides that a conveyance by a woman of property that is presumptively her separate property under § 803 is "conclusive in favor of any person dealing in good faith and for a valuable consideration with the married woman." The quoted language refers to a bona fide purchaser for value without notice (BFP). A BFP for value is protected from claims on property that the purchaser was unaware of at the time of the purchase.[21] Once a BFP for value purchases § 803 property from a woman, the separate property presumption is no longer rebuttable—the presumption is conclusive in favor of the BFP.

Section 803(b) provides that the separate property presumption applies when property was "acquired by the married woman and any other person." The word "any" includes the woman's husband.

When a married couple purchased property together prior to January 1, 1975 by an instrument in writing "in which they are described as husband and wife," the § 803(c) presumption is that the property is community property. This is straight forward when the deed said, "To Bill and Hillary Smith, husband and wife." But what if the deed said, "to Bill Clinton and Hillary Rodham in fee simple," and it turns out Bill and Hillary were married. Does § 803(c) apply? It does not seem so.

---

[21] *See* Vasquez v. LBS Financial Credit Union, 52 Cal. App. 5th 97, 265 Cal.Rptr.3d 78 (2020) ("It is black-letter law that a bona fide purchaser for value who acquires his or her interest in real property without knowledge or notice of another's prior rights or interest in the property takes the property free of such unknown interests. The elements of bona fide purchase are payment of value, in good faith, and without actual or constructive notice of another's rights. Conversely, it is an equally well-established principle of law that any purchaser of real property acquires the property subject to prior interests of which he or she has actual or constructive notice. Actual notice is defined as express information of a fact, while constructive notice is that which is imputed by law. A bona fide purchaser without notice may seek a legal determination through a quiet title action that the title it obtained remains free and clear of any adverse interest in the property.").

Chapter 6

PENSIONS AND OTHER EMPLOYMENT-RELATED BENEFITS

Analysis

§ 6.1	Pension as Community Property
§ 6.2	Government Retirement Systems
§ 6.3	Private Sector Retirement Systems
§ 6.4	Defined Benefit and Defined Contribution Plans
§ 6.5	Determining the Community Property Share of a Pension
§ 6.6	Lawyer's Responsibility Regarding Pensions
§ 6.7	Methods of Dividing Pensions
§ 6.8	Qualified Domestic Relations Order (QDRO) to Divide ERISA Pension
§ 6.9	QDRO to Collect Child or Spousal Support
§ 6.10	Joining Pension Plan as a Party
§ 6.11	Military Retirement
§ 6.12	Social Security Retirement
§ 6.13	*Gillmore* Election
§ 6.14	Disability Benefits
§ 6.15	Military Disability
§ 6.16	Early Retirement
§ 6.17	Is Employment-Related Health Insurance Community Property?
§ 6.18	Severance Pay
§ 6.19	Accrued Vacation and Sick Days
§ 6.20	Stock Options
§ 6.21	Life Insurance

The law of pensions is complicated. Miles Mason quips, "The entire process of dealing with pensions is a bugbear."[1]

§ 6.1 Pension as Community Property

In *Marriage of Brown*, 15 Cal. 3d 838, 544 P.2d 561, 126 Cal. Rptr. 633 (1976), the Supreme Court held, "Pension rights, whether or not vested, represent a property interest; to the extent that such rights derive from employment during coverture, they comprise a community asset subject to division in a dissolution proceeding. . . . The community owns all pension rights attributable to employment during the marriage."

§ 6.2 Government Retirement Systems

For government employees at federal, state, and local levels, employers have pension plans. Go online and search California Public Employees Retirement System—CalPERS. You will find a wealth of information on America's largest public employee retirement system. On the site, click on Marriage or Divorce and you will find information on how CalPERS pensions are divided on divorce. California teachers are covered by CalSTRS. Employees of California counties are covered by a statewide retirement system: CERS, the County Employees Retirement System. Cities have pension plans for police, fire, and other departments. Some local governments contract with CalPERS or the county system.

Federal civil service employees participate in the Federal Employees Retirement System (FERS). Members of the military have a retirement system. The federal Railroad Retirement Act provides pensions for railroad workers.

§ 6.3 Private Sector Retirement Systems

Workers in the private sector may or may not have a pension at work. For those without a work-related pension, pension-like savings plans are available. Most private sector pensions are

---

[1] Miles Mason, Sr., *Accounting Deskbook: A Practical Guide to Financial Investigation and Analysis for Family Lawyers*, p. 145 (2011).

covered by the federal Employee Retirement Income Security Act of 1974 (ERISA).[2]

§ 6.4 Defined Benefit and Defined Contribution Plans

Traditional pensions are either defined benefit plans or defined contribution plans.[3] Each has many permutations. With a defined benefit plan, an employer agrees to provide pension benefits upon retirement. The pension amount is tied to a formula that typically includes length of service to the employer and the employee's salary during the final years of employment.

With many defined benefit plans, the employee contributes a portion of her salary each pay period to the employee's pension. The

---

[2] David Clayton Carrad, *The Complete QDRO Handbook*, p. 1 (3d ed. 2009)("Before 1974, private pension plans were not regulated by the federal government and were only sporadically regulated by the states.").

[3] *See* Lee v. Lee, 775 N.W.2d 631 (Minn. 2009). In a concurring opinion, Justice Dietzen wrote:

> Retirement plans may be divided into two general categories: defined contribution and defined benefit. On the one hand, a defined contribution plan provides an individual account for each employee participant, with retirement benefits based on the amount contributed to the account and any income, expenses, gains, or losses to the account. A 401k retirement plan is an example of a defined contribution plan in which employer and employee have the opportunity to contribute amounts into an individual account for the benefit of the employee. The amounts contributed to the account are invested by the plan and the balance of the account, consisting of contributions and income earned on those contributions, is available to the employee upon retirement.
>
> On the other hand, a defined benefit plan provides qualified employees with monthly retirement benefits, the amount of which is calculated according to the plan and which are paid from plan assets as a whole. Although employees may contribute to the fund, the employer or other plan sponsor agrees to contribute as much as is required to generate the promised benefit. Thus, a defined benefit plan does not accumulate a principal amount for the employee, but rather "guarantees" a periodic payment to the employee upon retirement.
>
> The division of the marital portion of a defined contribution plan does not—indeed, cannot—involve the division of future payments from the plan. Because future payments from a defined contribution plan depend on future contributions and future returns on those contributions—amounts that are not known at the time of the judgment and decree—the division of the marital portion of a defined contribution plan requires the division of the plan balance itself, not the division of future payments from the plan.

employer also contributes. The pension upon retirement is determined by the formula, with the employee's contributions forming part of the calculation.

During the early years of employment, a defined benefit pension is typically unvested. If an employee leaves the job before a defined benefit pension vests, the employee may have no pension rights. After a number years with an employer, the pension vests, which means the employee has rights even if the employee leaves or is fired or laid off before normal retirement age. When an employee is eligible to retire, the pension is mature. If the employee retires, the pension is in "pay status." Many older workers keep working after their pension matures, postponing receipt of the pension.

With a defined contribution plan, each employee has a retirement account. Typically, the employee and the employer make regular contributions—*e.g.*, every payday—to the employee's account. At retirement, the employee's pension depends on the amount in the account. Typically, during the employee's working years, the money is invested according to the wishes of the employee.[4]

With a defined contribution plan, it is easy to tell how much money is in an employee's retirement account.[5] The plan administrator or the employee can tell at a glance the balance of the account. With the typical defined benefit plan, by contrast, the employee does not have an individual account containing a set amount of money.[6] Instead, the employee has a contractual promise that at retirement age the retirement plan will apply the formula and determine, *at that time*, the amount of the pension. With defined benefit plans it is generally not possible to tell precisely the value of a pension until the employee reaches retirement age.

---

[4] The following are defined contribution retirement tools: 401(k) plans, 403(b) tax sheltered annuity plans, employee stock bonus plans, employee stock ownership plans (ESOPs), and profit sharing plans.

[5] One should not get the impression there is actually money sitting in an employee's account. The pension plan invests the money it receives. Thus, the employee's money is "working" for the employee and other employee members of the plan.

[6] Some defined benefit plans do have an account for each employee.

As mentioned above, if a divorcing spouse has a defined contribution pension that is partly or wholly community property, it is simple to value the asset. The plan administrator can determine the value of the pension on the appropriate date. But how does one put a value on a defined benefit plan in a divorce *today*, when the employee spouse will not retire for years? Recall that with defined benefit plans there typically is no individual account with a running balance. Rather, there is a promise of benefits in the future—benefits that are tied to variables that are impossible to predict with certainty years before retirement. Determining the value *today* ("present value") of a defined benefit pension that is years from maturity requires an expert, typically an accountant or an actuary. The expert makes assumptions about when the employee will retire and what the employee's pension amount will likely be at retirement (this depends, of course, on the formula used by the retirement plan and assumptions about the employee's future salary, etc.). The likely pension amount is discounted to present value. The expert factors in the possibility the employee will die—the mortality discount. Needless to say, determining present value of a defined benefit pension that will not materialize for years—if it ever materializes—is not an exact science.

§ 6.5 Determining the Community Property Share of a Pension

A pension is community property to the extent it is acquired during marriage and prior to separation. Consider, for example, Mary, who enlisted in the Navy at age 18, right after high school. Mary served twenty years, and retired at 38 as a chief petty officer. At 39, Mary married Mike. Five years later, they divorce. Mary's Navy pension is entirely her separate property because it was acquired prior to marriage. The fact that Mary receives pension checks during marriage does not change the fact that the pension was earned before marriage. Now consider Sue and Tom, who fell in love and married during college. Following graduation, Sue entered the Navy at age 22, as an officer. After thirty years of service, Sue retired at 54, at the rank of vice admiral. Two years after retirement, Sue and Tom divorce. Sue's entire pension is community property because it was acquired entirely during marriage. Finally, consider John and Kim. Upon graduation from law school at age 26,

Kim was commissioned an officer in the Army Judge Advocate General's corps—an Army lawyer. Five years into her Army career, Kim married John, an Army officer. After twenty years' service, Kim retired from the Army at age 46, at the rank of colonel. A few years following retirement, Kim and John divorce. Kim's pension is part her separate property and part community property because part of the pension was acquired prior to marriage and part during marriage. To be precise, 75% of the pension is community, and 25% is Kim's separate property. In the divorce, Kim is entitled to the 25% that is separate, plus half the community portion of the pension. In the end, Kim will have 62.5% of the pension and John will have 37.5%.

When a defined contribution plan is part separate and part community, the proportions are calculated on divorce by characterizing the funds that contributed to the retirement account. Brett Turner writes, "The marital interest includes contributions from marital funds and contributions made by the employer as compensation for marital efforts, plus passive investment return. The separate interest includes contributions from separate funds, as well as contributions made by the employer as consideration for premarital or [post-separation] efforts, plus passive investment return."[7] The divorce judgment may provide that the administrator of the pension is to divide the pension by creating separate accounts for the employee and the non-employee. Each spouse obtains the benefit of appreciation on their respective account.

With defined benefit plans, division into separate and community components is typically accomplished with the "time rule," sometimes called the "coverture fraction." The numerator of the fraction is years of service during marriage.[8] The denominator is total years during which the pension was earned. For example, Sue retired after twenty years with the California Highway Patrol. During ten of those years, Sue was married to Paul. The numerator of the fraction is 10; the denominator is 20. Half of Sue's pension is her separate property. Half is community property. Sue owns half

---

[7] Brett R. Turner, *Equitable Distribution of Property*, § 6:24, pp. 143–144 (3d ed. 2005).

[8] With the time rule, it is possible to use years, months, or days.

of the community property portion. In the end, Sue is entitled to 75% of the pension, and Paul 25%.

In Sue's case, she was already retired at the time of the divorce. Thus, the denominator of the fraction—20—was established. In many divorces, the employee spouse is years from retirement. The employee may retire after 20 years of service or may continue working. The denominator of the fraction cannot be determined until the employee retires. In this scenario, the divorce judgment may contain the coverture fraction with the proviso that the denominator will be filled in when the employee retires.

Apply the time rule to the following cases:

1. Wendy began employment on January 2, 2000, while single. Wendy has a defined benefit pension through her employer. Wendy married Bill on January 2, 2010. Wendy and Bill separate on January 2, 2015. Their divorce is final January 2, 2016. Wendy retires on January 2, 2020, after twenty years' service. W = 87.5%. B = 12.5%.

2. Elenore went to work at the university in 2000. She married Mike in 2005. In 2010, Elenore took a two year leave of absence from the university, during which she earned nothing toward her university pension. In 2012, Elenore returned to the university. In 2016, Elenore and Mike separated. In 2025, Elenore retired.

§ 6.6 Lawyer's Responsibility Regarding Pensions

An important part of a lawyer's job in divorce is learning about all pension benefits of both parties. The lawyer determines whether pension benefits are separate or community. The lawyer educates the client about the impact of family law on pensions. In some cases, the law's impact comes as an unpleasant surprise to the client. Consider Joe, who has worked nineteen years at a job he hates, and who can't wait to retire. Joe's attorney tells Joe that nearly half his monthly pension belongs to his soon-to-be-ex-wife. In an angry voice, Joe says, "You mean to tell me I got to give half my pension to that woman?! I been going to that rotten job nearly twenty years while she stayed home with the kids having a great old time and not working at all. Now you're telling me half my pension belongs to her? I'm the one who earned that pension. Not her!" Sorry Joe, you acquired most of the pension during marriage, and that makes the pension community property. Offer Joe a cup of coffee and time to calm down.

If a pension is community property and is to be divided, the lawyer drafts the complex documents required to divide the pension. Many family law attorneys delegate the drafting of some of these documents to pension specialists (*See* § 6.8).

§ 6.7 Methods of Dividing Pensions

In addition to learning about a couple's pensions and calculating community property shares, attorneys help clients decide how to divide community pension interests. There are several ways divorcing couples can handle pensions.

§ 6.7(a) Dividing a Defined Contribution Pension

Dividing a defined contribution pension is typically pretty straight forward. As explained in § 6.4, the value of a defined contribution pension is usually simple to determine. If the employee is retired, periodic pension payments are divided according to the percentage of the pension that is community property. If the employee spouse is still working, the administrator of the pension plan informs the parties of the balance in the employee spouse's retirement account on a specific date. The divorce judgment divides the account in two—one account for each spouse.

§ 6.7(b) Dividing a Defined Benefit Pension: Cash out or Wait and See

When a defined benefit plan is in pay status—that is, the employee spouse is retired and drawing the pension—the pension can be dividing using the time rule. When the employee spouse is yet to retire, two methods are used to divide the pension: The cash out method and the wait and see method.

With cash out, the employee spouse keeps the entire pension and the non-employee spouse receives other property equal in value to the foregone pension—the non-employee is cashed out. Consider, Rita and Juan, who married while in college. Upon graduation, Rita became a police officer, Juan became a teacher. Both have defined benefit pensions. After five years of marriage, Rita and Juan divorce. They are many years from retirement. For this couple, the best solution may be for each to keep their entire pension. If there is a difference in present value between the pensions, the spouse with the less valuable pension can receive other community property to make up the difference. It is important to understand that the law does not insist that Rita and Juan leave the marriage with the same value in pension benefits. Divorcing couples are free to divide their community property as *they* see fit. If Rita's public safety pension is worth more than Juan's teaching pension, Juan is a free to say, "Rita, you keep your pension. I'll keep mine. I don't care if yours is worth more than mine." Although many people getting divorced are angry, hurt, and depressed, many—hopefully, most—still care about their partner, and want what is best for them. If Juan wants to give up his portion of Rita's more valuable pension, he is free to do so, so long as his decision is voluntary and informed. It is the responsibility of Juan's attorney to explain the rights Juan has and what he is giving up. In the final analysis, the law allows divorcing couples to arrange their property according to their own lights.

When a couple decides on the cash out method, it is necessary to determine the value of the pension at the time of divorce—present value. Present value must be determined in order to figure out how much money the employee spouse must give the non-employee spouse in order to cash out the non-employee spouse. As mentioned in § 6.4, determining the value today—present value—of a defined benefit pension that will not mature for years is not an exact science. Miles Mason writes, "The calculation of value is never 'accurate.' It is an estimate for at least two important reasons. First, no one knows exactly when the participant will die. Second, judgment is always involved when determining a discount rate.... There are two basic methods of estimating value. The mortality method takes into consideration probabilities of death, and is almost always handled by actuaries. The more common life expectancy method, also called the discounted to present value method, is the method more commonly used by forensic accountants."[9]

---

[9] Miles Mason, Sr., *Accounting Deskbook: A Practical Guide to Financial Investigation and Analysis for Family Lawyers*, pp. 147, 151 (2011). Mason continues: "To calculate present value, a discount rate must be chosen. Discount rates (and

One advantage to the employee spouse of keeping her entire pension, and the non-employee spouse taking other property, is that the parties can make a clean break from each other at the time of the divorce. With this approach, all pension rights are disposed of at divorce. As you will see momentarily, the other method of dealing with pensions has the potential to keep divorced spouses financially entangled for years. A second advantage to the employee spouse of retaining the entire pension is that when retirement rolls around, the employee has the entire pension and, thus, more money. Of course, this benefit for the employee ex-spouse disadvantages the non-employee ex-spouse.

The second method for dealing with a community interest in a defined benefit pension is to determine the interests in the pension at the time of divorce (the time rule), and then wait until the employee spouse retires for the non-employee spouse to start receiving their share of the pension.[10] The principle advantage of the wait and see method is that the non-employee spouse will have an income stream at a time in life when they need it—at or near retirement. There are disadvantages too. What if the employee spouse dies before retiring? There will be *no* pension! Or, suppose the employee retires, the non-employee starts getting checks, and the employee drops dead a few months later. The pension stops!

There are remedies for the possibility that the employee spouse dies prematurely. First, pension plans have survivor benefits, and the parties' marital settlement agreement (MSA) can specify that the non-employee spouse is entitled to such benefits. Sometimes, attorneys fail to state in the MSA that the non-employee spouse is entitled to survivor benefits. In *Marriage of Morris,* 810 N.W.2d 880 (Iowa 2012),[11] counsel failed to specify in the MSA that wife was entitled to survivor benefits under husband's Marine Corps pension. The Iowa Supreme Court warned, "This case should serve as a vivid reminder to attorneys practicing matrimonial law to specifically

---

interest rates, for that matter) reflect an assessment of risk. . . . The greater the discount rate, the less the estimated net present value of expected benefits." p. 153.

[10] *See* Thomson v. Thomson, 394 P.3d 604 (Alaska 2017).

[11] *Compare* Marriage of Morris, 810 N.W.2d 880 (Iowa 2012) (attorney failed to mention survivor benefits in property settlement agreement (PSA)), *with* Craig v. Craig, 59 Va. App. 527, 721 S.E.2d 24 (2012)(attorney specifically mentioned survivor benefits in PSA).

address survivor rights when dividing retirement benefits."[12] An attorney's failure to secure all available pension benefits, including survivor benefits, is malpractice.

The second remedy in case the employee spouse dies is to incorporate into the MSA a requirement that the employee spouse buy life insurance with the non-employee spouse as beneficiary.

With the wait and see method, the nonemployee spouse postpones receipt of her share until the employee spouse retires. With this approach, it is usually unnecessary to determine the present value of the pension. The community property percentage of the pension is determined at the time of divorce using the time rule, and the former spouse waits until retirement to split whatever the final pension amount turns out to be.

§ 6.8 Qualified Domestic Relations Order (QDRO) to Divide ERISA Pension

When a divorcing couple divides the community property interest in a pension governed by ERISA, an important drafting responsibility falls to the attorneys, typically the attorney for the non-employee spouse. The attorney drafts a "domestic relations order" (DRO) that becomes part of the divorce judgment.[13] A DRO specifies the spouses' interests in the pension, and describes how the interests are to be divided. The DRO is submitted to the pension plan, which—if everything is in order—approves the DRO,

---

[12] The Iowa Supreme Court wrote in *Marriage of Morris*, 810 N.W.2d 880 (Iowa 2012): "Other courts in this situation [where the decree does not specify whether the non-employee spouse gets survivor benefits] have adopted a default rule by holding that a decree dividing retirement benefits includes survivorship benefits. Several of these courts have allowed post-dissolution orders compelling the retiree to designate his former spouse as the survivor to effectuate the division of retirement benefits in the original degree. Other courts, however, have refused to allow postdissolution orders awarding a former souse survivorship rights when the decree does not expressly contemplate the survivorship benefit."

[13] ERISA and the Internal Revenue Code define "domestic relations order" as follows: "The term 'domestic relations order' means any judgment, decree, or order (including approval of a property settlement agreement) which—(i) relates to the provision of child support, alimony payments, or marital property rights to a spouse, former spouse, child, or other dependent of a participant, and (ii) is made pursuant to a State domestic relations law (including a community property law)." 26 U.S.C. § 414(p)(1)(B); 29 U.S.C. § 1056(d)(3)(B)(ii).

Many retirement plans will examine draft DROs to see if they are acceptable.

transforming it into a Qualified Domestic Relations Order or QDRO. As mentioned, the QDRO becomes part of the divorce judgment.

ERISA provides that pension benefits of employees (participants) cannot be alienated by participants.[14] Absent an exception to ERISA's anti-alienation provision, a participant's retirement benefit cannot be awarded (alienated) in a divorce to a non-employee spouse.[15] In *Ablamis v. Rober*, 937 F.2d 1450 (9th Cir. 1991), the Ninth Circuit explained the anti-alienation provision of ERISA:

> To secure the financial well-being of employees and their dependents, ERISA contains a spendthrift provision. That provision states that the benefits provided under the retirement plan may not be assigned or alienated.... ERISA's prohibition on the assignment or alienation of pension benefits reflects a considered congressional policy choice, a decision to safeguard a stream of income for pensioners (and their dependents), even if that decision prevents others from securing relief for the wrongs done them. If exceptions to this policy are to be made, it is for Congress to undertake that task.... Congress did make one important exception, however. Congress was ... concerned with the inequities that might be suffered by women who are the economic victims of divorce or separation. To protect their interests, the [Retirement Equity Act] REA creates an express statutory exception to the prohibition on assignment and alienation in the case of distributions made pursuant to certain state court orders: ERISA's spendthrift provisions are not applicable to a qualified domestic relations order (QDRO). A court may divide spousal rights in pension benefits through the mechanism of a QDRO and award the non-employee spouse her appropriate share of those benefits—but only if

---

[14] 29 U.S.C. § 1056(d)(1) ("Each pension plan shall provide that benefits provided under the plan may not be assigned or alienated."). There are some exceptions to ERISA's anti-alienation provision. *See* 29 U.S.C. § 1056(d)(2).

See David Clayton Carrad, *The Complete QDRO Handbook*, p. 2 (3d ed. 2009)("From its enactment in 1974, ERISA has required that each pension plan ensure that the benefits it provides are not 'assigned or alienated.' ").

[15] ERISA is federal law, and federal law trumps state law.

the domestic relations order is a qualified one as defined in the REA.

Under REA, a QDRO is any judgment, decree, or order made pursuant to a state domestic relations law (including community property law) which (1) "creates or recognizes the existence of an alternate payee's right to, or assigns to an alternate payee the right to, receive all or a portion of the benefits payable with respect to a participant under a plan," and (2) "relates to the provision of child support, alimony payments, or marital property rights to a spouse, former spouse, child, or other dependent of a participant." Only "qualified" domestic relations orders are exempt from ERISA's spendthrift provisions; other domestic relations orders are expressly made subject to the anti-assignment provision and are, as a result, preempted. Thus, in the case of QDROs the REA provides a "limited exception" to the anti-assignment provision for certain specified types of domestic relations property allocations.

In ERISA parlance, the non-employee spouse is an alternative payee. As mentioned above, ERISA contains an exception to anti-alienation. An alternative payee *can* receive a share of a participant's retirement pursuant to a QDRO.[16] Thus, it is critical that the provisions of the divorce judgment fulfill ERISA's requirements for a QDRO. Only QDROs escape ERISA's anti-alienation provision.[17]

---

[16] *See* Quijano v. Quijano, 347 S.W.3d 345, 353–354 (Tex. Ct. App. 2011)("The purpose of a QDRO is to create or recognize an alternate payee's right, or to assign an alternate payee the right, to receive all or a portion of the benefits payable to a participant under a retirement plan.").

[17] 29 U.S.C. § 1056(d)(3)(A) provides: "Paragraph (1) [the anti-alienation provision] shall apply to the creation, assignment, or recognition of a right to any benefit payable with respect to a participant pursuant to a domestic relations order, except that [the anti-alienation provision] shall not apply if the order is determined to be a qualified domestic relations order. Each pension plan shall provide for the payment of benefits in accordance with the applicable requirement of any qualified domestic relations order."

What are the requirements for the all-important QDRO? A QDRO is a DRO that satisfies the following requirements of federal law:

> (C) A domestic relations order meets the requirements of this subparagraph only if such order clearly specifies—
>
>   (i) the name and last known mailing address (if any) of the participant and the name and mailing address of each alternative payee covered by the order.
>
>   (ii) the amount or percentage of the participant's benefits to be paid by the plan to each such alternative payee, or the manner in which such amount or percentage is to be determined,
>
>   (iii) the number of payments or period to which such order applies, and
>
>   (iv) each plan to which such order applies.
>
> (D) A domestic relations order meets the requirements of this subparagraph only if such order—
>
>   (i) does not require a plan to provide any type or form of benefit, or any option, not otherwise provided under the plan,
>
>   (ii) does not require the plan to provide increased benefits (determined on the basis of actuarial value), and
>
>   (iii) does not require payment of benefits to an alternate payee which are required to be paid to another alternative payee under another order previously determined to be a qualified domestic relations order.[18]

It is not difficult for a lawyer drafting a DRO to obtain names and mailing addresses. Nor is it particularly challenging to specify "the amount or percentage of the participant's benefits to be paid by the plan to" the alternative payee. The tricky bit is ensuring that

---

[18] 29 U.S.C. § 1056(d).

the DRO does not require the plan to pay any type of benefit that is not authorized by the plan. The Indiana Court of Appeals explained in *Evans v. Evans*, 946 N.E.2d 1200, 1206 (Ind. Ct. App. 2011), "A QDRO must comply with ERISA. . . . A QDRO cannot require the plan administrator to provide any type or form of benefit, or any option, not otherwise provided under the plan." The only way to be sure this requirement for a valid QDRO is satisfied is obtain the actual pension plan—perhaps hundreds of pages long—and to read and understand precisely what the plan does and does not provide. The difficulty with this requirement—studying the entire plan—is the reason many family law attorneys do not draft their own QDROs, referring the task to QDRO specialists.

Government pensions, including CalPERS and CalSTRS, are not governed by ERISA. An ERISA QDRO is not used to divide a government pension. Rather, the lawyer drafts a domestic relations order that complies with requirements established by CalPERS, CalSTRS, and other government pensions.

§ 6.9 QDRO to Collect Child or Spousal Support

QDROs divide pensions. Additionally, a QRDO can be used to collect child or spousal support.

§ 6.10 Joining Pension Plan as a Party

A state pension should be joined as a party to the divorce case (Family Code § 2021(b)). Pensions under CalPERS, CalSTRS, University of California Retirement System, and certain other pensions must be joined. *See* FL-318 for an Information Sheet on what pensions must be joined. Federal government pensions are not joined. Joining a pension plan as a party means the court's orders are binding on the pension plan.

§ 6.11 Military Retirement

Members of the active duty military have a defined benefit retirement plan. Members of the reserve and National Guard also have a retirement system.

In 1981, in *McCarty v. McCarty*, 453 U.S. 210, 101 S. Ct. 2728 (1981), the U.S. Supreme Court ruled that state family courts could not divide military pensions. Congress abrogated *McCarty* with passage of Uniformed Services Former Spouses' Protection Act (USFSPA).[19] USFSPA allows family courts to divide military pensions on divorce. Mark Sullivan writes, "State courts can order the direct pay of pension division awards through Defense Finance and Accounting Service (DFAS) when there is ten years' overlap between the marriage and creditable military service."[20] The details of military pension law are many, and Colonel Sullivan's book is an excellent guide.

§ 6.12 Social Security Retirement

Social Security retirement is available to workers who reach a set age and who have paid the required amount of payroll tax under the Federal Income Contributions Act (FICA). Federal Social Security retirement benefits are not subject to division on divorce.

In *Marriage of Peterson*, 243 Cal. App. 4th 923, 197 Cal. Rptr. 3d 588 (2016), the Court of Appeal grappled with a scenario that challenges courts to reach fair results. John and Annette married in 1994. They separated in 2010. John is an attorney in private practice. John contributes to Social Security, and will receive Social Security retirement. Annette is a deputy district attorney. Annette has a defined benefit plan with the county. Under Annette's plan, she does not pay Social Security taxes. Thus, Annette will not receive Social Security retirement.

On divorce, John keeps 100% of his Social Security.[21] To the extent Annette's pension is community property, John gets 50% of her pension. Annette argues this result is unfair, and that her pension should be divided in a way that accounts for the unfairness. John argues that although the result might be unfair, federal law requires he receive 100% of his Social Security and California Family Code § 2550 requires equal division of Annette's pension.

---

[19] 10 U.S.C. § 1408.

[20] Mark E. Sullivan, *The Military Divorce Handbook: A Practical Guide to Representing Military Personnel and Their Families* 484 (2d ed. 2011).

[21] The *Peterson* Court wrote, "Although retirement benefits are generally community property under California law, federal law mandates that Social Security is separate property. The supremacy clause of the United States Constitution establishes a constitutional choice-of-law rule, makes federal law paramount, and vests Congress with the power to preempt state law. California law on this issue is preempted."

The Court of Appeal concluded it had no choice but to accept John's position. The Court wrote, "The Family Code does not allow courts to make unequal awards of community assets. Because [Anette's pension] benefits are community assets, the court was required to divide the benefits equally.... We sympathize with Annette's situation, and recognize that the result of California's strict policies on the division of property, intended to protect spouses (see § 2580), did not produce an equitable result in the situation before us. But it is not our role to change or defy California law."

§ 6.13 *Gillmore* Election

Fran and Dave divorce in 2015. Dave has a defined benefit pension at work. Dave's pension is part community property. In the divorce, the time rule determines the community interest in the pension. A QDRO is entered, dividing the pension. Fran will begin receiving her share of the pension when Dave retires, and the pension is in pay status. Dave's pension matures in 2022, when Dave is eligible to retire. When 2022 arrives, Dave decides to keep working. Thus, his pension does not start. Fran would like to receive her share of the pension. Fran has two choices—called the *Gillmore* election.[22] First, Fran can wait until Dave retires and start receiving her share at that time. By waiting until Dave retires, Fran participates in any increase in Dave's pension during the years he continues working. Second, Fran can insist that she begin receiving her share in 2022, when Dave *could* retire. The pension plan will cut checks to Fran, starting in 2022, or, if the pension does not provide for that method, Dave will have to dig into his pocket and pay Fran the amount she would receive each month if Dave retired in 2022. If Fran decides she wants to start getting her share in 2022, the amount she receives is fixed as of 2022, and she does not participate in any increases in Dave's pension after 2022.

§ 6.14 Disability Benefits

Disability benefits have caused California courts considerable difficulty. In his treatise titled *Bassett on California Community Property Law,* William Bassett observed, "Case law fluctuates

---

[22] Marriage of Gillmore, 29 Cal. 3d 418, 629 P.2d 1, 174 Cal. Rptr. 493 (1981).

between analogizing disability payments to income or to personal injury lump sums or installment payout recoveries . . . ."[23]

Sometimes, a person who is entitled to retire with a regular retirement pension has the option to select a disability pension instead of regular retirement. To the extent a pension that is labeled "disability" serves the function of regular retirement, a court ignores the label and treats the pension as regular retirement unless federal or state law prohibits the court from doing so.

In *Marriage of Saslow*, 40 Cal. 3d 848, 710 P.2d 346, 221 Cal. Rptr. 546 (1985), during marriage, husband purchased disability insurance with community property. The Supreme Court concluded trial courts should treat disability benefits as separate property if the benefits were intended to replace post-separation earnings that would have been separate property. Trial courts consider the spouses' intent at the time disability policies were purchased and renewed. Did the parties intend the benefits to serve the function of a retirement pension that would be community property? Or did the parties intend the benefits to compensate for lost future income, which would be separate property? Often, of course, the parties' intent is unknown.

In *Marriage of Elfmont*, 9 Cal. 4th 1026, 891 P.2d 136, 39 Cal. Rptr. 2d 590 (1995), husband, during marriage, used community funds to purchase disability insurance. After the couple separated, husband renewed the policies with his separate property. The Court ruled the disability insurance was husband's separate property.

In *Marriage of Marshall*, 23 Cal. App. 5th 477, 487, 232 Cal. Rptr. 3d 819 (2018), the Court of Appeal wrote: "The character of those proceeds will usually follow the character of the disabled spouse's earnings: If during the marriage an insured spouse becomes disabled, the benefits received are community property because they replace community earnings. If the benefits continue after the spouses have separated, they are the separate property of the insured spouse whose earning they replace."

Attorneys for divorcing parties should ask whether the parties have disability insurance. If so, planning is needed to document the

---

[23] William W. Bassett, *Bassett on California Community Property Law* § 7:37, p. 784 (2017 edition).

parties' intent about the insurance and how the insurance should be characterized on divorce.

§ 6.15 Military Disability

Military retired benefits can be divided on divorce, similar to civilian pensions. Military disability benefits cannot be divided on divorce.

A service member can retire after 20 years' service. As mentioned above, a service member's retirement pension can be divided on divorce. However, if the military determines that a service member, at the time of retirement or later, has a service-related disability, the service member can elect to receive disability benefits. Regular military retirement is taxable whereas disability benefits are not taxable. Understandably, most retirees who qualify opt for disability benefits to save taxes. The service member cannot receive both regular retirement and disability benefits, so the service member gives up regular retirement equal to the amount of disability benefits.

In *Howell v. Howell,* 137 S. Ct. 1400 (2017), John and Sandra divorced in 1991. At the time of the divorce, John was nearing the end of his career in the Air Force. In the divorce, Sandra received part of John's pension when he retired. John retired in 1992, and started receiving his pension, which was shared with Sandra pursuant to the divorce. Thirteen years later, the Department of Veterans Affairs determined that John was 20% disabled due to a service-related shoulder injury. John elected to receive disability benefits, and had to give up about $250 each month of his regular retirement. The result was that Sandra got less money each month. Sandra went to family court in Arizona and asked the court to enforce the original divorce judgment by ordering John to pay Sandra the amount she lost each month because John elected to receive disability. The Arizona courts ordered John to make up the difference, requiring John to indemnify or reimburse Sandra the lost funds. The case went to the U.S. Supreme Court, which reversed the state court decisions. The U.S. Supreme Court reiterated that military disability is not divisible on divorce. The Court ruled: "We see nothing in this circumstance that makes the reimbursement of Sandra any less an award of the portion of military retirement pay that John waived in order to obtain disability benefits. . . . Neither can the State avoid [the Court's ruling] by describing the family court order as an order requiring John to 'reimburse' or to 'indemnify' Sandra."

The United States military has three disability programs: (1) Veterans Administration (VA) disability; (2) Military disability retired pay; and (3) Combat-Related Special Compensation.[24] When a service member is sufficiently disabled that she can no longer perform assigned duties, the service member may receive disability pay. No portion of a former service member's disability benefit can be divided in a divorce.[25]

Service members who are not sufficiently disabled to qualify for military disability pay, or whose disability is detected after retirement, may qualify for VA disability benefits. The service member gives up a portion of regular retirement benefits to obtain VA disability benefits. A state court cannot divide the retired pay that a service member gives up to receive VA disability.[26]

Combat-related Special Compensation (CRSC) is available to service members who are at least 10% disabled and whose disability is related to the award of a Purple Heart or to combat. CRSC is not divisible on divorce.

§ 6.16 Early Retirement

Occasionally, an employee approaching retirement is offered "early retirement." Such benefits are also called a "golden parachute" or "enhanced early retirement." The purpose is typically to encourage an employee to retire early so the company can reduce staff. If early retirement is based on employment during marriage, the early retirement money is community property.[27]

---

[24] *See* Mark E. Sullivan, *The Military Divorce Handbook: A Practical Guide to Representing Military Personnel and Their Families*, p. 509 (2d ed. 2011).

[25] Mark E. Sullivan, *The Military Divorce Handbook: A Practical Guide to Representing Military Personnel and Their Families*, p. 509 (2d ed. 2011).

[26] Mark E. Sullivan, *The Military Divorce Handbook: A Practical Guide to Representing Military Personnel and Their Families*, p. 513 (2d ed. 2011).

[27] *See* Marriage of Hehman, 18 Cal. 4th 169, 955 P.2d 451, 74 Cal. Rptr. 2d 825 (1988).

§ 6.17 Is Employment-Related Health Insurance Community Property?

One of the most valuable benefits of employment is health insurance for employees and their dependents. Is employment-related health insurance property subject to valuation and division on divorce? In *Burts v. Burts*, 266 P.3d 337 (Alaska 2011), the Alaska Supreme Court wrote, "We have repeatedly recognized that health insurance benefits earned during the marriage are a marital asset of the insured spouse . . . ." In *Burts*, husband retired after 20 years in the military. Husband was eligible for TRICARE—health insurance for the rest of his life. The Alaska court ruled husband's TRICARE health insurance was marital property.

The California Court of Appeal concluded in *Marriage of Elli*, 101 Cal. App. 4th 400, 124 Cal. Rptr. 2d 719 (2002) that husband's postretirement participation in his employer's health care plan was not property subject to division on divorce.

§ 6.18 Severance Pay

When certain employees resign or are laid off, the employee receives a "severance package." In divorce, is severance money community or separate? What purpose did the severance serve? If the severance was a reward for past service to the employer, and the employee was married during the period of service, then the severance is community property. On the other hand, if the severance was intended to replace lost future income after the couple separated, the severance is the separate property of the employee.

§ 6.19 Accrued Vacation and Sick Days

In some jobs, employees can accrue unused vacation and sick days. In California, accrued vacation pay earned during marriage is community property.[28] For example, Sue consults you about her desire for a divorce. Sue has been married twenty years, and during the entire marriage, Sue worked for the same company. Sue never

---

[28] *See* Suastez v. Plastic Dress-Up Co., 31 Cal. 3d 774, 647 P.2d 122, 183 Cal. Rptr 846 (1982). Family Code § 80 includes vacation pay in the meaning of "employee benefit plan."

missed a day's work due to sickness. Nor did she take any vacation. Fortunately for Sue, her employer allows employees to accrue unused sick and vacation days. The company does not have a "use it or lose it" policy for these benefits. Sue has accumulated nearly $100,000 in accrued sick/vacation days. Advise Sue on the proper characterization of the vacation and sick days.

§ 6.20 Stock Options

Some employers offer stock options as part of an employee's compensation package. Stock options earned for work during marriage and before separation are community property. If stock options are earned partly during marriage and partly following separation, the time rule is employed to allocate between separate and community portions of the options.[29]

§ 6.21 Life Insurance

A life insurance policy is a community asset to the extent the policy is paid for with community property. A term life policy covers a specific term, for example a year. With a term policy, there is no cash surrender value. At the end of the term, there is no value unless the policy is renewed for another term. When an insured dies during a term paid for with community property, the proceeds of the policy are community property. If a couple divorces, the insured spouse is, of course, alive. Thus, there are no proceeds of the policy.

California courts have struggled with whether a term life insurance policy paid for with community property has value to be divided on divorce. In *Marriage of Lorenz*, 146 Cal. App. 3d 464, 194 Cal. Rptr. 237 (1983), the Court of Appeal held that term life insurance with no cash surrender value was not a divisible community asset. The court in *Marriage of Gonzalez*, 168 Cal. App. 3d 1021, 214 Cal. Rptr. 634 (1985), disagreed with *Lorenz*. The Supreme Court has yet to resolve the issue.

---

[29] If stock options are nonassignable, they must be awarded to the employee spouse on divorce. To reach equal division of community property, other community property would be awarded to the non-employee spouse. *See* Marriage of Steinberger, 91 Cal. App. 4th 1449, 111 Cal. App. 2d 521 (2001); Marriage of Hug, 154 Cal. App. 3d 780, 201 Cal. Rptr. 676 (1984).

A whole life insurance policy, unlike term insurance, has a cash surrender value in addition to the proceeds of the policy on death. The cash surrender value builds up from premiums. To the extent the cash surrender value is earned with community property, it is community property, divisible on divorce.

In *Marriage of Steiner,* 17 Cal. App. 5th 1165, 225 Cal. Rptr. 3d 880 (2017), husband was in the military and had a life insurance policy under the Servicemen's Group Life Insurance Act. In the divorce, husband and wife stipulated that husband would maintain wife as the beneficiary of the insurance. The stipulation became a court order. Despite the order, following divorce husband changed the beneficiary to his sister. After husband died, the question was whether the proceeds of the insurance belonged to the ex-wife or the sister. Federal law allows service members the unfettered right to select the beneficiary. The Court of Appeal agreed with the trial judge that federal law—allowing husband to change the beneficiary—preempted the California court order to the contrary. The Court wrote, "A necessary consequence of the Supremacy Clause is that a state divorce decree, like other laws governing the economic aspects of domestic relations, must give way to clearly conflicting federal enactments."

Chapter 7

A POTPOURRI OF CHARACTERIZATION ISSUES

Analysis

§ 7.1   Business as Community or Separate Property
§ 7.2   Increased Value of Business
§ 7.3   Goodwill
§ 7.4   Educational Degrees
§ 7.5   Gambling Proceeds
§ 7.6   Intent of the Lender—a Tracing Method to Rebut the Community Property Presumption
§ 7.7   Commingled Bank Accounts
§ 7.8   Improvements
§ 7.9   Personal Injury Damages
§ 7.10 Are Pets Property?
§ 7.11 Collectibles
§ 7.12 Wedding Gifts
§ 7.13 Engagement Ring

This chapter discusses a variety of community property issues.

§ 7.1   Business as Community or Separate Property

A business can be separate property or community property. For example, Ann and Alex marry while earning engineering degrees. Upon graduation they start a business: A & A Electron Systems (AAES). Together, they invent a new method of communication—the next Facebook. Within ten years the business is worth millions. Their marriage, however, is on the rocks. In their divorce, AAES is community property—property acquired during marriage through the time, effort, energy, and skill of Ann and Alex. The business will be valued according to the fair market value.[1]

Change the facts. Ann started Allied Electron Systems (AES) before she met Alex. Ann met and married Alex five years *after* AES had become a profitable business. Because AES was owned by Ann prior to marriage, it is her separate property. During their ten year marriage, Ann devoted countless hours to AES, serving as its chief executive officer. Over the course of the marriage, AES tripled in value. When the parties divorce, how should AES be characterized? Does AES remain entirely Ann's separate property? Is it part separate and part community—pro rata apportionment? If AES is Ann's separate property, what about the increased value during marriage? Does the increased value belong in whole or part to the community? (*See* § 7.2).

Consider Bill and Tamara. When they married 10 year ago, Bill already owned a large and profitable stock portfolio he inherited from his parents. The portfolio is separate property. During marriage, Bill did little to manage the portfolio. Bill entrusted the portfolio to a stock broker. Periodically, Bill met briefly with the stock broker, but apart from these meetings Bill ignored the portfolio and simply enjoyed the checks sent to him by the stock broker. Between marriage and divorce, the portfolio doubled in value. Who owns the portfolio? What about the increased value during marriage? Change the facts. Bill managed the stock portfolio himself, devoting many hours a day to research and stock trades. Who owns the portfolio? The increased value?

§ 7.2 Increased Value of Business

When a business increases in value due to the efforts of one or both spouses, it is necessary to characterize the increased value.

---

[1] *See* Nuveen v. Nuveen, 795 N.W.2d 308, 313 (N.D. 2011) ("The fair market value of a business is ordinarily the proper method for valuing property in a divorce. Fair market value is the price a buyer is willing to pay and the seller is willing to accept under circumstances that do not amount to coercion.").

§ 7.2(a) Increased Value of Separate Property Business—*Van Camp* or *Pereira*

When a spouse owns a separate property business or asset that increases in value during marriage due in part or in whole to the efforts of the owner spouse, California provides that the increased value is part community property and part separate property. The business itself remains separate property. It is the increased value attributable to efforts of the owner spouse that is divided.[2]

In California, if the increased value of a separate property business is due entirely to natural growth, then the entire increase is the separate property of the owner spouse (*See* Family Code § 770—rents, issues, and profits of separate property are separate property). However, if the owner spouse expended more than *de minimus* effort on the business, and if at least part of the increased value is attributable to the owner spouse's efforts, then the increased value is divided between community property and separate property.[3] When the increased value is due primarily to the efforts of the owner spouse, the lion's share of the increase is community property. On the other hand, if the owner's efforts account for only a small portion of the increase—market forces account for most of the increase—most of the increase is separate property.

---

[2] *See* American Law Institute, *Principles of the Law of Family Dissolution: Analysis and Recommendations*, § 4.05, p. 663 (2000) ("(1) A portion of any increase in the value of separate property is marital property whenever either spouse has devoted substantial time during marriage to the property's management or preservation. (2) The increase in value of separate property over the course of the marriage is measured by the difference between the market value of the property when acquired, or at the beginning of the marriage, if later, and the market value of the property when sold, or at the end of the marriage, if sooner. (3) The portion of the increase in value that is marital property under Paragraph (1) is the difference between the actual amount by which the property has increased in value, and the amount by which capital of the same value would have increased over the same time period if invested in assets of relative safety requiring little management.").

[3] *See* Marriage of Dekker, 17 Cal. App. 4th 842, 851, 21 Cal. Rptr. 2d 642 (1993).

In most cases, it is the owner of the business who devotes time and effort to the business. In some cases, however, the non-owner spouse devotes effort to the business. In still other cases, both spouses are involved in the business. Courts apportion increased value in all these scenarios.

Two cases guide decision making in this area: *Van Camp v. Van Camp*, 53 Cal. App. 17, 199 P. 885 (1921) and *Pereira v. Pereira*, 156 Cal. 1, 103 P. 488 (1909). If the trial judge concludes the increase in value is due primarily to the efforts of the owner spouse, the judge uses *Pereira*. The judge allocates a fair return on the owner spouse's business (typically the legal interest rate), and allocates the rest of the increased value as community property arising from the owner's efforts. On the other hand, if most of the increase in value is due to market forces, the judge uses *Van Camp*.[4] With *Van Camp*, the judge determines the reasonable value of the owner spouse's services to the business and allocates that amount as community property. The remainder of the increase is separate property.[5] The judge is not tied rigidly to *Van Camp* or *Pereira*. In *Marriage of Brandes*, 239 Cal. App. 4th 1461, 192 Cal. Rptr. 3d 1 (2015), the trial court used *Van Camp* for some years and *Pereira* for other years.

How should the judge decide the following case? Two weeks prior to marrying Wendy, Hank registered a domain name in his name to develop a website. During marriage, Hank worked many hours a week on the web-based business, which prospered. Most income to support the family came from the website business. After a five year marriage, Wendy and Hank are divorcing. The domain name and website dramatically increased in value during marriage. Who owns the domain name and website? Should the increased value of the domain name and website be considered partly community property? If so, should the court employ *Pereira* or *Van Camp*? If you are Hank's attorney, which approach will you advocate to the court? What if you are Wendy's attorney? Which approach best serves your client's interests? *See Robertson v. Robertson*, 78 So. 3d 76 (Fla. Ct. App. 2012).

---

[4] For a useful discussion of *Van Camp see* Marriage of Brooks, 33 Cal. App. 5th 576, 244 Cal. Rptr. 3d 910 (2019).

[5] With *Van Camp*, after the amount of community property is calculated, the traditional view is that the court deducts from the community share family expenses over the course of the marriage. Family expenses are not deducted when the court uses *Pereira*. In *California Practice Guide: Family Law*, Retired Judge William Hogoboom and Retired Justice Donald King argue that family expenses should not be deducted from community property under *Van Camp* any more than under *Pereira* (Section 8:346, pp. 8–137).

§ 7.2(b) Increased Value of Community Business After Separation

When a married couple owns a community property business and the couple separates, it is common for one spouse to continue running the business. A married person's post-separation efforts generate separate property. If the business increases in value due in whole or part to the separated spouse's efforts, it is necessary to apportion the increased value. Courts use *Pereira* or *Van Camp* in reverse. Under *Pereira,* a fair return on the community property business is allocated to the community. The rest of the increased value is separate property. Under *Van Camp,* the court determines the reasonable value of the spouse's services, minus salary paid to the spouse, and allocates that amount as separate property. The balance of the increase is community property.

§ 7.3 Goodwill

You graduate from law school, pass the bar, and enter practice. After a few years in the legal trenches you realize your true passion is not the courtroom but the kitchen. You hang up your shingle, donate your fancy suits to charity, and move to Paris. You get a little apartment on the Left Bank with a view of the Eifel Tower, wile away the hours sipping coffee at quaint sidewalk cafes, mingle with artists, and enroll in the famous Le Cordon Bleu school of French cooking. (Hmm, sounds pretty good right about now, doesn't it?) Upon graduation from Le Cordon Bleu you return home to start your career as a chef. Most novices go to work at the bottom of the ladder in a restaurant and work their way up, but not you! You decide to buy a popular French restaurant. What will you pay? If the current owner owns the building, you will pay for that. Obviously, you will pay for the furniture and fittings of the restaurant—stoves, pots and pans, china, etc. But that's not all. A substantial portion of the purchase price will be "goodwill."

The California Business and Professions Code defines goodwill as "the expectation of continued public patronage." (§ 14100). In *In re Lyons,* 27 Cal. App. 2d 293, 81 P.2d 190, 193 (1938), the Court of Appeal defined goodwill as "the advantage or benefit which is acquired by an establishment beyond the mere value of the capitol stock, funds or property therein, in the consequence of the general public patronage and encouragement it receives from constant or habitual customers, on account of its local position, or common celebrity, or reputation for skill or affluence, or punctuality, or from other accidental circumstances, or necessities, or even from ancient partialities or prejudices." In *McReath v. McReath*, 800 N.W.2d 399 (Wis. 2011), the Wisconsin Supreme Court offered several definitions of goodwill:

> In its broadest sense the intangible asset called good will may be said to be reputation; however, a better description would probably be that element of value which inheres in the fixed and favorable consideration of customers arising from an established and well-conducted business.
>
> The advantage or benefit which is acquired by an establishment beyond the mere value of the capital stock, funds, or property employed therein, in consequence of the general public patronage and encouragement which it receives from constant or habitual customers on account of its local position, or common celebrity, or reputation for skill or affluence, or punctuality, or from other accidental circumstances or necessities, or even from ancient partiality or prejudices.
>
> Goodwill is a business's reputation, patronage, and other intangible assets that are considered when appraising the business, especially for purchase; the ability to earn income in excess of the income that would be expected from the business viewed as a mere collections of assets.
>
> Simply stated, goodwill is an asset of recognized value beyond the tangible assets of a business.[6]

The goodwill of a traditional commercial business (*e.g.*, a laundry) is often relatively simple to value: What would a willing buyer pay for the business, including goodwill?[7] Commercial

---

[6] 800 N.W.2d at 408.

[7] *See* American Law Institute, *Principles of the Law of Family Dissolution: Analysis and Recommendations*, § 4.07, p. 699 (2000) ("Accounting conventions usually ascribe goodwill to a business only when it is sold, at which time it is defined as the difference, if there is any, between the sale price of the business and the value

goodwill is often called enterprise goodwill. Courtney Beebe writes, "Enterprise goodwill attaches to a business entity and is associated separately from the reputation of the owners. Product names, business locations, and skilled labor forces are common examples of enterprise goodwill. The asset has a determinable value because the enterprise goodwill of an ongoing business will transfer upon sale of the business to a willing buyer."[8] To the extent enterprise goodwill is acquired during marriage, it is community property.

Professionals, including attorneys, accountants, physicians, dentists, engineers, and architects, can acquire goodwill. Professional goodwill is community property if it is acquired during marriage.[9]

Some courts divide professional goodwill into two components: personal goodwill and enterprise goodwill.[10] Enterprise goodwill is the goodwill of the professional practice itself. Personal goodwill is unique to the individual.[11] In *May v. May*, 214 W. Va. 394, 589 S.E.2d 536, 545–546 (2003), the West Virginia Supreme Court

---

of the business's tangible assets. Standard accounting practice thus gives goodwill a purely operational definition: it is no more (or less) than the amount by which the market value of a going concern exceeds the total value of its tangible assets ('asset value'). If the market value does not exceed the asset value, the business has no goodwill; if it does, it has goodwill in an amount precisely equal to that excess.").

[8] Courtney E. Beebe, *The Object of My Appraisal: Idaho's Approach to Valuing Goodwill as Community Property in* Chandler v. Chandler, 39 Idaho Law Review 77, 83–84 (2002).

[9] *But see* Von Hohn v. Von Hohn, 260 S.W.3d 631, 638 (Tex. Ct. App. 2008)("Professional goodwill attaches to the person of the professional man or woman as a result of confidence in his or her skill and ability, and would be extinguished in the event of the professional's death, retirement, or disablement. Such professional goodwill is not property in the estate of the parties and, therefore, not divisible upon divorce. To the extent that goodwill exists in the professional practice separate and apart from the professional's personal ability and reputation, that goodwill has a commercial value and is community property subject to division upon divorce.").

[10] *See* Ahern v. Ahern, 938 A.2d 35, 38 (Me. 2008) ("Most jurisdictions embrace a framework that distinguishes between 'enterprise' goodwill and 'personal' goodwill.").

[11] *See* Von Hohn v. Von Hohn, 260 S.W.3d 631, 638 (Tex. Ct. App. 2008)("Professional goodwill attaches to the person of the professional man or woman as a result of confidence in his or her skill and ability, and would be extinguished in the event of the professional's death, retirement, or disablement. Such professional goodwill is not property in the estate of the parties and, therefore, not divisible upon to divorce. To the extent that goodwill exists in the professional practice separate and apart from the professional's personal ability and reputation, that goodwill has a commercial value and is community property subject to division upon divorce.").

wrote: "There is a split of authority on whether enterprise goodwill and/or personal goodwill in a professional practice may be characterized as marital property and thus equitably distributed. Three different approaches have developed. A large number of courts make no distinction between personal and enterprise goodwill. These jurisdictions have taken the position that both personal and enterprise goodwill in a professional practice constitute marital property.... On the other hand, a minority of courts have taken the position that neither personal nor enterprise goodwill in a professional practice constitutes marital property.... The majority of states differentiate between enterprise goodwill and personal goodwill. Courts in these states take the position that personal goodwill is not marital property, but that enterprise goodwill is marital property." The American Law Institute's *Principles of the Law of Family Dissolution* have this to say: "Professional goodwill earned during marriage is marital property to the extent [it has] value apart from the value of spousal earning capacity, spousal skills, or post-dissolution spousal labor."[12]

Generally, expert testimony is needed to place a value on goodwill. Accountants use several formulas to calculate goodwill, and California courts permit any generally accepted accounting approach.

Do movie stars and professional athletes have goodwill?—celebrity goodwill? What is the value of a name like Serena or Venus Williams, LeBron James, Namar, Jennifer Lopez, Tom Hanks, or Matt Damon? To these star athletes and actors, their name is worth millions. But does a celebrity have goodwill that can be valued and divided on divorce? California is home to Hollywood. Given the divorce rate among actors it is surprising to learn that the issue of celebrity goodwill did not reach a California appellate court until 2006. In *Marriage of McTiernan and Dubrow*, 133 Cal. App. 4th 1090, 35 Cal. Rptr. 3d 287 (2005), the Court of Appeal ruled celebrity goodwill is not property for purposes of divorce. Courts in New

---

[12] American Law Institute, *Principles of the Law of Family Dissolution: Analysis and Recommendations* § 4.07(3), p. 694 (2000).

Jersey and New York rule celebrity goodwill can be property subject to equitable distribution.[13]

§ 7.4 Educational Degrees

In California, a college or graduate degree is not property subject to division on divorce. Family Code § 2641 creates a limited right to reimbursement for community contributions to the attainment of a degree. Section 2641(b)(1) provides that "the community shall be reimbursed for community contributions to education or training of a party that substantially enhances the earning capacity of the party." If a divorce occurs more than ten years after a degree was earned, the law presumes the community has benefitted sufficiently from the degree that reimbursement is unwarranted.

§ 7.5 Gambling Proceeds

Gambling usually results in debt not profit. On the rare occasion that gambling results in an asset, California courts characterize the asset by tracing to the funds used to gamble. Thus, if community property paid for a winning lottery ticket the winnings are community property. In *Marriage of Wall*, 29 Cal. App. 3d 76, 105 Cal. Rptr. 201 (1972), a separated spouse used separate property to buy the winning ticket for the Irish Sweepstakes. The money was hers. In *Marriage of Shelton*, 118 Cal. App. 3d 811, 173 Cal. Rptr. 629 (1981), Husband and Wife were separated. Husband took $10,000 of community property to Nevada to gamble. He won $21,000. With $31,000 burning a hole in his pocket, he bought a Ferrari. At the divorce trial, wife argued the car was entirely community property. Husband argued pro rata apportionment should apply. According to Husband, $10,000 worth of the car was community property, and $21,000 worth was his separate property because he used his post-separation time and talent to win the $21,000. The Court of Appeal held the car was entirely community property, reasoning that gambling depends more on luck that skill. Thus, the Court looked to the source of the funds.

---

[13] *See* Piscopo v. Piscopo, 232 N.J. Super. 559, 557 A.2d 1040 (1989); Elkus v. Elkus, 169 A.D.2d 134, 572 N.Y.S.2d 901 (1991).

§ 7.6 Intent of the Lender—a Tracing Method to Rebut the Community Property Presumption

When a married person or a married couple acting together takes out a loan, it may be necessary on divorce to characterize the proceeds of the loan. Is the money separate property or community property? Assuming the loan was acquired during marriage and prior to separation, the proceeds fall under the general community property presumption (Family Code § 760).

If the loan was used to purchase property—*e.g.*, a car—the car falls under general community property presumption. The general community property presumption persists if title to the car is put in one spouse's name alone.[14] If the spouses took title jointly, § 2581 applies on divorce to characterize the car as community property. If one spouse wants to claim that the car is separate property, the separatizer has to rebut the community property presumption. The general community property presumption is rebutted by tracing to separate property. The § 2581 presumption is rebutted by tracing *plus* a writing sufficient to rebut the presumption. (*See* § 5.17).

The tracing technique used to rebut the community property presumption with loans, items purchased with loans, and credit acquisitions, is the intent of the lender test.[15] The separatizer offers evidence that the lender relied for repayment on separate property. If the lender relied on separate property for repayment, then the loan was separate property, and items purchased with the loan are traceable to separate property, rebutting the community property presumption.

---

[14] If the couple has a written transmutation agreement regarding the car, the agreement will control.

[15] *See* Marriage of Bonvino, 241 Cal. App. 4th 1411, 1423, 194 Cal. Rptr. 3d 754 (2015)("The character of property acquired on credit is determined by whether the lender intended to rely on separate or community property. Loan proceeds acquired during marriage are presumed to be community property. This presumption can be rebutted by showing the lender intended to rely on the spouse's separate property alone. Loan proceeds secured by separate property are also separate property. However, the proceeds of a loan made on a spouse's personal credit are considered community property. Without satisfactory evidence of the lender's intent, the general [community property] presumption prevails.").

There are two formulations of the intent of the lender test, each derived from a case. In 1953, the Supreme Court ruled in *Gudelj v. Gudelj,* 41 Cal. 2d 202, 259 P. 656 (1953) that the community property presumption is rebutted with evidence the lender relied primarily on separate property to repay the loan. In 1985, the Court of Appeal ruled in *Marriage of Grinius,* 166 Cal. App. 3d 1179, 212 Cal. Rptr. 803 (1985) that rebuttal of the community property presumption requires evidence the lender relied solely on separate property for repayment.

It is nearly impossible to satisfy the *Grinius*—solely relied on— test because lenders rely on a person's creditworthiness as a critical factor in extending a loan. A married person's creditworthiness belongs to the community. Thus, it is difficult to imagine a scenario in which a lender relied solely on a person's separate property for repayment. The *Gudelj*—primarily relied on—test is easier on the separatizer than *Grinius.* With *Gudelj,* the separatizer need only prove that the lender relied primarily on separate property for repayment. But even with *Gudelj,* the separatizer has an uphill fight because, again, lenders rely on creditworthiness, which belongs to the community.

If the separatizer cannot satisfy *Gudelj* or *Grinius,* the community property presumption prevails.

§ 7.7 Commingled Bank Accounts

A bank or savings and loan account may be in one spouse's name or it may be a joint account. California's Multi-Party-Accounts Law (Probate Code §§ 5100 et seq.) defines a joint account as "an account payable on request to one or more of two or more parties . . ." (Probate Code § 5130). Contributions by married persons to a joint account are presumed to be community property (Probate Code § 5305(a)). The community property presumption established by § 5305(a) can be rebutted by tracing to separate property,[16] unless the couple has a written agreement that the funds in the account are community property.

Commingling refers to a situation in which community property funds and separate property funds are deposited in a bank

---

[16] Do not apply Family Code § 2581 to joint bank accounts.

account. Commingling does not change the character of money in an account. Thus, if $1,000 of separate property, and $1,000 of community property are deposited in an account, the funds retain their character as separate property and community property.[17]

In a divorce, money in a commingled account typically falls under the general community property presumption (§ 760). If a spouse wants to claim some or all of the money in the account is separate property, the spouse has to trace the money to separate property deposits in order to rebut the general community property presumption.

If items were purchased during marriage with funds from a commingled account, the items typically fall under the general community property presumption (§ 760) or under a form of title presumption (*e.g.*, § 2581). If a spouse claims the money used to purchase an item was separate property, the spouse must trace the money back to the bank account, and then to separate property deposits in the account.

Two methods are used to trace money in a commingled account to separate property. In other words, there are two ways to uncommingle a commingled account. The methods are called direct tracing and indirect tracing. Indirect tracing is also called the exhaustion method.

§ 7.7(a) Direct Tracing

The theory of direct tracing is simple, at least in theory: The spouse seeking to prove money withdrawn from a commingled account was separate property proves two things: (1) At the moment the withdrawal was made sufficient separate funds were available in the account to cover the withdrawal, and (2) The spouse intended to withdraw separate funds.[18]

In most cases it is difficult to meet the first requirement of direct tracing—sufficient separate funds in the bank—because most

---

[17] *See* Marriage of Bonvino, 241 Cal. App. 4th 1411, 1423, 194 Cal. Rptr. 3d 754 (2015)(commingling does not change the status of property as separate or community).

[18] For a case where a spouse was successful in using direct tracing, see the unpublished decision in Marriage of Antoniadis, 2016 WL 675548 (Cal. Ct. App. 2016).

people do not keep adequately detailed financial records to prove what funds were in an account on a particular day. What is required is *not* just proof of the account balance on a particular day—that is easy to prove. What is required is proof of exactly how much community property and separate property was in the account on the day of the withdrawal. Judges Hogoboom and King describe the necessary record keeping, "Direct tracing requires specific records reconstructing each separate and community deposit and each separate and community payment or withdrawal as it occurs."[19] Most people don't keep such detailed financial records.

§ 7.7(b) Indirect Tracing—Exhaustion Method

The exhaustion method of uncommingling a commingled account rests on the presumption that family expenses are paid from available community property rather than available separate property.[20] Family expenses are the routine costs of maintaining a household and family. The party seeking to prove that separate property was withdrawn from a commingled account proves that at the moment of the withdrawal all community property had been used—exhausted—to pay family expenses. Since all community property was exhausted on family expenses, the money remaining in the account was, by process of elimination, separate property. When family expenses are paid with separate property there is no right to reimbursement of the separate property unless the parties agreed to reimbursement.

The exhaustion method is simple in theory, but, like direct tracing, very difficult to prove in court. As with direct tracing, people simply do not maintain the kinds of financial records that are necessary to reconstruct what funds—separate or community, and in what amounts—were in an account on a given day, perhaps years earlier.

In *See v. See*, 64 Cal. 2d 778, 415 P.2d 776, 51 Cal. Rptr. 888 (1966), Husband sought to use indirect tracing to prove that items of property acquired from a commingled account during a long

---

[19] William P. Hogoboom & Donald B. King, *California Practice Guide: Family Law* § 8:528, p. 8–204 (2017).

[20] The family expense presumption is a judge made presumption; it is not found in statute.

marriage were purchased with his separate property funds. Husband did not have the financial records to prove that on the days when the items were purchased community funds were exhausted by family expenses. Husband sought to overcome this failure of proof with evidence that over the course of the entire marriage, family expenses were greater than deposits of community property in the account, a method called total recapitulation accounting. The Supreme Court rejected Husband's effort because total recapitulation tells the court *nothing* about the only relevant issue: At a particular moment in time, was all the community property in a commingled account exhausted by family expenses?

§ 7.7(c) Simple Samples

In real marriages, it is often impossible to use direct or indirect tracing to uncommingle a commingled account because adequate financial records are not available. To give you some idea of how direct and indirect tracing work on drastically oversimplified facts, consider two cases.

1. Mary and Richard are married. During marriage, Mary opened a bank account in her name, and made the following deposits and withdrawals:

January—Deposit $50,000 income from employment during marriage.

May—Withdraw $20,000 to redecorate the family home.

June—Withdraw $20,000 to purchase Apple stock.

July—Deposit $10,000 income from employment.

August—Deposit $30,000 from sale of Mary's separate property.

September—Withdraw $50,000 to pay for Richard's medical care.

October—Deposit $10,000 from employment.

Mary and Richard are divorcing. Characterize the Apple stock. Characterize the money in the account, following the October deposit.

2. Rachel and Tom are married. On their wedding day, Tom had a bank account that contained his $20,000 inheritance from his aunt Minnie. During marriage, Tom makes the following deposits and withdrawals:

January 1—Withdraw $1,000 to pay rent on Rachel and Tom's apartment.

January 20—Withdraw $2,000 to pay Rachel's medical bill.

February 3—Deposit $2,000 paycheck from work.

February 20—Deposit $1,000 paycheck from work.

March 3—Deposit $1,000 paycheck from work.

April 1—Withdraw $1,000 for a new suit for Tom.

May 23—Withdraw $3,000 to purchase Apple stock.

May 30—Deposit $2,000 paycheck from work.

June 5—Withdraw $1,000 to pay for trip for Rachel and Tom.

July 6—Deposit $2,000 paycheck from work.

July 25—Withdraw $6,000 to purchase stock in Xerox.

Rachel and Tom are divorcing. Character the suit Tom bought. Characterize the Apple stock. Characterize the Xerox stock.

§ 7.8 Improvements

Husband owns Blackacre as separate property. Without consulting Wife, Husband uses $14,000 of community property to add a swimming pool to Blackacre. When Wife finds out she is upset. Does she have a remedy? Consider another case. Wife and husband own a farm as community property. Husband uses $25,000 of his separate property to add a barn. Wife and husband are divorcing. Is husband entitled to be reimbursed the separate property he used to pay for the barn? Does Husband's expenditure of $25,000 give him a separate property ownership interest in the farm?

These scenarios play out frequently in divorce litigation, and involve a set of rules dealing with improvements. An improvement is a permanent addition to property. Examples include adding a building to land, installing wall-to-wall carpeting, replacing a water heater, adding a swimming pool or hot tub, and repairing a roof.

Personal property that is sufficiently affixed to land becomes part of the realty and is called a fixture (Civil Code § 660). Personal property becomes a fixture when: (1) It is annexed to reality; (2) It is adapted or applied to the realty; and (3) The addition is intended to become a permanent accession to the realty. The fact that an item (*e.g.*, water heater; cabinets) can be removed without damaging the real property does not necessarily mean the item is not a fixture. *Aljabban v. Fontana Indoor Swap Meet, Inc.,* 54 Cal. App. 5th 482, 501, 268 Cal. Rptr. 3d 25 (2020).

Spending money to improve land or add fixtures generally does *not* acquire an ownership interest in the land. One acquires an ownership interest by paying the mortgage, not by adding an improvement. Thus, improvements do not trigger pro rata apportionment of ownership. Recall the situation above where Husband used community property to add a swimming pool to his separate property. The property remains entirely Husband's separate property. The issue is whether the spouse who did not consent to adding the pool with community funds can claim reimbursement.

The improvement issue arises in the following scenarios:

- One spouse uses her/his separate property to improve the other spouse's separate property.

- One spouse uses community property to improve the other spouse's separate property.

- One spouse uses community property to improve her/his own separate property.

- One spouse uses her/his separate property to improve community property.

- One spouse uses her/his separate property to improve her/his own separate property.

§ 7.8(a) One Spouse Uses Her/His Separate Property to Improve the Other Spouse's Separate Property

Prior to January 1, 2005, when one spouse used their separate property to improve the other spouse's separate property, there was no right of reimbursement. After January 1, 2005, the improving spouse is entitled to reimbursement (Family Code § 2640(c)).

Question: Wife owns Purpleacre as separate property. Husband uses his separate property to add a swimming pool. Who owns Purpleacre? If the couples divorces, is Husband entitled to reimbursement?

§ 7.8(b) One Spouse Uses Community Property to Improve the Other Spouse's Separate Property

Traditionally, when one spouse used community property to improve the other spouse's separate property, the improving spouse had no right to reimbursement. The Court of Appeal, in *Marriage of Wolfe*, 91 Cal. App. 4th 962, 110 Cal. Rptr. 2d 921 (2001), expressed dissatisfaction with the traditional rule. The court concluded there is "no logical basis for denying a spouse reimbursement for a community funded improvement to the other spouse's separate property."[21] The community is reimbursed half the cost of the improvement.

Question: Husband inherited a farm from his mom. Wife used $100,000 of community property to add a barn and an orchard. The marriage is ending. Who owns the farm? What rules govern the improvements?

§ 7.8(c) One Spouse Uses Community Property to Improve Her/His Own Separate Property

If spouses agree to expend community funds to improve one spouse's separate property, there is no problem. The agreement amounts to a transmutation, and should be in writing to satisfy the requirement of Family Code § 852(b). But what if the spouse making

---

[21] 91 Cal. App. 4th at 971. *Accord*, Marriage of Allen, 96 Cal. App. 4th 497, 116 Cal. Rptr. 2d 887 (2002).

the improvement with community property does not consult the other spouse to obtain their consent? In this scenario, courts order reimbursement to the community. Reimbursement is the amount of community funds expended or the increased value due to the improvement, whichever is greater.

§ 7.8(d) One Spouse Uses Her/His Separate Property to Improve Community Property

When a spouse uses their separate property to improve community property after January 1, 1984, Family Code § 2640 requires reimbursement of the separate property. See § 5.19 for discussion of § 2640.

§ 7.8(e) One Spouse Uses Her/His Separate Property to Improve Her/His Own Separate Property

No special rules apply here. A married person can do what they like with their separate property, including spending it on improvements to their separate property. The other spouse has no complaint.

§ 7.9 Personal Injury Damages

A married person may commit a tort and owe money to the injured party. On the other hand, a married person may be injured and receive money. The first scenario creates a debt, the second creates an asset. Different rules govern each situation.

§ 7.9(a) Personal Injury Award—Injured Spouse

When a spouse is injured and receives money damages, the money is community property if the cause of action arose during marriage and prior to separation (§ 780). If the cause of action arose after separation, the money is separate property (§ 781). If one spouse injures the other, money paid to compensate for the injury is separate property of the injured spouse (§ 781(c)).

In divorce proceedings, if the parties cannot agree on how to divide community property, the court divides the community property equally (§ 2550). When personal injury damages are community property because the cause of action arose during marriage and before separation, Family Code § 2603(b) creates an exception to the equal division requirement. Section 2603(b) mandates that 100% of the community property personal injury money be assigned to the injured spouse. The idea behind § 2603(b) is that the injured spouse's need for the money outweighs the principle of equal division of community property. Section 2603(b) allows the judge to depart from the rule that 100% of community property personal injury damages must be awarded to the injured spouse when circumstances indicate the injured spouse does not need the money. The court considers how much time has gone by since the injury as well as the economic circumstances and needs of each spouse. In any event, the injured spouse must receive at least half the money.

§ 7.9(b)   Personal Injury Debt—Injuring Spouse

When a spouse commits a tort and has to pay damages, the damages constitute a debt (Family Code § 902). Satisfaction of such debts is discussed in § 9.3.

§ 7.10   Are Pets Property?

Sue and Sam are divorcing. For the three years prior to divorce, Sue and Sam enjoyed the companionship of their two miniature dachshunds, Bindy and Chibby. Sue and Sam dearly love Bindy and Chibby, and the dogs are very attached to their owners and each other. In the divorce, Sue and Sam cannot agree on who should get the dogs. In a divorce case, are family pets property subject to division under principles of community property law? Or are pets akin to children, which means the judge should apply a "best interests of the pet" test? Courts traditionally treated pets as property.[22] In 2018, the Legislature added Family Code § 2605. Under this section the court, at the request of a party, can assign sole or joint ownership of pets.

Three articles on pets and divorce may be of interest. Heidi Stroh, Puppy Love: Providing for the Legal Protection of Animals

---

[22] *See* Eric Kotloff (Note), *All Dogs Go To Heaven . . . Or Divorce Court: New Jersey Un"Leashes" a Subjective Value Consideration to Resolve Pet Custody Litigation in* Houseman v. Dare, 55 Villanova Law Review 447 (2010); Moore v. Knower, 214 So. 3d 165 (La. Ct. App. 2017).

When Their Owners Get Divorced, 2 *Journal of Animal Law and Ethics* 231 (2007); Diane Sullivan & Holly Vietzke, An Animal is Not an iPod, 6 *Journal of Animal Law* 41 (2008); John DeWitt Gregory, Pet Custody: Distorting Language and the Law, 44 *Family Law Quarterly* 35 (2010).

§ 7.11 Collectibles

People collect just about anything you can imagine: cars, china, baseball cards, stamps, dolls, art, jewelry, jukeboxes, clocks, beer cans, barbed wire (yes, barbed wire; check out *Barbed Wire Collector Magazine*). You name it; people collect it. Some collections are worth millions (consider late-night talk show host Jay Leno's car collection), while others are only of sentimental value. To the extent acquired during marriage, collections are community property. Valuing a collection may require an expert.

§ 7.12 Wedding Gifts

On your wedding day, you are not (hopefully) thinking about divorce. The guests arrive bearing gifts—ten pancake makers, five toasters, six waffle irons, etc. Hopefully, some guests give you cash. Suppose the marriage doesn't last. Are wedding gifts community property? It depends on the intent of the donor. If Aunt Minnie intended the toaster to belong to you and you alone, it is your separate property. Most of the time, however, there is no clear evidence of donative intent.[23] In *Coppola v. Farina*,[24] the Connecticut Superior Court wrote: "Treatises have stated that if the donor's intent is not clear, there are two basic approaches for classifying wedding gifts. Those two approaches are referred to as

---

[23] *See* American Law Institute, *Principles of the Law of Family Dissolution: Analysis and Recommendations* 658 (2000) ("Wedding gifts are sometimes said to present a special problem because they are typically received before the marriage. The usual rule classified gifts and premarital acquisitions as separate property, yet one normally assumes that wedding gifts are intended for the couple jointly. The question is whether and under what circumstances this assumption should govern. One line of cases follows an approach, sometimes called the New York rule, that treats wedding gifts as marital unless they are earmarked by the donor for one spouse alone, or consist of an item appropriate for only husband or wife. The competing approach, sometimes called the English rule, treats the source of the gift as dispositive where the donor's intent is ambiguous or uncertain, allocating it to the spouse whose relative or friend provided it.").

[24] 50 Conn. Supp. 11, 910 A.2d 1011, 1016–1018 (Sup. Ct. 2006).

the New York rule and the English rule. The New York rule presumes that a wedding gift is intended as a joint gift unless the gift is appropriate for the use of only one spouse or is peculiarly earmarked for one particular spouse. . . . Under the English rule, the donor is presumed to have given the gift to the party to whom he is more closely related."

§ 7.13 Engagement Ring

Two people are in love, and one asks, "Will you marry me?" The answer is "yes." They are engaged! A small box emerges from a pocket and is opened to reveal a diamond engagement ring. Unfortunately, the engagement is broken off, and the couple does not marry. Does the one who gave the engagement ring have a right to its return? In California, the answer is generally, yes.[25] Civil Code § 1590 provides: "Where either party to a contemplated marriage in this State makes a gift of money or property to the other on the basis or assumption that the marriage will take place, in the event that the donee refuses to enter into the marriage as contemplated or that it is given up my mutual consent, the donor may recover such gift or such part of its value as may, under all of the circumstances of the case, be found by a court or jury to be just." If a couple marries and later divorces, an engagement ring is generally considered a gift to the donee.[26]

---

[25] *See* Priebe v. Sinclair, 90 Cal. App. 2d 79, 202 P.2d 577 (1949).
[26] *See* Randall v. Randall, 56 So. 3d 817 (Fla. Ct. App. 2011).

Chapter 8

TRANSMUTATIONS

Analysis

§ 8.1	Pre-1985 Transmutations
§ 8.2	Writing Requirement for Post-1985 Transmutations
§ 8.3	Transmutations and Fiduciary Duties
§ 8.4	Uniform Voidable Transactions Act

During marriage, a couple is free to change the character of property.[1] Thus, a couple may change separate property to community property, community property to separate property, or separate property of one spouse to separate property of the other (Family Code § 850). Such changes are called transmutations.

§ 8.1 Pre-1985 Transmutations

Prior to January 1, 1985, a transmutation could be written or oral.[2] In one pre-1985 case, for example, Husband owned real estate and personal property as separate property.[3] After Husband died, his widow claimed that during the marriage, Husband transmuted the property to community property. The widow testified that Husband told her, "Now that we are married, we are partners, and marriage is a partnership. Everything I have is ours, and everything you have in ours. We are partners. Everything is 50–50." The court

---

[1] Marriage of Valli, 58 Cal. 4th 1396, 1400, 324 P.3d 274, 171 Cal. Rptr. 3d 454 (2014) ("Married persons may, through a transfer or an agreement, transmute—that is change—the character of property from community to separate or from separate to community.").

[2] In re Brace, 9 Cal. 5th 903, 470 P.3d 15, 266 Cal. Rptr 3d 298 (2020) (in a rare case, a pre-1985 transmutation might even be inferred from the conduct of the parties).

[3] Estate of Rapheal, 91 Cal. App. 2d 931, 206 P.2d 391 (1949).

ruled this language sufficient to transmute Husband's separate property into community property.

Normally, a transfer of real property requires a writing to comply with the statute of frauds. A pre-1985 oral transmutation of land was an exception to the statute of frauds.

§ 8.2 Writing Requirement for Post-1985 Transmutations

Effective January 1, 1985, transmutations must be in writing.[4] Oral transmutations entered before January 1, 1985 remain valid (§ 852(e)). Any transmutation entered after January 1, 1985 must be in writing. Family Code § 852(a) describes the writing required for a valid post-January 1, 1985 transmutation: "A transmutation of real or personal property is not valid unless made in writing by an express declaration that is made, joined in, consented to, or accepted by the spouse whose interest in the property is adversely affected."

The writing required by § 852(a) for a transmutation is specific. In *Estate of MacDonald*, 51 Cal. 3d 262, 794 P.2d 911, 272 Cal. Rptr. 153 (1990), the Supreme Court held that a writing is not an "express declaration" for § 852(a) purposes unless it contains language which expressly states that the characterization or ownership of property is being changed." The writing must be signed by the party economically disadvantaged by the change in characterization. The Supreme Court wrote, "A writing signed by the adversely affected spouse is not an 'express declaration' for the purposes of [§ 852(a)] *unless* it contains language which expressly states that the characterization or ownership of the property is being changed."[5]

In *Marriage of Barneson*, 69 Cal. App. 4th 583, 81 Cal. Rptr. 2d 726 (1999), Husband had a stroke and was not sure he would

---

[4] The Legislature changed transmutation law to require a writing because, when transmutations could be oral, it was too easy to slip into a transmutation during casual conversation, or through an offhand remark. An oral communication is easily misinterpreted. Memories fade about words that were spoken, or their meaning. Indeed, there was concern that some purported oral transmutations never really happened, and that angry or greedy spouses created so-called transmutations out of whole cloth. To put an end to this "invitation to litigation," the Legislature required transmutations after January 1, 1985 to be in writing. *See* Marriage of Valli, 58 Cal. 4th 1396, 1401, 324 P.3d 274, 171 Cal. Rptr. 3d 454 (2014).

[5] 51 Cal. 3d at 272.

survive. Husband instructed various stock brokers, in writing, to "transfer" his separate property stock to his wife. Husband recovered but the marriage ended in divorce. In the divorce, Wife claimed Husband's written instructions to "transfer" stock to her satisfied the writing requirement of § 852(a). The Court of Appeal disagreed because the writing did not expressly state that ownership of the stock was being changed.

In *Estate of Bibb*, 87 Cal. App. 4th 461, 104 Cal. Rptr. 2d 415 (2001), Husband singed a deed transferring his separate real property to himself and his wife as community property. A deed, signed by the grantor and accepted by the grantee, is an express declaration that ownership is changed, satisfying § 852(a).[6]

When a third party property owner signs a deed conveying property to a married couple as joint tenants, the conveyance creates a joint tenancy that is presumptively community property under Family Code § 760. Could one spouse successfully argue that the deed constitutes a transmutation of part of the property to the spouse's separate property? In *In re Brace*, 9 Cal. 5th 903, 912, 470 P.3d 15, 266 Cal. Rptr 3d 298 (2020), the Supreme Court said no, writing, "[J]oint tenancy titling of property acquired by spouses using community funds on or after January 1, 1975 is not sufficient by itself to transmute community property into separate property."[7]

In *Estate of MacDonald*, the Supreme Court made clear that extrinsic evidence is not admissible to aid in the interpretation of a purported transmutation.

A transmutation does not have to use the word "transmutation."[8] What is important is that the writing clearly state that ownership interests are being changed.

Family Code § 853(a) provides, "A statement in a will of the character of property is not admissible as evidence of a transmutation of the property in a proceeding commenced before the

---

[6] *See* Marriage of Wozniak, 59 Cal. App. 5th 120, 273 Cal. Rptr. 3d 421 (2020) (to be effective, a deed must be accepted by the grantee).

[7] The Court wrote, "joint tenancy property acquired with community funds before January 1, 1975 is presumptively separate property." 9 Cal 5th at 912.

[8] Estate of MacDonald, 51 Cal. 3d 262, 794 P.2d 911, 272 Cal. Rptr. 153 (1990) ("We do not hold that section [852(a)] requires use of the term 'transmutation' or another particular locution.").

death of the person who made the will." A will does not "speak" until death. A will can be changed or revoked during the lifetime of the testator. Thus, a statement in a will about changing property does not qualify as a transmutation. However, when the testator dies, the will speaks and an otherwise valid transmutation in the will is enforceable.

§ 8.3 Transmutations and Fiduciary Duties

A transmutation agreement is subject to the fiduciary standards set forth in Family Code § 721(b). (*See* § 10.7). A transmutation agreement that advantages one spouse over the other is presumed to have been induced by undue influence. To rebut the presumption of undue influence, the advantaged spouse must prove by a preponderance of the evidence that the disadvantaged spouse: (1) freely entered into the transmutation; (2) had full knowledge of the facts; and (3) understood the legal implications of the agreement.

§ 8.4 Uniform Voidable Transactions Act

A transmutation is subject to the Uniform Voidable Transactions Act (UVTA).[9] In addition to applying to transmutations, the UVTA applies to premarital agreements and marital settlement agreements.[10]

The UVTA is found at Civil Code § 3439. The Act is intended to protect unsecured creditors from property transfers by debtors that impede creditor rights.[11] For example, Debby Debtor realizes that her creditor is about to take her home to enforce a debt. To avoid this, Debby deeds the home to her sister for $1.00. This transfer is fraudulent as to the creditor. The transaction can be set aside.

The UVTA provides a remedy for two types of fraudulent transfers: Actual fraud and constructive fraud. A transfer

---

[9] *See* Nagel v. Westen, 59 Cal. App. 5th 740, 274 Cal. Rptr. 3d 21 (2021); Aghaian v. Minassian, 59 Cal. App. 447, 273 Cal. Rptr. 3d 561 (2020); Strum v. Moyer, 32 Cal. App. 5th 299, 243 Cal. Rptr. 3d 556 (2019).

[10] *See* Strum v. Moyer, 32 Cal. App. 5th 299, 243 Cal. Rptr. 3d 556 (2019) (UVTA can apply to premarital agreement).

[11] A secured creditor does not need the UVTA because a transfer of the debtor's property does nothing to the lien, which can be foreclosed while the property is in the hands of the transferee.

§ 8.4   UNIFORM VOIDABLE TRANSACTIONS ACT   143

constitutes actual fraud when it is made "with actual intent to hinder, delay, or defraud any creditor of the debtor" (Civil Code § 3439.04(a)(1)). Constructive fraud occurs when a debtor conveys property without receiving reasonably equivalent value in exchange, and the transfer renders the debtor insolvent (Civil Code § 3439.04(a)(2)).

In *State Board of Equalization v. Woo*, 82 Cal. App. 4th 481, 98 Cal. Rptr. 2d 206 (2000), Husband owed state taxes. Wife and Husband learned the Board of Equalization intended to garnish Wife's wages to pay Husband's tax debt. Wife's wages are community property, and community property is liable for the debts of either spouse (Family Code § 910) (*See* Chapter 9). To avoid the tax collector, Wife and Husband entered a transmutation agreement converting wife's wages to her separate property. Separate property is generally not liable for the debts of the spouse (§ 913(b)(1)). The tax collector argued that the transmutation violated the UVTA, and the Court of Appeal agreed. The purpose of the transmutation was to avoid paying a debt.

In *Mejia v. Reed*, 31 Cal. 4th 657, 74 P.3d 166, 3 Cal. Rptr. 3d 390 (2003), husband had an affair, and his lover had a baby. Wife and husband divorced. They entered a marital settlement agreement (MSA) in which husband transferred all his interest in jointly held property to his wife. Lover sued, claiming the purpose of the MSA was to get property out of husband's ownership so he could not be forced to pay child support. The Supreme Court ruled the UVTA can apply to an MSA that works a fraud on creditors.

Question: Sue is a local restaurateur. She owns and operates a popular eatery. In addition to being a regular patron at Sue's restaurant, you have occasionally reviewed contracts for her. Recently, while you are enjoying a coffee at Sue's restaurant, Sue sits at your table and says, "May I ask you a legal question?" You reply, "Sure." Sue relays the following: Sue and her husband Phil own the real estate housing the restaurant. They own it as joint tenants. A year ago, a customer slipped and fell in the restaurant and broke her hip. Sue recently received a demand letter from an attorney representing the injured customer. The letter demands that Sue pay the customer $500,000 or the customer will sue. Unfortunately, at the time the accident happened, Sue did not have insurance to cover the accident. After relating these facts, Sue says, "Phil and I are thinking we should sell the restaurant to my mom for a nominal amount so we don't own it if this lady sues us. If the lawsuit goes against us, the property won't be ours, and we won't lose it. Can we do that?" How should you answer Sue's question?

Chapter 9

DEBTS

Analysis

§ 9.1	Four Sets of Debt Rules
§ 9.2	Debts During Marriage
§ 9.3	During Marriage, Priority of Payment of Tort Debts
§ 9.4	During Marriage, Protecting Paycheck from Spouse's Premarital Debts
§ 9.5	Necessaries During Marriage
§ 9.6	Support Debt from Previous Relationship
§ 9.7	Characterization of Debts on Divorce
§ 9.8	Exam Questions on Debts

§ 9.1 Four Sets of Debt Rules

As you learn the law regarding debts, it is important to understand there are four sets of debt rules. One set governs payment of debts during marriage (Family Code §§ 910–914). A second set of rules governs characterization of debts on divorce (Family Code § 2620 et seq.). The third set consists of a single rule (Family Code § 916. See § 11.4) that specifies what property is liable for debts after the divorce court divides the property. The fourth set of rules is found in the Probate Code and applies when marriage ends in death (Probate Code §§ 13550, 11444). Chapter 9 focuses on debts during marriage and characterization of debts on divorce.

Family Code § 902 defines debt as "an obligation incurred by a married person before or during marriage, whether based on contract, tort, or otherwise." Contract debts are incurred when the contract is made. Tort debts are incurred when the tort is committed. Other debts are incurred when the obligation arises. (Family Code § 903).

§ 9.2 Debts During Marriage

Married couples incur debt. Generally, couples pay their debts and no one gives a thought to the community property aspects of debt. Suppose, however, that a debt is not paid and a creditor takes legal action to collect a debt. When this happens, the question becomes what property can a creditor take to satisfy a debt? Can a creditor take community property? Separate property of the debtor spouse? Separate property of the non-debtor spouse? What if both spouses incur a debt? The answers are found in Family Code §§ 910 to 914.

§ 9.2(a) During Marriage, Liability of Community Property

During marriage, community property is liable for debts incurred by either spouse before or during marriage.[1] Section 910 provides:

> **§ 910. Community estate; liability for debts**
>
> (a) Except as otherwise expressly provided by statute, the community estate [community property and quasi-community property] is liable for a debt incurred by either spouse before or during marriage, regardless of which spouse has the management and control of the property and regardless of whether one or both spouses are parties to the debt or to a judgment for the debt.
>
> (b) "During marriage" for purposes of this section does not include the period after the date of separation, as defined in Section 70, and before a judgement of dissolution of marriage or legal separation of the parties.[2]

Examples: Nancy and Ron are married. During marriage, Ron incurs a debt. Family Code § 910 provides that all of the community property is liable for the debt—Not half, all. Before marriage, Nancy incurred a debt. All the community property is liable for the debt.

---

[1] See In re Brace, 9 Cal. 5th 903, 938, 470 P.3d 15, 266 Cal. Rptr 3d 298 (2020).

[2] A debt incurred after separation is the obligation of the debtor, and is not chargeable against community property.

§ 9.2(b) During Marriage, Liability of Separate Property

Turning from community property to separate property, the separate property of the debtor spouse is liable for payment of the debtor's debts. The separate property of the non-debtor spouse generally is *not* liable for debts incurred by the other spouse.[3] These principles find expression in Family Code § 913:

> **§ 913. Separate property of married person; liability for debt**
>
> (a) The separate property of a married person is liable for a debt incurred by the person before or during marriage.
>
> (b) Except as otherwise provided by statute:
>
> (1) The separate property of a married person is not liable for a debt incurred by the person's spouse before or during marriage.
>
> (2) The joinder or consent of a married person to an encumbrance of community estate property to secure payment of a debt incurred by the person's spouse does not subject the person's separate property to liability for the debt unless the person also incurred the debt.

Sometimes, a married person signs a document creating an encumbrance on property without also incurring the debt that is secured by the encumbrance. Family Code § 913(b)(2) provides that in such cases the signing spouse's separate property is not liable for the debt. The signing spouse's separate property is liable only if the spouse incurs the debt.

§ 9.2(c) Questions on Debts During Marriage

In the following hypotheticals, what property can a creditor take to satisfy a debt?

---

[3] *See* Direct Capital Corp. v. Brooks, 14 Cal. App. 5th 1168, 222 Cal. Rptr. 3d 601, 603 (2017) ("Generally, a spouse's separate property is not liable for debts incurred by the other spouse during marriage.").

1. Prior to marriage, Beth incurred $20,000 in credit card debt. Beth and Tom marry. If the debt is not paid, what property can the creditor look to satisfy the debt? CP, B's SP

2. During marriage, Beth and Tom both sign loan documents to refinance their home. If the loan is not repaid, what property can the creditor take to satisfy the debt? CP + SP

3. During marriage, Tom buys a boat on credit. The debt remains unpaid. What property can the creditor go after to satisfy the debt? CP, T's SP

§ 9.3 During Marriage, Priority of Payment of Tort Debts

The rules for payment of tort debts are similar to the rules for contract and other debts. All community property is liable for a tort debt (§ 910). Separate property of the tortfeasor spouse is liable for the debt (§ 913(b)(1)). Separate property of the non-tortfeasor spouse is not liable for the debt (§ 913(a)).

Family Code § 1000 establishes an order of payment for tort debts. Section 1000 does not change the fact that the creditor can collect out of community property and the separate property of the tortfeasor. What § 1000 does is dictate which source of funds the creditor must look to *first*. Section 1000 provides, in part:

> **§ 1000. Liability for injury or damage caused by spouse; property subject to satisfaction of liability; satisfaction out of insurance proceeds; limitation on exercise of reimbursement right**
>
> (a) A married person is not liable for any injury or damage caused by the other spouse except in cases where the married person would be liable therefore if the marriage did not exist.
>
> (b) The liability of a married person for death or injury to person or property shall be satisfied as follows:
>
> > (1) If the liability of the married person is based upon an act or omission which occurred while the married person was performing an activity for the benefit of the community, the liability shall first be satisfied from the

community estate and second from the separate property of the married person.

(2) If the liability of the married person is not based upon an act or omission which occurred while the married person was performing an activity for the benefit of the community, the liability shall first be satisfied from the separate property of the married person and second from the community estate.

An activity for the benefit of the community is one that supports or enhances the community. Thus, going to work is an activity for the benefit of the community, as is driving to the store to buy milk for the baby. Obviously, committing a tort is not an activity for the benefit of the community, but Section 1000 focuses not on the tort, but on whether the tort occurred during an activity benefitting the community. If so, the tort debt is satisfied first out of community property. If there is not sufficient community property to fully pay the debt, the creditor turns for the balance to the tortfeasor's separate property. If the tort occurred while the tortfeasor spouse was performing an activity not for the benefit of the community (*e.g.*, driving to a drug dealer to buy illegal drugs), payment comes first from the tortfeasor's separate property and second from community property.

Subsection (a) of § 1000 requires a word of explanation. In modern tort law, one spouse is not vicariously liable for torts committed by the other spouse. The first part of § 1000(a) reflects this principle by stating, "A married person is not liable or any injury or damage caused by the other spouse . . . ." However, in limited circumstances, one person is liable for a tort committed by another. The most common scenario involves the tort of negligent entrustment. The owner of a car loans the car to a friend who is obviously drunk. The drunk gets in an accident. The injured person sues the driver *and* the car owner. The driver is sued for negligence. The car owner is sued for negligent entrustment. The same scenario plays out when a married person negligently entrusts the car keys to an obviously drunk spouse who commits mayhem on the road. Subsection (a) of § 1000 acknowledges this possibility when it states that a married person is liable "in cases where the married person would be liable therefore if the marriage did not exist."

§ 9.4 During Marriage, Protecting Paycheck from Spouse's Premarital Debts

Family Code § 910 provides that 100% of community property can be taken by a creditor to satisfy premarital debts. Section 911 allows a non-debtor spouse to protect their paycheck, which is community property, from liability for the debtor spouse's premarital debts.[4] Section 911 states:

> **§ 911. Earnings of married persons; liability for premarital debts; earnings held in deposit accounts**
>
> (a) The earnings of a married person during marriage are not liable for a debt incurred by the person's spouse before marriage. After the earnings of the married person are paid, they remain not liable so long as they are held in a deposit account in which the person's spouse has no right of withdrawal and are uncommingled with other property in the community estate, except property insignificant in amount.
>
> (b) As used in this section:
>
> > (1) "Deposit account" has the meaning prescribed in paragraph (29) of subdivision (a) of Section 9102 of the Commercial Code.
> >
> > (2) "Earnings" means compensation for personal services performed, whether as an employee or otherwise.

Section 911 carves out an exception to the rule that a creditor can take all of the community property to satisfy a debt. The non-debtor spouse can shield her paycheck from liability for the debtor spouse's premarital debts by putting the paycheck in a bank account in the non-debtor spouse's name alone. Although the paycheck is community property, Section 911 shields it from the debtor spouse's premarital debts. The non-debtor must take care not to deposit the debtor spouse's income in the account. Doing so forfeits the protection of Section 911.

---

[4] *See* Strum v. Moyer, 32 Cal. App. 5th 299, 243 Cal. Rptr. 3d 556 (2019).

§ 9.5 Necessaries During Marriage

The word "necessaries" refers to items needed to survive: food, clothing, medical care, and shelter.[5] During marriage, debts for necessaries fall under Family Code §§ 910 and 913. That is, all of the community property can be taken to pay a debt for necessaries. The separate property of the debtor can be taken. When it comes to the separate property of the non-debtor spouse, Family Code § 914 comes into play, discussed, below.

California law defines two types of necessaries: (1) common necessaries of life, and (2) necessaries of life. Common necessaries of life are basic food, clothing, medical care, and shelter.[6] Necessaries of life depend on one's station in life, that is, how rich or poor is the person?[7] Membership in an expensive country club is not a common necessary of life, but it might be a necessary of life for a rich person. An old California case ruled that a maid was a necessary of life for a wealthy family.[8] In *Direct Capital Corp. v. Brooks*, 14 Cal. App. 5th 1168, 222 Cal. Rptr. 3d 601 (2017), the Court of Appeal ruled that office computer equipment is a necessary of life for an attorney.

As you know, normally a non-debtor's separate property is not liable for a debt incurred by the non-debtor's spouse. Family Code § 914 is an exception to the rule that a non-debtor's separate property is not liable for a debt incurred by the debtor spouse. Section 914 provides:

---

[5] It is a misdemeanor to fail to provide one's spouse and children common necessaries of life. Penal Code §§ 270, 270a.

[6] *See* Direct Capital Corp. v. Brooks, 14 Cal. App. 5th 1168, 1174, 222 Cal. Rptr. 3d 601 (2017) ("common necessaries are those that *all* families need (e.g., food, clothing, & shelter).

[7] *See* Direct Capital Corp. v. Brooks, 14 Cal. App. 5th 1168, 1174, 222 Cal. Rptr. 3d 601 (2017) ("what constitutes necessaries depends on the circumstances of the particular marriage. . . . The station in life test looks to the marital standard and mode of living.").

[8] Wisnom v. McCarthy, 48 Cal. App. 697, 192 P. 337 (1920).

§ 914. Personal liability for debts incurred by spouse; separate property applied to satisfaction of debt; statute of limitations

(a) Notwithstanding Section 913, a married person is personally liable for the following debts incurred by the person's spouse during marriage:

> (1) A debt incurred for necessaries of life [and common necessaries] of the person's spouse before the date of separation of the spouses.
>
> (2) Except as provided in Section 4302,[9] a debt incurred or common necessaries of life of the person's spouse after the date of separation of the spouses.

(b) The separate property of a married person may be applied to the satisfaction of a debt for which the person is personally liable pursuant to this section. If separate property is so applied at a time when nonexempt property in the community estate or separate property of the person's spouse is available but is not applied to the satisfaction of the debt, the married person is entitled to reimbursement to the extent such property was available.

* * *

(d) For purposes of this section, "date of separation" has the name meaning as set forth in Section 70.

When Section 914 states that "a married person is personally liable," the statute means the person's separate property is liable to pay for necessaries incurred by the person's spouse.

The basic rule of § 913(b)(1) is that a non-debtor's separate property is *not* liable for a debt incurred by the person's spouse. Debts for necessaries, however, are an exception to this rule, not in all cases, but in some. (Family Code § 914(a)).

A good way to understand Section 914 and liability for necessaries is to create a timeline like the one in Figure 1. Along the

---

[9] Family Code § 4302 provides: "A person is not personally liable for support of the person's spouse when the person is living separate from the spouse by agreement, unless support is stipulated in the agreement."

timeline, place the date of marriage, the date of separation, and the date the judgment of divorce is granted.[10] Looking at the timeline, you see debts incurred before marriage, debts incurred during marriage and prior to separation, debts incurred after separation and before the divorce judgment is signed. When you have placed debts at the right spots on the timeline, you can apply § 914 to determine whether the separate property of the non-debtor spouse is liable for a debt.

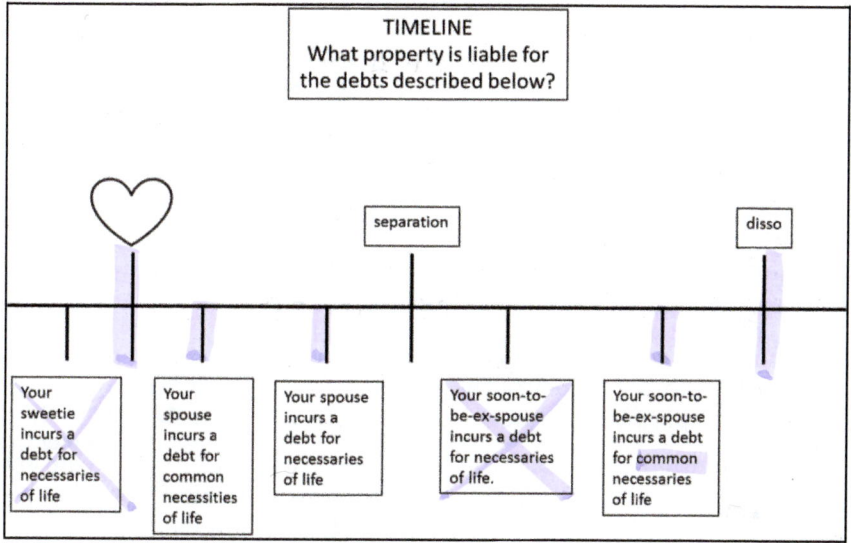

Figure 1
Debt—Necessaries Timeline

Referring to Figure 1, a non-debtor spouse's separate property is not liable for a debtor-spouse's premarital debt. At the other end of the relationship, a non-debtor's separate property is not liable for debtor-ex-spouse's debt incurred following divorce. During marriage and before separation, a non-debtor's separate property is liable debts incurred by the debtor-spouse for common necessaries of life and necessaries of life. After separation and prior to divorce, the non-debtor spouse is liable debts incurred by the debtor-spouse for

---

[10] With some divorces, the divorce is not final on the date a judge signs the judgment of divorce.

common necessaries of life of the debtor-spouse, but not for necessaries of life of the debtor-spouse.

Try your hand at the following questions regarding Mary and Abe, a married couple:

1. During marriage and prior to separation, Abe injures his back surfing and incurs medical bills of $5,000. What property is liable for the debt? CP, both SP

2. During marriage and prior to separation Abe purchases a fancy sports car on credit and puts title in his name alone. What property is liable for the debt? CP, A's SP

3. Prior to marriage Abe is injured in a car accident and incurs medical bills of $10,000. What property is liable for the debt? CP, A's SP

4. Mary and Abe have a ten-year-old son, Todd. During marriage and prior to separation, Mary incurs a debt of $5,000 to pay for braces for Todd's teeth. Let's agree that braces are not a common necessary of life. Are braces a necessary of life? What property is liable for the debt? CP, both SP

5. Referring to question 4, what if Mary and Abe separate on January 1 and Mary incurs the debt for braces the following March 15th? What property is liable for the debt? CP, M's CP, A's SP if common nec.

As mentioned in § 9.1, there are four sets of debt rules. One set governs payment of debts during marriage. A second set of rules characterizes debts on divorce. Section 914(a) can cause confusion because it refers to payment for necessaries after a couple separates. Because § 914 deals with separation, you might think § 914 is among the rules dealing with characterization of debts on divorce. That is not correct. Section 914 is part of the set of rules dealing with debts during marriage.

§ 9.6 Support Debt from Previous Relationship

Family Code § 915 contains a reimbursement provision for child and spousal support debts from previous relationships. Section 915 states in relevant part:

§ 915. Child or spousal support obligation not arising out of marriage; reimbursement of community

(a) For the purpose of this part, a child or spousal support obligation of a married person that does not arise out of the marriage shall be treated as a debt incurred before marriage, regardless of whether a court order for support is made or modified before or during marriage and regardless of whether any installment payment on the obligation accrues before or during marriage.

(b) If property in the community estate is applied to the satisfaction of a child or spousal support obligation of a married person that does not arise out of the marriage, at a time when nonexempt separate income of the person is available but is not applied to the satisfaction of the obligation, the community estate is entitled to reimbursement from the person in the amount of the separate income, not exceeding the property in the community estate so applied.

A premarital debt for child or spousal support from a different relationship is like any other debt. All the community property is liable for the debt (§ 910). The separate property of the obligor/debtor spouse is liable for the debt (§ 913(a)). The separate property of the non-debtor spouse is not liable for the debt (§ 913(b)(1)). Section 915 applies when the creditor satisfies the debt out of community property rather than taking available separate property of the debtor. When this happens, the non-debtor spouse may seek reimbursement of the community property used to pay the obligation.

§ 9.7 Characterization of Debts on Divorce

Recall from § 9.1 that there are four sets of rules regarding debts: (1) Debts during marriage, (2) Characterization of debts on divorce, (3) Property subject to debts after court divides community property, and (4) Debts when a marriage ends in death. This section focuses on characterization of debts on divorce.

When a marriage ends in divorce, part of the family law attorney's job is characterizing assets as community property or separate property. The rules concerning characterization of assets are addressed in earlier chapters. Most married couples have debts as well as assets. Like assets, debts are characterized on divorce. Debts are characterized as separate debts or community debts. Family Code § 2551 states, "The court shall characterize liabilities as separate or community . . . ." The Family Code sections dealing with characterization of debts on divorce are 2621 to 2625. The statutes follow:

§ 2621. Premarital debts; confirmation

Debts incurred by either spouse before the date of marriage shall be confirmed without offset to the spouse who incurred the debt.

§ 2622. Marital debts incurred before the date of separation; division

(a) Except as provided in subdivision (b), debts incurred by either spouse after the date of marriage but before the date of separation shall be divided as set forth in Section [2550 requiring equal division of community estate] and Sections 2601 to 2604 [setting forth rules on how to allocate debts on divorce].

(b) To the extent that community debts exceed total community and quasi-community assets, the excess of debt shall be assigned as the court deems just and equitable, taking into account factors such as the parties' relative ability to pay.

§ 2623. Marital debts incurred after the date of separation; confirmation

Debts incurred by either spouse after the date of separation but before entry of a judgment of dissolution of marriage or legal separation of the parties shall be confirmed as follows:

(a) Debts incurred by either spouse for the common necessaries of life or the necessaries of life [and common necessaries] of the children of the marriage for whom support may be ordered, in the absence of a court order or written agreement for support or for the payment of these debts, shall be confirmed to either spouse according to the parties' respective needs and abilities to pay at the time the debt was incurred.

(b) Debts incurred by either spouse for nonnecessaries of that spouse or children of the marriage for whom support may be ordered shall be confirmed without offset to the spouse who incurred the debt.

§ 2624. Marital debts incurred after entry of judgment of dissolution or after entry of judgment of legal separation; confirmation

Debts incurred by either spouse after entry of a judgment of dissolution of marriage but before termination of the parties' marital status or after entry of a judgment of legal separation of the parties shall be confirmed without outset to the spouse who incurred the debt.

§ 2625. Separate debts incurred before date of separation; confirmation

Notwithstanding Sections 2620 and 2624, inclusive, all separate debts, including those debts incurred by a spouse during the marriage and before the date of separation that were not incurred for the benefit of the community, shall be confirmed without offset to the spouse who incurred the debt.

§ 2626. Reimbursements

The court has jurisdiction to order reimbursement in cases it deems appropriate for debts paid after separation but before trial.

Before discussing characterization of debts on divorce, two terms in §§ 2621–2625 require clarification. The words "confirmed to" mean a debt is ordered to be paid by a spouse. The debt is confirmed to the spouse. The words "without offset" refer to the process by which the court reaches an equal division of community property by offsetting assets and debts to reach equality. When a debt is confirmed to a spouse "without offset," the debt plays no role in the overall equal division of the community estate. Community debts *do* figure into overall division.

§ 9.7(a) Premarital Debts Are Separate Debts—§ 2621

Debts incurred before marriage are separate debts. (§ 2621). Premarital debts are confirmed to the debtor and do not factor into the overall equal division of property on divorce.

§ 9.7(b) Debts Before Judgment Is Final Are Separate Debts—§ 2624

Debts incurred after a divorce judgment is signed by a judge, but before the divorce is final, are separate debts (§ 2624). In some divorces, the judgment is final on the day the judge signs the judgment. In other cases, a period of weeks or months must pass after the judgment is signed before the divorce is final. These differences are explained by the fact that in California, a divorce does not become final until at least six months have passed since the date the respondent spouse was served with the summons and petition, or made a general appearance (§ 2339). When a divorce proceeds swiftly to judgment, the six months may not have expired. The judgment is not final until the six months passes. The judgment form (FL-180) has a place that specifies the date the judgment is final (*See* § 2340).

Debts incurred after the judgment is signed but before it is final are separate debts. Such debts are not included in the overall equal division of property.

§ 9.7(c) Debts Incurred After Separation and Prior to Judgment for Non-Necessaries Are Separate Debts—§ 2623(b)

Debts incurred after separation and prior to signing of the Judgment for non-necessaries are separate debts (§ 2623(b)). Here, the term "necessaries" has the same two meanings you learned in § 9.5: Common necessaries of life and necessaries of life.

For example, after separation and prior to signing of the Judgment, husband buys a race car on credit. A race car is not a common necessary of life. Even for a rich person a race car is probably not a necessary of life. Thus, the debt for the race car is a separate debt and is confirmed without offset to husband (He gets the car and the debt).

How about this case: Following separation, and prior to signing of the Judgment, wife incurs a debt to send the couple's ten-year-old daughter to a football camp in Brazil. Is this a separate debt? Football camp in Brazil is not a common necessary of life. It might be a necessary of life. If it is a necessary of life, then the debt is a community debt. If it is not a necessary of life, it is wife's separate debt.

§ 9.7(d) Debts Incurred After Separation and Prior to Judgment for Necessaries— § 2623(a)

Debts incurred by either spouse after separation and prior to judgment for necessaries are neither separate debts nor community debts. Family Code § 2623 provides that debts incurred during this period for the common necessaries of life of either spouse, or for the common necessaries of life[11] *and* necessaries of life of the children, are confirmed to the spouse in the best position to pay at the time the debt was incurred.

You encountered necessaries in the discussion of Family Code § 914, regarding debts during marriage (*See* § 9.5). The meaning of necessaries is the same in § 914 and § 2623(a).

Following separation, and before the judge signs the divorce judgment, wife incurs a debt of $4,000 to pay for a visit to the emergency room after wife cut her hand gardening. This debt is for common necessaries of life and is assigned to the spouse in the best position to pay.

Change the facts. Following separation, and before the judge signs the divorce judgment, wife incurs a debt of $14,000 for elective cosmetic surgery for herself. Let's agree the surgery is not a common necessary of life. If it is a necessary at all, it is a necessary of life. Section 2623(a) only covers common necessaries of life for the

---

[11] Section 2623(a) doesn't actually say common necessaries of life of the kids. The section only mentions necessaries of life for the kids. However, when it comes to the kids, the section includes both types of necessaries.

spouses. Thus, the debt for the cosmetic surgery is wife's separate debt.

Change the facts again. Following separation, and before the judge signs the divorce judgment, wife incurs a debt of $5,000 to pay for private school for the couple's child. How should this debt be characterized in the divorce? Is private school a common necessary of life? No. Is private school a necessary of life? This depends, of course, on how rich or poor the family is.

§ 9.7(e) Debts Incurred During Marriage and Prior to Separation Can Be Separate or Community

Debts incurred during marriage and before separation can be community debts or separate debts. (Family Code §§ 2622, 2625, 2627). Contract debts for the benefit of the community create community debts. If a contract debt is not for the benefit of the community, it creates a separate debt (§ 2625). A loan to the community creates a community debt.[12] Tort debts based on a spouse's conduct in the performance of an activity for the benefit of the community (*e.g.*, driving to the store for milk) create a community debt. Conduct in the performance of an activity not for the benefit of the community creates a separate debt (§ 2627).

§ 9.7(f) Timeline for Debts on Divorce

The easiest way to characterize debts on divorce is to use a timeline like the one in Figure 2. The debt characterization sections of the Family Code are placed at the appropriate places on the timeline. You can examine the facts of your case and determine where a debt fits along the timeline and apply the correct law.

---

[12] *See* Marriage of Crimes and Mou, 45 Cal. App. 5th 406, 422, 258 Cal. Rptr. 3d 576 (2020).

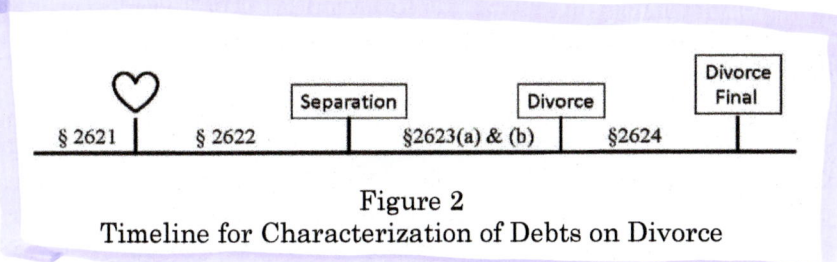

Figure 2
Timeline for Characterization of Debts on Divorce

§ 9.7(g) After the Family Court Divides Community Property, What Property Can a Creditor Take to Satisfy Debt?—Family Code § 916

Chapter 11 describes how the family court arrives at an equal division of community property when a divorcing couple has debts as well as assets. After the court allocates assets and debts, Family Code § 916 establishes the property a creditor looks to satisfy debt. Section 916 is explained in § 11.4 of Chapter 11.

§ 9.8 Exam Questions on Debts

The rules on debts during marriage and on divorce are enough to give you a headache or put you to sleep or both. This confusing area of community property law makes more sense when you think through exam questions where debt issues arise. Take a look at the July 2016 Bar Exam question, at page 205 of this book, and Law School Exam Question 3 at page 227.

Chapter 10

MANAGEMENT AND CONTROL

Analysis

§ 10.1 Equal Management and Control
§ 10.2 Gifts of Community Property
§ 10.3 Gifts Between Spouses
§ 10.4 Furniture of the Home; Mobile Home
§ 10.5 Spouse Operating a Community Property Business
§ 10.6 Management and Control of Community Real Property
§ 10.7 Spouses Are in a Fiduciary Relationship Regarding Community Property
§ 10.8 Remedies for Breach of Fiduciary Duty
§ 10.9 Bank Account in One Spouse's Name

This chapter discusses decisionmaking authority regarding community property, typically called management and control.

§ 10.1 Equal Management and Control

Married couples share equal management and control (M&C) of community real and personal property (Family Code §§ 1100(a), 1102(a). *See* pp. 261–263). Prior to January 1, 1975, only husbands had M&C of community property. Today, equal M&C applies regardless of whether property was acquired before or after January 1, 1975.

Family Code § 721(a) provides, "either spouse may enter into any transaction with the other, or with any other person, respecting property, which either might if unmarried." A spouse can sell community personal property without the consent of the other spouse. Section 1100(a) refers to this authority as "like absolute power of disposition." Regarding community real property, both spouses must execute any instrument that conveys such property (§ 1102(a)).

When a spouse dies, she can dispose of her half of community property. A deceased spouse has no authority to dispose of the half that belongs to the surviving spouse.

§ 10.2 Gifts of Community Property

A spouse cannot give away community personal or real property without the written consent of the other spouse (§ 1100(b)). A non-consenting spouse can set aside an unauthorized gift in its entirety during the lifetime of the donor spouse. If the donor has died, one-half of the unauthorized gift can be set aside.

An unauthorized gift of personal property must be returned. Thus, if husband gives his sister a community property painting, and wife moves to set the gift aside, the sister has to return the painting. If a gifted item is used up, destroyed, lost, or, in the case of money, spent, the non-consenting spouse has a cause of action against the donor spouse for half the value of the item.

If real property is given away without authorization, the grantee/donee can be forced to return the land during the lifetime of the donor. After the donor's death, the non-consenting spouse can set the gift aside as to one-half, becoming a tenant in common with the grantee/donee.

A spouse who does not consent to a gift of community property may ratify the gift through words or conduct. Similarly, a non-consenting spouse may be estopped to claim that a gift was invalid. For example, Husband, without consulting Wife, used community funds to purchase a home for his mom. Wife helped her mother-in-law move in to the home, and drove her to the county recorder of deeds office to record the deed. When Wife and Husband divorced, Wife was estopped to object to the gift.

§ 10.3 Gifts Between Spouses

One spouse can give community property to the other spouse. A gift between spouses is a transmutation. Transmutation is discussed in Chapter 8. Normally, transmutations must be in writing, but the writing requirement "does not apply to a gift between the spouses of clothing, wearing apparel, jewelry, or other tangible articles of a personal nature that is used solely or principally by the spouse to whom the gift is made and that is not substantial in value taking into account the circumstances of the marriage" (§ 852(c)).[1]

For example, Sandy and Ben are married. For their anniversary, Sandy paid $10,000 of community property for a man's Rolex watch as a gift for Ben. On divorce, Ben claims the watch is his separate property. Sandy says the gift was an invalid transmutation, and the watch is community property. Ben argues § 852(c) validates the gift. A watch is jewelry. Only Ben wears the watch. The question is whether $10,000 is substantial in value, taking into account the circumstances of the marriage. Basically, the question is how rich or poor is the couple? For most people, ten thousand dollars for a watch is a lot of money. If Sandy and Ben are well off, however, the watch may not be substantial in value for them, rendering the gift valid.

In *Marriage of Buie and Neighbors,* 179 Cal. App. 4th 1170, 102 Cal. Rptr. 3d 387 (2009), the Court of Appeal ruled that a car is not a tangible article of a personal nature within the meaning of § 852(c).

§ 10.4 Furniture of the Home; Mobile Home

Family Code § 1100(c) provides that "a spouse may not sell, convey, or encumber community personal property used as the family dwelling [mobile home], or the furniture, furnishings, or fittings of the home, or the clothing or wearing apparel of the other spouse or minor children which is community personal property, without the written consent of the other spouse." A purported sale or encumbrance in violation of § 1100(c) is void, and can be set aside in its entirety.

---

[1] Marriage of Steinberger, 91 Cal. App. 4th 1449, 111 Cal. Rptr. 2d 521 (2001) (ring given to wife was substantial in value given the couple's finances).

§ 10.5 Spouse Operating a Community Property Business

In many marriages, one spouse manages a community property business. Family Code § 1100(d) acknowledges this reality, and provides that the manager spouse has primary management and control of the business. The manager can make the day-to-day decisions needed to operate the business. The one thing § 1100(d) forbids the manager to do is sell the business or go out of business without advance notice to the non-manager spouse.

§ 10.6 Management and Control of Community Real Property

Both spouses have M&C of community real property (Family Code § 1102(a)). Both spouses must join in any instrument by which the property is sold, encumbered, or leased for longer than a year (§ 1102(a)).

If community real property, title to which is in one spouse's name alone, is conveyed, a non-signing non-consenting spouse has a year after the deed is recorded to avoid the conveyance (§ 1102(d)). The transaction is avoided in its entirety during the lifetime of the grantor spouse. The grantee has to re-convey the land, but is entitled to repayment. If the non-consenting spouse waits until the grantor has died, the conveyance is set aside as to one half the property.

§ 10.7 Spouses Are in a Fiduciary Relationship Regarding Community Property

In matters of community property, spouses owe each other complete honesty and fair dealing.[2] Neither spouse may take unfair advantage of the other. Spouses are fiduciaries to each other. Family Code § 721(b) specifies, "This confidential relationship is a fiduciary relationship subject to the same rights and duties of nonmarital business partners, as provided in . . . the Corporations Code."

Each spouse must allow the other access to financial information (§ 721(b)(1)). Upon request by one spouse, the other

---

[2] *See* Marriage of Schleich, 8 Cal. App. 5th 267, 213 Cal. Rptr. 3d 665 (2017).

must provide accurate and complete information about transactions affecting community property (§ 721(b)(2)).

If a spouse engages in a transaction with community property without the consent of the other spouse, any profits must be held as a trustee (§ 721(b)(3)).

When a spouse invests community property and the investment fails, does the failure constitute a breach of fiduciary duty? In many cases the answer is, no. The fact that an investment does not turn a profit does not necessarily mean the investing spouse was careless or negligent. Even if the investing spouse was negligent, California courts generally hold that negligence is not a breach of fiduciary duty. On the other hand, if a spouse acted with gross negligence or recklessness, a court is likely to find a breach of fiduciary duty. In *Marriage of Duffy*, 91 Cal. App. 4th 923, 940, 111 Cal. Rptr. 2d 160 (2001), the Court of Appeal wrote, "[A] spouse generally is not bound by the Prudent Investor Rule and does not owe to the other spouse the duty of care one business partner owes to another."

Section 1100(e) repeats the requirements of Section 721(b) and adds that the fiduciary obligation between spouses continues *after* separation, until the community property is divided by the parties or the court.[3] The family law attorney emphasizes to clients that the duty of honesty and fair dealing continues uninterrupted following separation, a time when one spouse might be inclined to take advantage of the other.

§ 10.8   Remedies for Breach of Fiduciary Duty

Family Code § 1101 sets forth detailed remedies for breach of fiduciary duty. A spouse can sue the other spouse for such breach (§ 1101(a)). Issues of breach of fiduciary duty typically arise in divorce litigation.

In an action for breach of fiduciary duty, the court may order an accounting (§ 1101(b)). With limitations, the court may order a spouse's name added to the title of community property (§ 1101(c)).

---

[3] *See* Marriage of Desouza, 54 Cal. App. 5th 25, 32, 266 Cal. Rptr. 3d 890 (2020) ("The fiduciary duty continues after separation.").

Section 1101(d) creates a three year statute of limitations for actions for breach of fiduciary duty.[4]

Section 1101(g) sets forth the monetary remedy for a breach of fiduciary duty that impairs an interest in community property. The normal remedy is 50% of the value of the community property plus attorney fees. Section 1101(h) provides that if the breaching spouse acted with malice, oppression, or fraud, the remedy is 100% of the value of the community property.

§ 10.9 Bank Account in One Spouse's Name

When a bank account is in one spouse's name, the other spouse cannot access the account. Financial Code § 851 provides, "A bank account . . . in the name of a married person shall be held for the exclusive right and benefit of the person [and] shall be free from the control or lien of any other person except a creditor." If the account contains community property, the account holder has a fiduciary duty to account for the money in the account.

---

[4] *See* Yeh v. Li-Cheng Tai, 2017 WL 6523571 (2017) (thorough discussion of statute of limitations and laches under § 1101).

Chapter 11

DIVISION OF PROPERTY ON DIVORCE

Analysis

§ 11.1	Marital Settlement Agreement (MSA)
§ 11.2	Division by the Court Following Trial
§ 11.3	Omitted Assets
§ 11.4	What Property Can Creditors Attach After the Divorce Court Divides Community Property?
§ 11.5	Property Division Is *Res Judicata*
§ 11.6	Out of State Community Property
§ 11.7	Authority Regarding Jointly Held Separate Property
§ 11.8	*Epstein* Credits and *Watts* Charges
§ 11.9	Reimbursement Summary
§ 11.10	Relationship Between Spousal Support and Property Division: The Problem of Double Dipping
§ 11.11	Property Problems

In previous chapters you learned to characterize assets and debts. Now it is time to divide the community assets and debts and finalize the divorce.

§ 11.1 Marital Settlement Agreement (MSA)

A divorcing couple can divide their property however they wish—equally or unequally. In most cases, couples agree on how to divide property and debts. The agreement is reduced to writing, called a marriage settlement agreement (MSA). The MSA is attached to the Judgment of Divorce (FL-180), and incorporated into the Judgment.[1] Once a judge signs the Judgment, the MSA is

---

[1] *See* Marriage of Minkin, 11 Cal. App. 5th 939, 218 Cal. Rptr. 3d 407 (2017).

transformed from a contract to a court order, and is enforceable as such. If the parties cannot agree on division of property, a trial is held at which the court divides the community estate equally (Family Code § 2550).

§ 11.2 Division by the Court Following Trial

When a divorcing couple cannot agree on division of property, a trial ensues. The court characterizes assets and debts as separate or community. When necessary, the court determines the value of assets. Assets are valued as near as practicable to the time of trial unless a different valuation date is appropriate (§ 2552). The court divides the community property equally (§ 2550).

§ 11.2(a) Exceptions to Equal Division

There are several exceptions to the requirement of equal division. First, community property personal injury damages must be awarded entirely to the injured spouse unless economic circumstances justify a different division (§ 2603, *see* § 7.9(a)). Second, where one spouse deliberately conceals or misappropriates community assets, the court may award some of the wrongdoer spouse's community property to the innocent spouse (§ 2602). Third, when the value of the community estate is less than $5,000 and the respondent spouse can't be located and the case proceeds to default judgment the court can award all of the community property to the petitioner (§ 2604). Fourth, when one spouse successfully sues the other for domestic violence, damages can be paid out of the abuser's share of community property. Fifth, a spouse who has been convicted of attempting to murder their spouse, or convicted of sexually assaulting the spouse, receives no share of the victim's pension.

§ 11.2(b) Court Divides Property at Time of Divorce

The court divides community property at the time of divorce. With certain items of property, the court may postpone possession or enjoyment of property to a later time. This can occur with pensions. For example, the court determines the community interest in the pension at the time of divorce, but orders the non-employee spouse to wait until the employee spouse retires to begin receiving checks.

§ 11.2(c) Methods to Achieve Equal Division

To divide the community estate equally, the court has several options. The court can order a community asset sold and the proceeds divided. Alternatively, the court can confirm a community asset to one spouse with equal and offsetting community property to the other spouse (§ 2601).[2] A spouse can be ordered to make an "equalizing payment" to the other spouse. In appropriate cases, to reach equal division, the court orders one spouse to execute a promissory note to the other spouse. The note should bear interest and be of relatively short duration. At the end of the process, the value received by each spouse must be equal, or as nearly so as possible.

Most divorcing couples have community debts as well as community assets. The court factors community debts into the overall division to reach a net equal division. A simple example illustrates how a judge might arrive at equal division:

Mary and Jim are divorcing. They own the following community property:

Boat worth $50,000.

Car worth $100,000.

Stock worth $20,000.

Jim's pension—community share worth $200,000.

Mary's pension—community share worth $180,000.

Home worth $100,000.

Mary and Jim have the following separate property. Separate property does not factor into the equal division. Separate property is mentioned here to give you a complete picture of the couple's financial situation, and to

---

[2] When the court awards specific community assets to one spouse, with other assets or cash to the other spouse, it is necessary to value the various assets. Simply ordering assets sold, and the proceeds divided, avoids the expense of valuing assets. The judge has broad discretion to decide the best way to reach net equal division.

remind you that much of the family law attorney's job is characterizing assets and debts as community or separate:

Mary's trust fund.

Mary's pension—separate property share.

Jim owns Blackacre.

Mary and Jim have the following community debt:

Credit card: $10,000.

Judgment against both: $20,000.

Mary and Jim have the following separate debt. Separate debt does not factor into the equal division:

Mary: $25,000 premarital contract debt.

Jim: $5,000 premarital contract debt.

Jim: $20,000 student loan debt.

The court divides the assets as follows:

Mary is awarded: boat ($50,000); stock ($20,000); her share of Jim's pension ($100,000); her share of house ($50,000). Total: $220,000.

Jim is awarded: car ($100,000); his share of Mary's pension ($90,000); his share of house ($50,000). Total: $240,000.

Jim's community property is $240,000, while Mary's is $220,000. To arrive at equal division, the court does the following with the community debt:

The court assigns the $20,000 judgment and $5,000 of credit card debt to Jim, rendering his total award $215,000. The court assigns $5,000 of credit card debt to Mary, rendering her total award $215,000. Equality!

In *Marriage of Honer*, 236 Cal. App. 4th 687, 186 Cal. Rptr. 3d 607 (2015), the Court of Appeal approved a trial court's division of property. Tom and Penny were married 27 years. When they divorced, they owned two profitable grocery stores as well as rental properties. They lived on a 52 acre ranch. They owned IRA and 401(k) accounts and a profit sharing plan. All the property belonged to the community. Tom worked full time running the community property businesses. Penny had some involvement in the business but primarily worked as a teacher. The parties separated in 2009. In the same year, Penny was diagnosed with multiple sclerosis and stopped working. Penny moved to Texas. Tom continued living on the ranch and working full time. The couple's total net worth was $6,667,040. The trial court divided the property as follows:

To Tom: (1) Business assets worth $3.18 million; (2) rental property valued at $4,072,500, with equity of $1,687364; (3) the ranch, valued at $1.01 million, with equity of $137,832; (4) profit sharing plan valued at $207,539.

Total awarded to Tom, after calculation of *Epstein* credits and *Watts* charges: $4,909,712.

To Penny: (1) a home worth $375,000, with no debt on the home; (2) real property valued at $385,000, with equity of $185,000; (3) life insurance policy valued at $180,949; (4) 401(k) accounts valued at $430,250; (4) profit sharing plan valued at $216,647; (5) IRA accounts valued at $60,319.

Total awarded to Penny: $1,757,329.

Tom was ordered to make an equalizing payment to Penny of $1,576,192 within 90 days after the judgment of divorce. The Court of Appeal wrote, "When the equalizing payment is considered (*i.e.*, deducted from Tom's award and added to Penny's), Penny's total award was $3,333,521 and Tom's award was $3,333,520."

§ 11.3 Omitted Assets

Occasionally, a community property asset is overlooked in the divorce. When the asset is later discovered, Family Code § 2556 gives the court jurisdiction to divide the asset.[3]

---

[3] *See* Marriage of Huntley, 10 Cal. App. 5th 1053, 216 Cal. Rptr. 3d 904 (2017).

§ 11.4 What Property Can Creditors Attach After the Divorce Court Divides Community Property?

You recall there are four sets of rules regarding debts: (1) Debts during ongoing marriage (§ 9.2), (2) Characterization of debts on divorce (§ 9.7), Debts when marriage ends in death (§ 13.5), and liability of community property after the divorce court divides the community property (§ 11.4).

During marriage, a creditor can take *all* the community property to satisfy a debt incurred by either spouse before or during marriage (§ 910). After the court divides community property on divorce, § 916 provides that the half of the community property awarded to the non-debtor spouse is *not* subject to attachment by the creditors of the debtor spouse.[4]

§ 11.5 Property Division Is *Res Judicata*

Once a divorce is final, some aspects of the divorce are subject to modification on a showing of changed circumstances. Thus, child custody, child support, and spousal support can be modified when post-divorce circumstances change.[5] By contrast, property division is *res judicata*. As the Court of Appeal put it in *Marriage of Thorne and Raccina*, 203 Cal. App. 4th 492, 136 Cal. Rptr. 3d 887 (2012):

> Generally, once a marital dissolution judgment has become final, the court loses jurisdiction to modify it later. Under the doctrine of *res judicata*, if a property settlement is incorporated in the divorce decree, the settlement is merged with the decree and becomes the final judicial

---

[4] *See* CMRE Financial Services, Inc. v. Parton, 184 Cal. App. 4th 263, 268–269 109 Cal. Rptr. 3d 139 (2010) ("Our conclusion a dissolution judgment relieves a spouse of liability imposed by section 914 is of course supported by the express terms of section 916, which make all other provisions of that chapter of the Family Code, including section 914, subject to the protection section 916 provides to former spouses following dissolution of marriage. . . . In sum, as we interpret sections 914 and 916, although spouses have an obligation to support each other while separated, they can avoid that obligation by way of agreement between themselves. (§ 914.) Moreover, any liability for support which arose during the parties' separation ceases following dissolution of the marriage, unless the court orders it extended. (§ 916, subd. (a)(2)).

[5] The parties can agree that there will be no spousal support, and this agreement is *res judicata*.

determination of the property rights of the parties. In short, marital property rights and obligations adjudicated by a final judgment cannot be upset by subsequent efforts to modify the judgment. . . .

There are three exceptions to the general rule. First, a judgment may contain an express reservation of jurisdiction authorizing the court to subsequently modify it. . . . Second, the court may divide a community property asset not mentioned in the judgment. . . . And third, the trial court may give equitable relief from an otherwise valid judgment for extrinsic fraud or mistake.

§ 11.6 Out of State Community Property

A California Superior Court judge who is dividing community property can enter orders that change title to California community real property. A California judge cannot change title to out of state real property. Regarding out of state community property, Family Code § 2660(a) provides, "The court shall, if possible, divide the community property and quasi-community property in such a manner that it is not necessary to change the nature of the interests held in [out of state] real property." The court can order the parties to convey out of state property, and impose sanctions for failing to obey the court's order.

§ 11.7 Authority Regarding Jointly Held Separate Property

When a married couple acquires property in joint form, Family Code § 2581 states that on divorce the property is presumptively community property (§ 5.17). The § 2581 presumption is rebuttable. When the presumption is rebutted, the interests of the spouses in the property are separate property. Generally, the family court has no jurisdiction over separate property. Section 2650, however, allows the divorce court to adjudicate the spouses' interests in jointly held separate property.

§ 11.8 *Epstein* Credits and *Watts* Charges

After a couple separates, it is common for one spouse to remain in the family home. Assume the home is community property, and paid off. The spouse lives in the home for a year before the couple's divorce is final. The couple could have rented the house for the year and the rental income would have been community property. Of course, since one spouse remained in the home there was no rental income. The spouse who moved out might say, "You stayed in the home rent free for a year, while I paid for an apartment. We could have rented the house and I would have gotten half the rental income. In our divorce, your share of the community property should be reduced by half the rental value of the house for the year you lived in it." The court has authority to order such a charge against a spouse's share of community property, called *Watts* charges, when one separated spouse has exclusive use of community property before trial. (*Marriage of Watts*, 171 Cal. App. 3d 366, 217 Cal. Rptr. 301 (1985)).

Epstein credits can be awarded to reimburse a separated spouse who uses separate property to pay community debt prior to trial. (*Marriage of Epstein*, 24 Cal. 3d 76, 592 P.2d 1165, 154 Cal. Rptr. 413 (1979)).

What should happen in the following case? Wife and Husband separate on January 1. Husband remains in the community property family home with the kids. Wife moves out. Their case comes on for trial one year later. The reasonable rental value of the home is $2,000 a month. During the year between separation and trial, Husband paid the monthly mortgage payment of $1,500 every month from his post-separation income from employment.

Change the facts. During the year after separation it was Wife who paid the monthly mortgage payment with her post-separation income from employment.

In *Marriage of Mohler,* 47 Cal. App. 5th 788, 791, 261 Cal. Rptr. 3d 221 (2020), husband owned a home prior to marriage. During marriage, mortgage payments were made with community property, necessitating *Moore/Marsden* apportionment. (*See* § 5.21). After separation, husband lived in the home and made mortgage payments with separate property for six years before the couple divorced. The Court of Appeal ruled, "*Watts* charges may be levied against a spouse for his or her post-separation occupation of a property where the property is not entirely community property, but rather is treated as partially community property due to the *Moore/Marsden* rule."

§ 11.9 Reimbursement Summary – memorize!

A right to reimbursement, or lack of such right, is a theme running throughout community property law. This section briefly recapitulates reimbursement.

- Family Code § 915(b) allows reimbursement of community property used to pay child support arising out of a previous relationship.

- Family Code § 916 addresses reimbursement after debts have been divided on divorce and a former spouse's separate property is used to pay a debt that the divorce Judgment assigned to the other former spouse.

- Family Code § 920 establishes how much reimbursement is allowed in the context of payment of debts.

- Family Code § 1000 deals with reimbursement for payment of tort debts.

- Family Code § 2640 requires reimbursement of separate property contributions to community property. The § 2640 right to reimbursement can be waived in writing. Section 2640 is not retroactive prior to January 1, 1984.

- Family Code § 2641 requires reimbursement to the community of contribution to education or training.[6]

- Family Code § 2626 gives the family court authority "to order reimbursement in cases it deems appropriate for debts paid after separation but before trial."

---

[6] *See* Marriage of Mullonkal and Kodiyamplakkil, 51 Cal. App. 5th 604, 265 Cal. Rptr. 3d 285 (2020) (community funds used to pay student loans for medical school).

- Absent an agreement, there is no right to reimbursement when separate property pays family expenses.

- Improvements are discussed in § 7.8. After January 1, 2005, a spouse who uses their separate property to improve the other spouse's separate property has a right to reimbursement (Family Code § 2640(c)). After 2001, the community is entitled to reimbursement when one spouse uses community property to improve the other souse's separate property. The community is entitled to reimbursement when a spouse uses community property without the consent of the other spouse to improve the spouse's separate property.

§ 11.10 Relationship Between Spousal Support and Property Division: The Problem of Double Dipping

Property division and spousal support serve different purposes. An issue at the intersection of property and support is whether income from property awarded to one spouse on divorce should be considered income for purposes of support.[7] In *Sampson v. Sampson*,[8] the Massachusetts Appeals Court wrote, "Commentators use the phrase 'double dipping' to describe the seeming injustice that occurs when property is awarded to one spouse in an equitable distribution of marital assets and is then also considered as a source of income for purposes of imposing support obligations. Courts and commentators have often disagreed, as to what constitutes double-dipping, whether double-dipping ought to be prohibited as a matter of law, and if not so prohibited, whether it is inequitable in the circumstances of the particular divorce settlement."

---

[7] *See* Grunfeld v. Grunfeld, 94 N.Y.2d 696, 731 N.E.2d 142, 709 N.Y.S.2d 486 (2000) ("The primary issue on appeal in this divorce action is whether the Appellate Division erroneously based both its equitable distribution award of one half the value of defendant's law license and his obligation to pay maintenance on the same projected professional earnings. McSparron v. McSparron, 87 N.Y.2d 275, 286, 639 N.Y.S.2d 265, 662 N.E.2d 745, prescribed a rule against such double counting of income.").

[8] 62 Mass. App. 366, 816 N.E.2d 999, 1006 (2004).

§ 11.10 RELATIONSHIP BETWEEN SPOUSAL SUPPORT AND PROPERTY DIVISION

Consider Sue and Tom who were married 20 years. They divorced five years ago. During the marriage, Sue worked for the Acme Company for 15 years, and had a defined benefit pension through Acme. On divorce, the pension, which was community property, was valued at $100,000, and was awarded to Sue. Tom received $50,000 in other community property to equalize the property division. In the divorce, Sue was ordered to pay spousal support to Tom in the amount of $500 per month. Sue recently retired from Acme after twenty years' service and started drawing her pension. Because Sue retired, her income decreased, and Sue filed a motion in family court seeking to eliminate her $500 per month spousal support obligation. In reply, Tom argues that Sue's pension is income, and when her pension income is combined with other income, Sue has enough income to continue paying $500 a month spousal support. Sue argues it would be wrong to count her pension as income because she was awarded the pension in the division of property five years earlier. To count her pension as income now would count the pension twice, once at divorce and again at retirement.

Wisconsin courts have grappled with double counting pension awards.[9] The approach in Wisconsin is to allow the retired spouse to receive the value of the pension assigned to the spouse in the divorce—in Sue's case, $100,000—before the pension is considered income to determine support.[10]

California courts reject the double dipping argument in most scenarios. In *Marriage of White*, 192 Cal. App. 3d 1022, 237 Cal. Rptr. 764 (1987), for example, husband received his entire pension in the divorce, while wife got the family home. The Court of Appeal ruled it was proper to consider husband's retirement income for purposes of determining spousal support. The court wrote, " 'Double counting' of a pension occurs only on those occasions when jurisdiction is reserved over the pension, and it is divided 'in kind' as payments fall due. Then each spouse is, properly speaking, an owner of a portion of those benefits and it would be incorrect to attribute the whole to either spouse for alimony determination purposes. When, however, all marital property division is effected

---

[9] *See* McReath v. McReath, 800 N.W.2d 399 (Wis. 2011).
[10] *See* Olski v. Olski, 197 Wis.2d 237, 540 N.W.2d 412 (1995).

at divorce and one spouse is awarded the entire pension, it is not in any way improper to consider the pension benefits as entirely [the supporting spouse's] income for purposes of alimony determination.' "[11]

§ 11.11 Property Problems

1. Family Code § 761 provides that community property transferred into a revocable trust remains community property unless the trust instrument provides otherwise. When a married couple funds an irrevocable trust for the benefit of a third party, the trust property is not community property.

Elizabeth and William were married eighteen years when they divorced. During marriage, Elizabeth and William established "The Elizabeth and William Chamberlin Irrevocable Charitable Trust." They created the trust to gain tax benefits and generate income for donations to charity. All monies transferred to the trust during marriage were from Elizabeth and William's income from employment. At the time of divorce, the trust contains $1 million. In the divorce, William argues that the corpus of the trust is community property and should be awarded to Elizabeth, with other marital property of equal value awarded to him. Elizabeth argues that because the trust is irrevocable, the money in the trust does not belong to either of them, and is not community property. Who is correct? In *Matter of Chamberlin,* 155 N.H. 13, 918 A.2d 1 (2007). Wife

2. During marriage, Dan's parents conveyed to Dan four deeds for mineral rights. The mineral rights produce substantial dividends every year. More than 20 years ago, Rita commenced a divorce action against Dan. Dan was properly served in the divorce action, but he did not appear or participate in the divorce. The court divided the mineral rights 50–50, giving half to Dan and half to Rita. Dan did not appeal. Nor did he take any action regarding division of the mineral rights until recently, when he filed an action in court seeking a declaration that the mineral rights are his separate property because the rights were a gift to him from his parents. Dan seeks a ruling that the trial court erred 20 years ago in dividing the

---

[11] 192 Cal. App. 3d at 1027 (quoting Grace Blumberg, Intangible Assets: Recognition and Valuation. In J. McCahey (Ed.), V*aluation and Distribution of Marital Property* 1984.).

mineral rights 50–50. How should the judge rule on Dan's claim that the divorce court erred so long ago? *Pearson v. Fillingim,* 332 S.W.3d 361 (Tex. 2011). Res judicata applies

3. Theresa and Aftab have been married twenty years. They have six children, four of whom are minors. Theresa and Aftab hold masters degrees. Both worked in banking. Aftab was laid off five years ago, and has not sought work since, preferring to be a stay-at-home parent. During the marriage, Theresa started her own finance company, specializing in the management of fixed income assets. At the time of divorce, her company has approximately $250 million of assets under management, and Theresa's net yearly income is $1 million. The couple owns valuable real and personal property, including the family home worth more than $3 million, and two vacation homes. Throughout the marriage, Aftab was verbally and physically abusive to Theresa and the children. Two months ago, Theresa informed Aftab she planned to seek a divorce. Several days later, at 4:00 a.m., Aftab broke the lock on the door to Theresa's bedroom, where she slept separately from him. Aftab entered Theresa's bedroom wearing rubber gloves and carrying a metal barbell. Aftab pinned Theresa to the bed with his knee and began beating her viciously on the head, face, neck and hands with the barbell. Theresa observed her blood, teeth and bone spattering everywhere. Her screams brought their three daughters, aged 15, 12 and 10, into the room. Aftab told the girls he had killed her mother. As one of the children called 911, Aftab attempted to renew his attack on Theresa. The daughters held him off her until police arrived and arrested him. Theresa's injuries were severe. She suffered multiple contusions, a broken nose and jaw, broken teeth, multiple lacerations, and neurological damage. Her medical treatment included the surgical installation of a titanium plate over her eye, over 20 hours of painful dental procedures, and many other oral and facial surgical procedures over the next several months. Afterwards, she suffered pain, dizziness, headaches, nightmares, sleeplessness and post-traumatic stress disorder. Despite these problems, Theresa was back at work on a part-time basis three weeks after the attack. Aftab was indicted for attempted murder, pleaded guilty to assault in the first degree, and was sentenced to 8 years in prison. Theresa commenced divorce proceedings. The value of the community property is $13 million, including real property,

cash and securities, pension and retirement benefits, jewelry, and automobiles. Given the facts of this case, may/should the judge depart from the equal division rule? *Havell v. Islam*, 301 A.D.2d 339, 751 N.Y.S.2d 449 (2002). yes

4. Carole and George were married nearly twenty years. Carole is an attorney practicing personal injury law. At the time the couple divorced, Carole was handling five personal injury cases on a contingent fee basis. Carole had devoted hundreds of hours to the cases (*e.g.*, depositions, motions, trial preparation), but none of the cases had settled or gone to trial when it was time to divide Carole and George's property. George argues that any contingent fee Carole earns from the cases is community property because she worked on the cases during the marriage. Carole argues that any fee she earns will be received after the divorce is final, and is hers alone. Who is right? *Marriage of Kilbourne*, 232 Cal. App. 3d 1518, 284 Cal. Rptr. 201 (1991). CP, b/c earned before separation

5. Sue and Sam met during their first year of law school. They got married during the summer before their third year. During fall semester of her senior year, Sue registered for a class on complex civil litigation. Unfortunately, the subject was dull and the professor was duller. One day, while daydreaming in class, Sue came up with the idea for a novel about an attorney engaged in complex civil litigation. The nature of the attorney's work involved her in romance, adventure, drama, international intrigue, car chases, five star hotels, and enormous wealth. Over the course of the semester, Sue used class time to write an outline of the novel. During spring semester, Sue wrote the first half of the novel. Unfortunately, Sue and Sam separated shortly following graduation, and Sue filed for divorce. After studying for the July bar examination, Sue devoted herself to the novel. The divorce was granted in December. The divorce judgment did not mention the novel. Sue finished the novel in February of the next year. To Sue's delight, the novel was published by a major publisher and, within weeks, sat atop the *New York Times* best seller list. Large royalty checks started flowing to Sue. When Sam learned of the novel's success, he consulted an attorney to see whether he has a right to a portion of the royalties. Does he? *Marriage of Worth*, 195 Cal. App. 3d 768, 241 Cal. Rptr. 135 (1987). probably, he could try and get an apportionment

6. Farah and Irfan are citizens of Pakistan. They married in Pakistan pursuant to an arrangement between their families. On their wedding day, Farah was 18 and Irfan was 29. In accordance with Pakistani custom, on their wedding day, they signed a written marriage contract. The contract provided a dowry of 51,00 rupees, payment of which was deferred. The contract did not contain any provisions regarding marital property. Under Pakistan law, unless a contract provides otherwise, upon divorce, all property owned by the husband on the date of the divorce remains his property, and all property owned by the wife remains hers. Shortly following marriage, the couple moved to England where Irfan completed his Ph.D. at Oxford. They then moved to the United States, where Irfan began work at the World Bank. The couple lived nearly 20 years in the United States on diplomatic visas. Recently, Farah filed for divorce. While the divorce was pending, Irfan went to the Pakistan embassy and performed talaq (divorce under Islamic religious law and Pakistan secular law). At the embassy, Irfan executed a talaq that stated: "Now this deed witnesses that I, the said Irfan, do hereby divorce, Farah, daughter of Mahmood, by pronouncing upon her Divorce/Talaq three times irrevocably and severing all connections of husband and wife with her forever and for good. (1) I Divorce thee Farah, (2) I Divorce thee Farah, (3) I Divorce thee Farah." In the state court divorce action, Irfan argues that the talaq means he is divorced under the law of Pakistan, and that Pakistani law must be applied. Irfan emphasizes that nothing in the marriage contract alters Pakistani law. At the time of the divorce, Irfan's pension at the World Bank is valued at one million dollars. The couple owns a home valued at $850,000, title to which is in Irfan's name. Irfan argues that the state court is bound by Pakistan law, and lacks jurisdiction to characterize or divide the pension or the home. Does the state court have authority to characterize and divide the pension and the marital home? Or must the state recognize and enforce the talaq? *Aleem v. Aleem,* 404 Md. 404, 947 A.2d 489 (2008).

7. Afiya and Bello met while both were Ph.D. students in archeology working on a dig in the Middle East. They married 15 years ago. After completing their doctorates, both became professors of archeology at U.C. Berkeley. Ten years ago, Bello purchased a small gold goat. The goat is approximately 2,000 years old and was excavated from a site in Syria. It is worth $10,000. The goat is in a

glass case in Afiya and Bello's home. Both are very fond of it. It is their most prized possession. Afiya and Bello own their home. They paid the last mortgage payment last year. The home is worth $750,000. Their home is close to the university, so they don't need or own cars. They ride bikes to work. They are often abroad, months at a time, on archeological digs. Both have defined benefit pensions with the university. Their pensions are of equal value. In addition to the golden goat, they own other historical artefacts with a value of $50,000. Unfortunately, Afiya and Bello are divorcing. They cannot agree on the goat. Both want it, and neither seems willing to budge. The goat is the only thing holding up the divorce. They agree to sell the home and divide the profit. They also agree on how to divide the historical artefacts. They agree they each will keep their own pension. It would be a shame to go to trial over one item of personal property. Is there any way to help Afiya and Bello resolve this without litigation? If the case goes to trial, what should the judge do with the goat?

Chapter 12

ANNULMENT

Analysis

§ 12.1   Why Annulment Instead of Divorce?
§ 12.2   Basis for Annulment
§ 12.3   Void Marriage
§ 12.4   Voidable Marriage
§ 12.5   Putative Spouse
§ 12.6   Relation-Back Doctrine
§ 12.7   Questions on Annulment

Annulment ends marriage. The California Family Code uses the word "nullity" instead of annulment. This chapter uses the traditional word, annulment. A proceeding for annulment is started the same way as a divorce, by filing a petition, FL-100.

§ 12.1 Why Annulment Instead of Divorce?

Why do some people prefer annulment over divorce? Historically, complete divorce (divorce *a vinculo matrimoni*) was unavailable, and annulment was the only way to terminate an unhappy marriage. Today, no-fault divorce is available. Yet, some people prefer annulment because they can say with a straight face that in the eyes of the law they never married, and, thus, never divorced. (*See* "relation-back" doctrine § 12.6). Some people have religious reasons to prefer annulment. In the past, divorce was socially stigmatizing. Eyebrows rose when a woman was a "divorcee." Today, divorce is practically normative, and the stigma is disappearing.

§ 12.2 Basis for Annulment

Annulment is available only if grounds for annulment existed *on the day* a couple married.[1] That is, annulment is available only if there was a defect in the marriage on the wedding day. Problems arising *after* a couple marries are not grounds for annulment although they may be grounds for divorce.

§ 12.3 Void Marriage

Marriages subject to annulment are void or voidable. Incestuous and bigamous marriages are void. Family Code § 2200 provides in part: "Marriages between parents and children, ancestors and descendants of every degree, and between siblings of the half as well as the whole blood, and between uncles or aunts and nieces or nephews, are incestuous and void from the beginning . . . ." Section 2201(a) states: "A subsequent marriage contracted by a person during the life of his or her former spouse, with a person other than the former spouse, is illegal and void, unless: The former marriage has been dissolved or adjudged a nullity before the date of the subsequent marriage."

A void marriage is void from the beginning—void *ab initio*. The Court of Appeal, in *Marriage of Seaton*, 200 Cal. App. 4th 800, 133 Cal. Rptr. 3d 50 (2011), wrote, "In California, a void marriage is invalid for all purposes from the moment of its inception, whether or not it has been so declared in a court of law, and its invalidity may be shown collaterally in any proceeding in which the fact of marriage may be material."

Because a void marriage was never really a marriage, it is technically not necessary to bring an annulment action—there is nothing to annul; it was void *ab initio*. Yet, void marriages sometimes last years, and it is useful to bring a nullity proceeding (or a divorce) so a court can clarify the parties' marital status and adjudicate issues pertaining to children, support, and property.

§ 12.4 Voidable Marriage

A voidable marriage is *valid* unless it is annulled. In *Marriage of Seaton*, 200 Cal. App. 4th 800, 133 Cal. Rptr. 3d 50 (2011), the

---

[1] *See* Marriage of Garcia, 13 Cal. App. 5th 1334, 221 Cal. Rptr. 3d 319 (2017).

Court of Appeal wrote, "A voidable marriage is valid for all purposes until it is judicially declared a nullity, and may only be challenged by a party entitled by statute to assert its voidability." A voidable marriage can only be annulled during the lifetime of the parties. Once one spouse dies, a voidable marriage is immune from attack.

Family Code § 2210 sets forth the "defects" that render marriage voidable: (1) The party seeking annulment was too young to marry; (2) Either spouse was of unsound mind on the wedding day, thus lacking capacity to enter the marriage contract; (3) Consent to marry was obtained by fraud; (4) Consent was obtained by force (so-called "shotgun wedding"); (5) Either party was, at the time of the marriage, physically incapable of entering into the marriage state.

Fraud is a basis for annulment, but not all types of fraud suffice. In *Marriage of Ramirez*, 165 Cal. App. 4th 751, 81 Cal. Rptr. 3d 180 (2008), the Court of Appeal analyzed the fraud that justifies annulling a marriage. Lilia sought to annul her marriage to Jorge after she learned that prior to *and* during marriage, Jorge was cheating on Lilia with Lilia's sister! The Court wrote:

> A promise to be a kind, dutiful and affectionate spouse cannot be made the basis of an annulment. Instead, the particular fraudulent intention must relate to the sexual or procreative aspects of marriage. In the absence of this type of fraud, the longstanding rule is that neither party may question the validity of the marriage upon the ground of express or implied representations of the other with respect to such matters as character, habits, chastity, business or social standing, financial worth or prospects, or matters of a similar nature. Concealment of incontinence, temper, idleness, extravagance, coldness or lack of represented fortune will not justify an annulment.
>
> To [annul] a marriage, the fraud alleged must show an intention not to perform a duty vital to the marriage, which exists in the mind of the offending spouse at the time of marriage. Thus, historically, annulments based on fraud have only been granted in cases where the fraud relates in some way to the sexual, procreative or child-rearing aspects of marriage.

Here, the trial court specifically found that ... the fraud was based on Jorge's intent to continue the ongoing simultaneous sexual relationships with Lilia and Blanca at the time that he and Lilia entered into the 2001 marriage.

Today, in the era of no-fault divorce, there are no viable defenses to divorce. If one spouse wants a divorce, the other spouse can't stop it. The divorce-seeker alleges irreconcilable differences and the judge does not second guess the grounds. Not so with annulment. To obtain annulment, the moving party must plead and prove that a specific ground for annulment existed on the wedding day. Failure to carry the burden of proof means the judge denies annulment. The party can get a divorce, but not an annulment.

§ 12.5 Putative Spouse

In divorce, the court divides the community property. What happens in annulment? How does a court divide property when a marriage is void or voidable? California's answer is the putative spouse doctrine.[2] Family Code § 2251 provides:

> (a) If a determination is made that a marriage is void or voidable and the court finds that either party or both parties believed in good faith that the marriage was valid, the court shall:
>
> (1) Declare the party or parties, who believed in good faith that the marriage was valid, to have the status of putative spouse.
>
> (2) If the division of property is in issue, divide ... that property acquired during the union that would have been community property or quasi-community property if the union had not been void or voidable, only upon request of a party who is declared a putative souse under paragraph (1). This property is known as "quasi-marital property."

To qualify as a putative spouse, a person must have honestly believed they were validly married. The court considers all evidence

---

[2] Courts apply the putative spouse doctrine in annulment cases, probate proceedings, and wrongful death cases.

shedding light on the person's belief in the validity of the marriage. The leading case is *Ceja v. Rudolph & Sletten, Inc.*, 56 Cal. 4th 1113, 302 P.3d 211, 158 Cal. Rptr. 3d 21 (2013). The Supreme Court concluded:

> [The law] contemplates a subjective standard that focuses on the alleged putative spouse's state of mind to determine whether he or she maintained a genuine and honest belief in the validity of the marriage. Good faith must be judged on a case-by-case basis in light of all the relevant facts, such as the efforts made to create a valid marriage, the alleged putative spouse's background and experience, and the circumstances surrounding the marriage, including any objective evidence of the marriage's invalidity. Under this standard, the reasonableness of the claimed belief is a factor properly considered along with all other circumstances in assessing the genuineness of that belief. The good faith inquiry, however, does not call for application of a reasonable person test, and a belief in the validity of a marriage need not be objectively reasonable.

Section 2251(a)(2) provides for division of property in annulment cases. Because the marriage is annulled, the parties do not acquire community property. At the request of a putative spouse, the court divides property that would have been community property if the marriage had been valid. The property is called quasi-marital property and is treated the same as community property.

§ 12.6 Relation-Back Doctrine

The relation-back doctrine is a legal fiction under which a judgment of annulment is said to relate back in time to the date of marriage, and erase the marriage.[3] As the Court of Appeal put it in *Marriage of Seaton*, 200 Cal. App. 4th 800, 133, 133 Cal. Rptr. 3d 50 (2011), "A judgment of nullity has been said to relate back and erase the marriage and all its implications from the outset. At the same time, this legal fiction was fashioned by the courts to do substantial justice between the parties to a void or voidable marriage, and is

---

[3] *See* Sefton v. Sefton, 45 Cal. 2d 872, 291 P.2d 439 (1955).

desirable only when used as a device for achieving that purpose. In cases involving the rights of third parties, courts have been especially wary lest the logical appeal of the fiction should obscure fundamental problems and lead to unjust or ill-advised results respecting a third party's rights."

QUESTIONS: SHOULD RELATION BACK APPLY?

1. Sue and Bill were married fifteen years. They divorced three years ago. In the divorce, Sue was ordered to pay Bill spousal support of $4,000 per month. The divorce decree provided that spousal support would end on Bill's death or remarriage. A year ago, Bill married Beth. Upon Bill's marriage to Beth, Sue stopped paying spousal support. Recently, Bill obtained an annulment of his marriage to Beth. As soon as the annulment was final, Bill returned to family court and filed a motion requesting the judge to order Sue to resume spousal support. Bill relies on the relation-back theory. According to Bill, the annulment relates back and wipes out the marriage to Beth. In other words, Bill did not remarry and Sue owes him support. Not only does Bill seek resumption of ongoing support, Bill argues that since he never remarried, Sue owes him arrears for the months Sue did not pay support. Should Sue be ordered to resume paying support to Bill? How about arrears? No.

2. Following a 20 year marriage, Pat and Jeff divorced. Jeff was ordered to pay Pat monthly spousal support of $3,000 for 10 years or until Pat died or remarried. Two years after the divorce, Pat was in Las Vegas on vacation. While playing a slot machine, Pat met Tom. Pat and Tom "partied" the night away, Las Vegas style. At 3:00 a.m., while highly intoxicated, Pat and Tom decided to get married. They went to a local wedding chapel and tied the knot. By dawn, they were newlyweds! When Pat sobered up, she realized what a huge mistake she had made. She Facebooked her best friend and asked, "Can I undue this horrible mistake? I was so drunk, I didn't know what I was doing!" Jeff found out about the wedding because, despite the fact that advertisements on TV say, "What Happens in Vegas Stays in Vegas," It ain't necessarily so. Because Pat had remarried, Jeff stopped paying spousal support. Pat promptly annulled her marriage to Tom. Once annulled, Pat went to court to reinstate Jeff's support obligation. Should Jeff be ordered

to resume paying support to Pat? Is this case different from number 1? Yes, b/c here Pat did not have capacity to enter into marriage contract

§ 12.7 Questions on Annulment

1. Harold is in prison serving a sentence of life without the possibility of parole. Janet is a social worker for the state. Harold and Janet met and married inside prison. Prior to marriage, Harold told Janet he had applied for clemency from the governor and expected to be released in a year or two. According to Janet, Harold lied about applying for clemency. After a year of marriage, Janet commenced an action to annul the marriage based on fraud. Janet argues that she married Harold based on his false statements about applying for clemency. *Meadows v. Meadows*, 330 S.W.3d 798 (Mo. Ct. App. 2011). Annulled b/c fraud relating to sexual/procreation aspect

2. Janet and Steve were married 33 years when Janet filed for divorce. The divorce was finalized, and Steve was ordered to pay spousal support. A year after the divorce was entered, Steve filed a motion to vacate the divorce judgment. Steve had obtained an annulment from a Roman Catholic tribunal. The religious tribunal ruled that the marriage was based on fraud perpetrated by Janet. In state court, Steve argues the judge should vacate the divorce based on the religious tribunal's annulment of the marriage. With the marriage annulled, Steve argues his duty to pay spousal support should terminate. Is a ruling from a religious tribunal controlling in state court? *Age v. Age*, 340 S.W.3d 88 (Ky. Ct. App. 2011). No.

3. Howard, age 72, had terminal cancer and severe dementia caused by Alzheimer's disease. Howard had several adult children. Howard lived at home. His daughter Nancy was his primary caretaker. Nancy went on a one-week vacation and left Howard in the care of Nidia, age 58. During the one-week vacation, Nidia married Howard and transferred all his assets into her name. Howard died a few months later. Following Howard's death, Nancy brought an action seeking to have the marriage annulled because Howard was mentally incompetent to consent to marriage. Nancy's suit sought to nullify the transfers of property from Howard to Nidia. Howard's will was admitted to probate. The will left his property to his children. In probate court, Nidia filed a right of election as a surviving spouse seeking a portion of Howard's estate.

Howard's children and his doctors provided evidence that, at the time of the wedding, Howard had advanced Alzheimer's and was incompetent. Nidia provided evidence that she had known Howard 25 years and that he had proposed marriage several times. Nidia accepted the Howard's last proposal, which just happened to occur while Nancy was on vacation. The pastor who performed the marriage stated that if he had known about Howard's medical condition he would not have performed the marriage. Can the marriage be annulled? Should the transfers of property be set aside? Is Nidia entitled to an elective share of Howard's property as a surviving spouse? *Campbell v. Thomas*, 73 A.D.3d 103, 897 N.Y.S.2d 460 (2010). *[handwritten: No to anullment (since after his death)]*

4. Festus is a resident of the United States, originally from Ethiopia. Betelehem is Ethiopian. Betelehem and Festus met through an internet dating site. After some months of internet communication, Betelehem told Festus she loved him and wanted a marital relationship with children. The two were married after Betelehem arrived in the United States. A year after the wedding, and two days after receiving her "green card," Betelehem left Festus, claiming he abused her. Betelehem filed for divorce. Festus filed for annulment based on fraud. A cousin of Betelehem testifies that Betelehem told her, "I only married him to come to the United States." A friend of Festus testifies that Betelehem told him, "Before I came to America, I took a birth control injection because I did not want to have his baby." Is Festus entitled to an annulment? *Desta v. Anyaoha*, 371 S.W.3d 596 (Tex. Ct. App. 2012). Might Betelehem have something to worry about with immigration authorities?

[handwritten: Yes b/c of procreative aspects of marital relationship.]

Chapter 13

WHEN DEATH ENDS MARRIAGE

Analysis

§ 13.1 Testate or Intestate
§ 13.2 Probate Code Definition of Community Property
§ 13.3 Probate Code Definition of Quasi-Community Property
§ 13.4 Problems on Characterization
§ 13.5 Debts When Marriage Ends in Death

Death ends marriage (Family Code § 310(a)). The Probate Code (PC) governs proceedings when marriage ends in death.

§ 13.1 Testate or Intestate

A person who has a will dies testate. A person who has no will dies intestate. The PC provides that one-half of the community property and quasi-community property belongs to the surviving spouse. The other one-half belongs to the decedent (PC §§ 100(a) and 101(a)). Through a will, the deceased may dispose of her half of the community property as she wishes. If the deceased dies intestate, the survivor receives all of the community and quasi-community property (PC § 6401(a) and (b)). Through a will, a deceased spouse may do as she wishes with her separate property. If the deceased dies intestate, some or all of the deceased's separate property passes to the surviving spouse according to the law of intestate succession (PC § 6401(c)).

§ 13.2 Probate Code Definition of Community Property

The Probate Code defines community property in § 28 as follows:

Probate Code § 28. Community property

"Community property" means:

(a) Community property heretofore or hereafter acquired during marriage by a married person while domiciled in this state.

(b) All personal property wherever situated, and all real property situated in this state, heretofore or hereafter acquired during the marriage by a married person while domiciled elsewhere, that is community property, or a substantially equivalent type of marital property, under the laws of the place where the acquiring spouse was domiciled at the time of its acquisition.

The Probate Code and Family Code definitions of community property coincide when a married person acquired property while domiciled in California. Under PC § 28(a) and FC § 760, community property includes real or personal property wherever situated acquired by a married person during marriage while domiciled in California.

There is a difference between the Probate Code and the Family Code definitions of community property when a married person acquires property while domiciled outside California. It is necessary in that instance to determine whether, at the time of acquisition, the person was domiciled in another community property state (AZ, ID, LA, NM, NV, TX, WI, WA) or in a non-community property state. Probate Code § 28(b) defines community property to include personal property wherever situated acquired by a married person while domiciled in another community property state that is community property under the law of that state. The Law Revision Commission Comment to Probate Code § 28(b) provides an example: "Property is community property under subdivision (b) if it is the income of separate property and the income of separate property is community property under the laws of the place where the spouse owning the separate property is domiciled at the time the income is earned." A California probate court applies the law of the other community property state.

Probate Code § 28(b) also defines community property to include personal property wherever situated acquired during marriage by a married person while domiciled in a non-community property state if, under the law of the non-community property state, the property is the substantial equivalent of community property. Given that the definition of community property is increasingly similar to the equitable distribution definition of marital property, it seems likely under Probate Code § 28(b) that a California probate judge will define personal property acquired while domiciled outside California as community property regardless of where the parties were living.

Turning from personal property to real property, Probate Code § 28(b) defines community property to include California real property acquired while a married person was domiciled outside California in a community property state or a non-community property state where the property is the substantial equivalent of community property.

The Family Code definition of community property (§ 760) does not include personal or real property acquired when a married couple was domiciled outside California when the property was acquired. Under the Family Code, such property is quasi-community property (§ 125). Thus, under the Probate Code, some property acquired while domiciled outside California is community property, while the same property is defined under the Family Code as quasi-community property.

§ 13.3 Probate Code Definition of Quasi-Community Property

The Probate Code definition of quasi-community property is found in Probate Code § 66.

Probate Code § 66. Quasi-community property

"Quasi-community property" means the following property, other than community property as defined in Section 28:

(a) All personal property wherever situated, and all real property situated in this state, heretofore or hereafter acquired by a decedent while domiciled elsewhere that would have been community property of the decedent and the surviving spouse if the decedent had been domiciled in this state at the time of its acquisition.

Under Probate Code § 66, quasi-community property is limited to property that is not community property under Probate Code § 28 and that was acquired when a couple was domiciled in a non-community property state.

Suppose Husband and Wife live in Texas where they buy a valuable painting. They move to California, and Husband dies. Under Probate Code § 28(b), the painting is community property. If the marriage ended in divorce in California, Family Code § 125 characterizes the painting as quasi-community property.

In divorce cases, Family Code §§ 760 and 125 cover all property that is not separate property. When a marriage ends in death, however, Probate Code §§ 28 and 66 do not cover all real property that is not separate property. In some death scenarios, out-of-state real property is not separate property, community property, or quasi-community property. When this happens, a California probate court has no authority to adjudicate interests in the out-of-state property. The proper procedure is to start a probate case in California accompanied by an ancillary probate proceeding in the state where the property is located.

§ 13.4 Problems on Characterization

In the following problems, characterize the property (1) when the marriage ends in divorce, and (2) when the marriage ends in death.

1. Wife and Husband, living in Davis, California, buy Blackacre in Davis. Don't consider how title is held.

   (a) Characterize on divorce. —CP

   (b) Characterize on death. —CP

2. Wife and Husband, living in Davis, buy Blackacre in Davis, taking title as joint tenants with right of survivorship.

   (a) Characterize on divorce. — CP

   (b) Characterize on death. — not really a need to characterize, but it could be considered SP

§ 13.4   PROBLEMS ON CHARACTERIZATION   197

/CP state

3. Wife and Husband, living in San Luis Obispo, California, buy Orangeacre, in Utah. Don't consider how title is held.

(a) Characterize on divorce. – CP

(b) Characterize on Death. – CP

4. Wife and Husband, living in San Luis Obispo, buy Orangeacre, in Utah. They take title as joint tenants.

(a) Characterize on divorce. – CP

(b) Characterize on death. – don't need to characterize

5. Wife and Husband, living in Los Angeles, California, buy Niceacre, in Texas. Don't consider how title is held.

(a) Characterize on divorce.

(b) Characterize on death.

6. Wife and Husband, living in Los Angeles, buy Niceacre, in Texas. They put title in Wife's name alone.

(a) Characterize on divorce.

(b) Characterize on death.

7. Wife and Husband, living in Texas, buy Prettyacre, in Sacramento, California. Don't consider how title held.

(a) Characterize on divorce. – CP

(b) Characterize on death. – CP

8. Wife and Husband, living in Texas, buy Prettyacre in Sacramento, taking title as joint tenants.

(a) Characterize on divorce.

(b) Characterize on death.

9. Wife and Husband, living in Utah, buy Greenacre, in Utah. Later they move to California. Title to Greenacre is in Wife's name alone.

(a) Characterize on divorce. – QCP

(b) Characterize on death. –

10. Wife and Husband, living in Nevada, buy Redacre, in Nevada. Later, Wife moves to California, but Husband remains in

Nevada. Wife divorces Husband in a California court. Characterize on divorce.

11. Wife and Husband, living in Nevada, buy Redacre, in Nevada. Later, Wife moves to California, but Husband remains in Nevada. Wife dies in California. Characterize on death.

12. Wife and Husband, living in New Mexico, buy Purpleacre, in New Mexico. Later, they move to California, and divorce here. Characterize Purpleacre on divorce. Suppose the couple remains married until Wife passes away. Characterize on death.

13. Wife and Husband, living in Egypt, buy a vacation home on the California side of Lake Tahoe. Later, they move to California, and divorce here. What if the marriage lasts until Husband passes away. Characterize on death.

14. Wife and Husband, living in San Diego, buy a car. Characterize the car, ignoring how title is held.

(a) Characterize on divorce.

(b) Characterize on death.

15. Wife and Husband, living in Montana, buy a car in Montana, taking title as joint tenants. Later they move to California.

(a) Characterize on divorce.

(b) Characterize on death.

§ 13.5 Debts When Marriage Ends in Death

As mentioned in Chapter 9, there are four sets of rules regarding debts. One set deals with debts during marriage, and two sets concern debts on divorce. This section discusses debts when a marriage ends in death. The executor or personal representative of the estate inventories the deceased's property, pays the deceased's debts, and distributes the property (PC § 8000 et seq.). The deceased's creditors are given notice of the death and have a limited time to file a claim against the estate (PC § 9052).

When a deceased spouse's property is not subject to probate administration, but passes directly to the surviving spouse, PC § 13550 provides that a surviving spouse is personally liable for the debts of the deceased spouse described in § 13551.[1] Section 13551 limits the survivor's personal liability to the value of the survivor's half of the community and quasi-community property plus the decedent's separate property that passes to the survivor. Thus, all the community and quasi-community property is liable for the decedent's debts, as well as all of the decedent's separate property. The separate property of the surviving spouse is not liable for the decedent's debts.

By filing for administration of the deceased's estates, a surviving spouse can obtain a court order allocating debts between the estate and the surviving spouse. (Probate Code § 11440 et seq.).[2] Probate Code § 11444(b) provides that debts are characterized as separate or community according to the debt characterization rules found in the Family Code (FC § 2620 et seq.). Funeral expenses and the costs of the decedent's last illness are assigned to the estate (PC § 11446).

---

[1] *See* Dawes v. Rich, 60 Cal. App. 4th 24, 30–31, 70 Cal. Rptr. 2d 72 (1997).

[2] *See* Dawes v. Rich, 60 Cal. App. 4th 24, 30–31, 70 Cal. Rptr. 2d 72 (1997) ("Under Probate Code section 11444, the surviving spouse, the personal representative, or an interested party may petition the probate court for an allocation of debts between the surviving spouse and the estate of the deceased spouse.")

Chapter 14

COMMUNITY PROPERTY EXAM QUESTIONS

Analysis

§ 14.1 California Bar Exam Community Property Questions
§ 14.2 Law School Community Property Exams
§ 14.3 Analysis of Chapter Questions and Examples

Chapter 14 contains California Bar Examination essay questions and law school exams. The chapter also provides analysis of questions scattered throughout the book.

§ 14.1 California Bar Exam Community Property Questions

The California Bar Exam regularly tests community property. Three bar exam questions follow.

If you Google California State Bar, you will be taken to the State Bar home page. Click on Admissions. Then click on California Bar Examination. Then click on Past Exams. You can click on Essay Questions and/or Essay Questions and Selected Answers. For each essay question, the bar examiners select two candidate answers that received high grades from bar exam readers. For the July, 2016 and the July, 2015 community property essay questions reproduced below, you will find one of the Selected Answers for each essay.

July 2017—Question 1

Wanda, a successful accountant, and Hal, an art teacher, who are California residents, married in 2008. After their marriage, Wanda and Hal deposited their earnings into a joint bank account they opened at Main Street Bank from which Wanda managed the couple's finances. Each month, Wanda also deposited some of her earnings into an individual account she opened in her name at A1 Bank without telling Hal.

In 2010, Hal inherited $10,000 and a condo from an uncle. Hal used the $10,000 as a down payment on a $20,000 motorcycle, borrowing the $10,000 balance from Lender who relied on Hal's good credit. Hal took title to the motorcycle in his name alone. The loan was paid off from the joint bank account during the marriage.

At Wanda's insistence, Hal transferred title to the condo, worth $250,000, into joint tenancy with Wanda to avoid probate. The condo increased in value during the marriage.

On Hal's 40th birthday, Wanda took him to Dealer and bought him a used camper van for $20,000, paid out of their joint bank account, titled in Hal's name. Hal used the camper van for summer fishing trips with his friends.

In 2016, Wanda and Hal permanently separated, and Hal filed for dissolution. Just before the first hearing on the dissolution, Hal happened to discover Wanda's individual account, which contained $50,000.

What are Hal's and Wanda's rights and liabilities, if any, regarding:

1. The condo? Discuss.
2. The motorcycle? Discuss. *—debt incurred during marriage is CP*
3. The camper van? Discuss.
4. The A1 Bank account? Discuss.

Answer according to California law.

Issues on July, 2017 Essay

It would be best for you to answer the essay before you look at what follows, but you are a grown up, so peek if you must!

1. The condo. Hal inherited the condo, so it is separate property under Family Code § 770. At Wanda's insistence, Hal transferred the condo into joint tenancy. This transfer triggers application of § 2581, and the condo is transmuted into community property on divorce. Hal signed the deed transferring the property, so his signature will satisfy the writing requirement for a

transmutation. You should discuss the presumption that a transmutation that advantages one party is presumed to be the produce of undue influence (§ 8.3). There is no evidence of a writing that would rebut the § 2581 presumption. It is worth mentioning Wanda's "insistence" on the transmutation. Did Wanda coerce Hal into transmuting his property? Did Wanda overcome Hal's free will? I doubt these facts would support the argument that Hal's free will was overborn. The condo should be characterized as 100% community property on divorce.

 2. The motorcycle. Title in Hal's name alone does not control. The motorcycle was acquired during marriage, by a married person, while domiciled in California, thus the motorcycle falls under the general community property presumption (§ 760). The down payment was with Hal's separate property inheritance. The balance of the purchase was with a loan. If Hal wants to claim the loan was separate property, he needs to use the intent of the lender test (§ 7.6). There are two approaches to the intent of the lender: (1) The lender relied solely on separate property for repayment of the loan, the *Grinius* case, or (2) The lender relied primarily on separate property for repayment of the loan, the *Gudelj* case. Hal won't be able to meet either approach because the facts tell us that the lender relied on Hal's "good credit." A married person's credit worthiness belongs to the community. Hal won't be able to prove that the lender relied primarily or entirely on separate property. Thus, the loan was community property. The loan was repaid with community property. This is a pro rata apportionment issue (§ 5.10). The motorcycle is part separate and part community.

 3. The camper van. The camper van falls under the general community property presumption. The van was paid for with community property because the money in the account was community property. If Hal wants to claim the camper as his separate property, he will have to argue that Wanda transmuted her interest in the van by way of a gift to Hal. Hal will fail in his gift argument. Transmutations require a writing, signed by the party whose financial interest is adversely affected, in this case Wanda. There are no facts to suggest Wanda signed the necessary writing. Section 852(c) creates an exception to the writing requirement for gifts between spouses. (See § 10.3). Section 852(c) applies to gifts of clothing, jewelry, or other personal property of a personal nature. A

[handwritten margin note: but not under 852(c) for a gift of personal property.]

camper van is not clothing or jewelry. It might be considered personal property of a personal nature, but probably not in light of the Court of Appeal's decision in *Marriage of Buie and Neighbors*, 179 Cal. App. 4th 1170, 102 Cal. Rptr. 3d 387 (2009), where the Court ruled that a car is not a tangible article of a personal nature within the meaning of § 852(c).

4. The A1 Bank account. The money in the A1 account was community property because it was Wanda's income from work. The fact that the account is in Wanda's name alone does not change the fact that the money in the account is community property. The issue here is whether Wanda breached her fiduciary duty as a married person by not being honest with Hal about their finances (See § 10.7). The facts tell us Wanda, an accountant, handled the couple's finances. Perhaps Wanda was not trying to hide money from Hal. On the other hand, Hal didn't learn about the A1 account until after the divorce was filed, and the first court hearing was approaching. Hal can argue forcefully that Wanda was under a duty to disclose the A1 account and her failure to do was a breach of fiduciary duty. Family Code § 1100(e) requires spouses "to make full disclosure to the other spouse of all material facts and information regarding the existence, characterization, and valuation of all assets in which the community has or may have an interest . . . ." The fiduciary duty of honesty continues after a couple separates. If Wanda failed to disclose the A1 account in her preliminary declarations of financial disclosure (See § 1.7(c)), then Hal has a strong argument that Wanda deliberately hid this community asset. The remedy for deliberate violation of the fiduciary duty of honesty is contained in § 1101(h), and allows a court to award Hal 100% of the A1 account (See § 10.8).

July 2016—Question 5

In 2003, while planning their wedding, Harry and Wanda, a California couple, spent weeks discussing how they could each own and control their respective salaries. Sometime before their wedding, they prepared a document in which they stated, "After we marry, Wanda's salary is her property and Harry's salary is his property." At the same time, they prepared a separate document in which they stated, "We agree we do not need legal advice." They signed and dated each document. They subsequently married.

§ 14.1 CALIFORNIA BAR EXAM COMMUNITY PROPERTY QUESTIONS

In 2004, Harry used his salary to buy a condominium and took title in his name alone. [CP] Harry and Wanda moved into the condominium.

In 2005, Harry and Wanda opened a joint savings account at their local bank. Each year thereafter, they each deposited $5,000 from their salaries into the account. – CP

In 2015, Harry discovered that Wanda used money from their joint account to buy rental property and take title in her name alone.

In 2016, Harry and Wanda permanently separated and Wanda moved out of the condominium. Wanda thereafter required emergency surgery for a medical condition, resulting in a hospital bill of $50,000. Harry later filed a petition for dissolution of marriage. [Comm. debt]

What are Harry's and Wanda's rights and liabilities, if any regarding:

1. The condominium? Discuss.
2. The joint savings account? Discuss.
3. The rental property? Discuss.
4. The hospital bill? Discuss.

Answer according to California law.

July 2016 Bar Examination
Question 5: Selected Answer A

Community Property and Separate Property

California is a community property (CP) state. Property acquired during a valid marriage while domiciled in CA is presumed to be CP. Property acquired before marriage or after permanent separation is presumed to be separate property (SP). Property acquired during marriage through gift, bequest, devise or descent is also presumed to be SP. Under the source rule, tracing will be permitted to determine the source of the funds, and therefore the character of the asset as CP or SP. Upon divorce, CP will be divided equally in kind unless some special rule requires deviation from this equal division, or the spouses agree otherwise in writing or orally in open court.

Prenuptial Agreement

Spouses may deviate from the community property presumption by agreeing that their salaries, for instance, which normally would be a product of community labor during the marriage and thus CP, be SP. They may do so before the marriage through a written prenuptial agreement. Prenuptial agreements must be voluntary and not unconscionable. [On this point, I disagree. In California, an unconscionable prenup can be enforceable.] A court will find a prenup to be unconscionable if the terms are unfair, or if a spouse did not know the extent of the other spouse's property before signing the agreement. Additionally, prenuptial agreements must be in writing. A court will find that a prenup is not voluntarily executed if a spouse is not represented by counsel before signing the agreement. In order to rebut the presumption of involuntariness without counsel, the spouse not represented by counsel must be advised to seek the advice of counsel in writing, and must waive that right in writing, and if she does waive that right, she must be allowed 7 days between the presentation of a prenuptial agreement and the signing of it, and she must also write, in a separate writing, that she understands the rights she is giving up, and from whom she received the information regarding what the extent is of her spouse's property.

Here, while planning their wedding, Henry and Wanda, both California residents, spent "weeks" discussing "how they could each own and control their respective salaries." Although it is not clear how long before the wedding this occurred, merely, "sometime before their wedding," they jointly "prepared a document in which they stated, 'After we marry, Wanda's salary is her property and Harry's salary is his property.'" They both signed and dated this document. Simultaneously, they "prepared a separate document in which they stated, 'We agree we do not need legal advice,'" which was also signed and dated by both of them. After doing so, they married.

Formalities of Prenuptial Agreement Not Followed: Voluntariness and Unconscionability.

As discussed above, a prenuptial agreement must be in writing. It appears from the facts that Henry and Wanda were attempting to create a prenuptial agreement through the "document" that they prepared "sometime before their wedding" in which they agreed that

Wanda's salary is her "[separate] property" and Harry's salary is his "[separate] property." Although couples may choose to contract around the general CP presumption through a prenuptial agreement, they must do so voluntarily and it must not be unconscionable. Because neither spouse was represented by counsel, the agreement is presumed to be involuntary. As stated above, this presumption can be rebutted if the spouses who are not represented by counsel are advised to seek counsel and explicitly waive that in writing. Here, it appears that the couple attempted to waive this right to counsel by stating, "We agree we do not need legal advice." This may be a sufficient writing in a court's opinion to waive the right to counsel. Nonetheless, there is still a problem with voluntariness, here. Even if this right is waived in a signed writing, the unrepresented couple must still be given 7 days with which to mull over the prenuptial agreement.

Either spouse (depending on the asset discussed below) may argue that because they spent "weeks discussing how they could each own and control their respective salaries," this was more than enough to satisfy the 7 day rule. However, because the agreement was signed simultaneously with their waiver of counsel, and there is nothing in the facts to demonstrate that there was a period of 7 days AFTER presentation of the document and signing, given that the facts only state "sometime before their wedding" they prepared a document. If this document was prepared and signed 2 hours before the wedding, this would not be deemed voluntary, and may even be deemed unconscionable by a court given its unfairness.

Additionally, neither spouse executed an additional separate document stating that they understood the rights that they were giving up and that they stated the source where they got information about the other spouse's financial assets and liabilities. Therefore, this prenuptial agreement will not be deemed voluntary. However, it probably will not be deemed unconscionable because it does not appear that the terms were patently unfair, given that both spouses were attempting to transmute their salaries into SP, and it does not appear that either spouse was hiding substantial debts or liabilities or significant assets from the other spouse.

In sum, this prenuptial agreement is not likely effective. This will mean that the analysis below will reflect the fact that earnings during marriage will remain CP for purposes of the analysis. Nonetheless, I will still discuss the possibility that this agreement is valid within each spouse's argument, and how that may arguably alter the characterization of property, below.

What are Harry's and Wanda's rights and liabilities regarding:

1. The condominium

Title Presumption

Property titled in one spouse's name alone is not presumably SP in CA.

Here, Henry will argue that he took title in the condominium alone, and therefore it is his separate property.

Wanda will argue that this is not conclusive in California, because ownership does not necessarily follow title. Wanda has the stronger argument here. She will argue that the court must trace, using the source rule to determine the character of the condo.

General CP Presumption

Assets acquired during marriage are presumably CP.

Wanda will argue that because the condo was purchased during the marriage, in 2004, it was presumably CP. She will argue that it is irrelevant that the condo was titled in Henry's name alone, because the court can trace.

Tracing: Source Rule

Under the source rule, a court will trace the assets used to purchase a particular property during marriage to determine its character.

Wanda will argue that by tracing, the court will determine that the condo was purchased with Harry's salary during marriage, and therefore it is CP.

Harry will argue that the prenup was valid, in which they agreed that his salary during marriage would be his separate property, and therefore by purchasing the condo with his salary, which is SP, and since SP breeds SP, the condo is also his SP.

Harry's argument will likely fail because, as discussed above, the prenup is likely invalid and therefore the salaries of both spouses earned during marriage will be community property, and therefore by purchasing the condo with CP funds, the condo itself is CP and it is immaterial that it is titled in Henry's name alone.

Transmutation

Spouses may alter the character of property from CP to SP, or from one spouse's SP to the other spouse's SP, or from SP to CP. After the "easy transmutation period" ended, courts now require transmutations to be in writing, and consented to or accepted by the spouse whose property is changing in nature, and the writing must explicitly state that a change in property is occurring.

Harry will argue that a transmutation of the CP condo occurred when he titled it in his sole name. He will argue that this was a gift from the community to his separate property, and that titling it in his own name was sufficient for a transmutation.

Wanda will argue that this was not sufficient for a transmutation because she did not consent to the change of CP to SP and given that she is the adversely affected spouse, her consent or acceptance was required, and that there is also no writing in the title document stating that the property is changing in form from CP to SP. Wanda has the stronger argument here, and the title of the property will not be deemed a transmutation.

Gifts Between Spouses

As a last ditch effort, Harry will argue that the condo was a gift between spouses and therefore was a valid transmutation that did not need to be in writing. An exception to the writing requirement for valid transmutations is when a gift of a personal nature is given from one spouse to another, and that gift is used primarily by the recipient spouse and is not substantial in nature, taking into consideration the financial situation of the couple.

Wanda will argue that a condo is not tangible personal property, and a condo is also substantial in nature, financially, given that they did not come into the marriage with significant amounts of SP, and moreover, the condo was used by both of them because they both "moved into the condominium." Therefore, Harry's argument that the condo was a gift from CP to SP will fail.

Conclusion

The condo is CP because it was purchased with earnings during marriage and the prenup is likely invalid. Therefore, it will be subject to equal division in kind upon divorce and Harry and Wanda will each take 50% of the proceeds from the sale of the house, assuming it is sold.

2. The joint savings account

Jointly Titled Property CP Presumption

In CA, when title to property is taken in joint form, there is a presumption that the character of the property is CP unless in the title document or elsewhere it is stated that a portion or all of the property is to be reserved as an SP ownership interest. In this case, . . . , a court will not allow tracing to determine the funds used to purchase a jointly titled home through the source rule and the property will be deemed CP. However, this joint presumption does not apply to bank accounts. With bank accounts, a court will allow jointly titled bank accounts to be traced to determine the source of funds and how it should be characterized.

Tracing

Because both spouses deposited $5,000 each from their salaries during the valid marriage in 2005 into the account, and these salaries were earned during marriage, property earned during marriage through community labor during the economic community is CP. In light of the fact that the prenuptial agreement is likely not valid, both spouse's salaries would be CP, and therefore the court would trace to the source of these funds and determine that the bank account is CP. If, for some reason, the court found that the prenup was valid, and therefore each spouse's salary was SP, then the account would be comprised of $5,000 worth of Wanda's SP and $5,000 worth of Harry's SP. However, this is unlikely.

Conclusion

Presuming that the prenup was invalid, the characterization of the joint savings account would be 100% CP, and therefore should be subject to the equal division in kind rule upon divorce, and whatever is left in the account will be divided equally between the spouses.

3. The rental property

Title Presumption

Property titled in one spouse's name alone is not presumably SP in CA.

Here, Wanda will argue that she took title in the rental property alone, and therefore it is her separate property.

Harry will argue that this is not conclusive in California, because ownership does not necessarily follow title. Henry has the stronger argument here. He will argue that the court must trace, using the source rule to determine the character of the rental property.

General CP Presumption

Assets acquired during marriage are presumably CP.

Harry will argue that because the rental property was purchased during the marriage, in 2015, it was presumably CP. He will argue that it is irrelevant that the rental was titled in Wanda's name alone, because the court can trace.

Tracing: Source Rule

Under the source rule, a court will trace the assets used to purchase a particular property during marriage to determine its character.

Harry will argue that, by tracing, the court will determine that the rental was purchased with both spouses' salaries during marriage, and therefore it is CP. He will argue that because the funds were taken from the joint savings account, which is ordinarily CP if the prenup was invalid, therefore Wanda used CP funds to purchase the rental, and therefore since CP breeds CP, the rental property is also CP.

Wanda will unconvincingly argue that the prenup was valid, in stark contrast to her earlier argument, stating that the couple agreed that her salary during marriage would be her separate property, and therefore by purchasing the rental with her salary, which is SP, and since SP breeds SP, the rental is also her SP.

Wanda's argument will likely fail because, as discussed above, the prenup is likely invalid and therefore the salaries of both spouses earned during marriage will be community property, and therefore by purchasing the rental with CP funds held in the bank account, the rental itself is CP and it is immaterial that it is titled in Wanda's name alone.

Transmutation

Spouses may alter the character of property from CP to SP, or from one spouse's SP to the other spouse's SP, or from SP to CP. After the "easy transmutation period" ended, courts now require transmutations to be in writing, and consented to or accepted by the spouse whose property is changing in nature, and the writing must explicitly state that a change in property is occurring.

Wanda will argue that a transmutation of the CP rental occurred when she titled it in her sole name. She will argue that this was a gift from the community to her separate property, and that titling it in her own name was sufficient for a transmutation.

Harry will argue that this was not sufficient for a transmutation because he did not consent to the change of CP to SP and given that he is the adversely affected spouse, his consent or acceptance was required, and that there is also no writing in the title document stating that the property is changing in form from CP to SR Harry has the stronger argument here, and the title of the property will not be deemed a transmutation.

Gifts Between Spouses

Finally, Wanda will argue that the rental was a gift between spouses and therefore was a valid transmutation that did not need to be in writing. An exception to the writing requirement for valid transmutations is when a gift of a personal nature is given from one spouse to another, and that gift is used primarily by the recipient spouse and is not substantial in nature, taking into consideration the financial situation of the couple.

Harry will argue that a rental property is not tangible personal property, and a rental property is also substantial in nature, financially, given that they did not come into the marriage with significant amounts of SP.

Wanda will counter that she, alone, was using the rental property, and therefore that property and any income, profits, or rents derived from it should be her SP because it was used primarily by her. This argument will fail because it is not an item of tangible personal property and thus was not an exception to the transmutation in writing rule.

Wanda's argument that the rental was a gift from CP to SP will fail.

Rents, Issues and Profits

The rents, issues, and profits of CP will be CP, and the rents, issues, and profits of SP will be SP. Because the rental property is CP, any rental income that Wanda derives by renting it out (the facts are silent about whether she has a tenant) will be CP, and therefore will be subject to the equal division in kind rule. Half of rents must be therefore shared with Harry.

Equal Management and Control

Each spouse has equal ability to manage and control CP. However, this is subject to certain limitations. For instance, a spouse may not sell or encumber personal property in the home or CP clothing belonging to either spouse or children without consent of the other spouse.

Gifts of CP

Moreover, spouses may not make gifts of CP without the written consent of the other spouse. A spouse may void the gift upon finding out about it.

Harry will argue that he did not consent to Wanda sneaking off and using money from their joint savings account to purchase the rental property and take title in her name alone. He will argue therefore that he should be allowed to void this transaction within one year of finding out about it. He will also argue that he can void this transaction because Wanda disposed of the CP without his written consent.

Wanda will argue that because she has equal management and control of the property, she does not need his consent to purchase a rental property with money from their joint savings account because she has a community interest in both of their salaries, and therefore can do what she wants with the money given that she had equal withdrawal rights on the bank account. She will also argue that this was not a "gift" of CP because she got her substantial benefit of the bargain from it: namely, a rental in exchange for the funds.

Wanda, unfortunately, likely has the stronger argument here, and she did not need Harry's consent before purchasing the rental and he likely cannot void it and cause the seller to return any of the purchase price despite finding out about the sale/purchase within one year.

Breach of Fiduciary Duty

Spouses owe each other fiduciary duties similar to those of business partners. They owe each other the highest duty of good faith and to avoid self-dealing.

Harry will argue that Wanda breached her fiduciary duty to him as a spouse by going behind his back and taking their joint CP funds and buying a rental and titling it in her own name without his knowledge. He will argue that this breaches her duty of loyalty to him and that this act was not in good faith.

Harry likely has a strong argument here, and he may also argue that this lack of good faith should cause the court to deviate from the equal division in kind rule.

Conclusion

The rental is CP because it was purchased with earnings during marriage, which were held in the bank account which is CP, given that the prenup is likely invalid. Therefore, it will be subject to equal division in kind upon divorce and Harry and Wanda will each take 50% of the proceeds from the sale of the rental, assuming it is sold, and assuming the court does not find justification for deviating from this, in light of Wanda's lack of good faith and fair dealing when going behind Harry's back to purchase the rental.

4. The hospital bill

End of the Economic Community: Permanent Separation

The economic community begins during marriage, and ends upon permanent separation. Permanent separation is understood through physical separation plus an intent not to resume the marital relationship.

Separate Debts of Spouses

Debts acquired after permanent separation are SP and the debtor spouse will be liable to his creditors for such debt incurred.

Here, Harry will argue permanent separation occurred in 2016 per the facts when "Wanda moved out of the condo" demonstrating an intent to not resume the marital relationship, and therefore the hospital bill incurred is her SP and only she will be liable for it because the economic community had ended.

Wanda will argue that Harry had not yet evidenced an intent not to continue the marital relationship because he only filed for divorce after her surgery and therefore the economic community was still intact, and thus the debt is CP to be shared between both of them.

Harry has the stronger argument, because per the facts, Harry and Wanda had "permanently separated" prior to the surgery.

Necessaries of Life

Despite the general rule that debts incurred post-separation are the SP debt of the debtor spouse and that spouse only will be liable for that debt to creditors, there is an exception for the "[common] necessaries of life" and debts incurred on their behalf post-separation but before divorce, because of the duty spouses owe to each other to take care of each other during marriage.

Wanda will argue that her surgery was an "emergency surgery for a medical condition," and therefore was a [common] necessary of life similar to food and water. Harry will have a difficult time countering this, because a court is likely to hold that this is a necessary.

Therefore, despite Wanda being the debtor spouse, if she does not have sufficient SP to pay for the $50,000 hospital bill, the hospital can attach to the CP of either spouse, and Harry may also be required to pay for the debt using his SP, because of the duty owed to take care of one's spouse prior to divorce, even after separation for necessaries of life.

Conclusion

In sum, the condo is CP and subject to equal division, the bank account is CP and subject to equal division, the rental property is CP and subject to equal division unless the court finds that it should deviate from this rule because of Wanda's breach of her fiduciary duty, and the hospital bill, despite being Wanda's separate debt, is a necessary of life which Harry may be required to pay for with CP and/or his SP.

Author's Note: How the bar taker who wrote that answer got so much on paper in one hour is a mystery to me. I know that when I took the bar a thousand years ago, I could not have done nearly as much. Even today, having taught community property a long time, I'm pretty sure I could not perform at that level. I say this to reassure you that your community property essay answer does not have to be as long as the selected answer to earn a passing grade from a bar grader.

July 2015—Question 4

In 2008, Henry and Wendy married in California. Neither had saved any money before marriage. At the time of the marriage, Henry had a monthly child support obligation of $1,000, which was deducted from his salary, for a child from a prior relationship.

In 2010, Wendy accepted a job at Company. At that time, she was told that if she performed well, she would receive stock options in the near future.

In 2011, Henry inherited $100,000. He used $25,000 to buy a necklace that he gave to Wendy as a holiday present. He used the remaining $75,000 to buy a municipal bond that paid him $300 per month.

In 2012, Wendy was granted stock options by Company, which would become exercisable in 2014, in part because she had been a very effective employee. Later in 2012, Wendy was injured in a car accident and made a claim against the person responsible.

In 2013, Henry and Wanda permanently separate and Henry moved away.

In 2014, Wendy settled her accident claim for $30,000. Later in 2014, Wendy exercised her stock options and earned a profit of $80,000.

In 2015, Wendy filed for dissolution.

1. What are Wendy's and Henry's respective rights regarding:

    a. The necklace? Discuss. *H's SP*

    b. The car accident settlement proceeds? Discuss. *CP, but at divorce, PI awarded entirely to injured spouse.*

    c. The stock option profits? Discuss. *time rule*

2. Should Henry be required to reimburse the community for his child support payments and, of so, in what amount? Discuss. *not from 2008-2011, yes from 2011 - date of separation*

Answer according to California law.

California Bar Exam 2015
Question 4: Selected Answer A

Wendy and Henry's Rights at Divorce

General Principles

Henry and Wendy were married in California. California is a community property state. Property acquired during marriage is presumed to community property (CP). Property acquired before marriage or after permanent physical separation is presumed to be separate property (SP). In addition, property acquired by gift, bequest, or devise, is that spouse's SP. The character of property is determined by tracing back to the source of funds used to acquire that property.

At divorce, each CP asset is divided 50/50 in kind, unless a special rule requires deviation from the equal division requirement or if the spouses agree in writing or by oral stipulation in court. Each spouse's SP remains that spouse's SP.

a. The Necklace

Characterization

Property acquired during marriage is presumed to be CP. A spouse can rebut this presumption by tracing back to the source of the property and showing that SP was used to purchase the property.

Here, the necklace was acquired in 2011, while Henry and Wendy were still married. Thus, the necklace is presumed to be CP. However, Henry will be able to rebut this presumption by tracing back to the source of the funds used to purchase the necklace. Henry used $25,000 of his $100,000 inheritance to purchase the necklace. Since an inheritance is SP regardless of when it was acquired, Henry will be able to rebut the CP presumption by tracing his SP funds. The next issue is whether Henry and Wendy changed the character of the property when Henry gave the necklace to Wendy.

Transmutation

Spouses can change the character of any asset from CP to SP, SP to CP, or from one spouse's SP to another spouse's SP. This is called a transmutation. To be valid, there must be an express declaration in writing that is signed or assented to by the spouse whose property interest is adversely affected. The writing must expressly state that a change in the property ownership is being made.

Here, when Henry gave Wendy the necklace, no transmutation occurred because there was no express declaration in writing signed by Henry that stated that a change in the ownership interest in the necklace was being made. However, there is an exception to the transmutation rule for gifts of a personal nature.

Exception—Gift of Personal Nature

A transmutation [writing] is not necessary to change the character of an item when there is a gift from one spouse to another of an item of personal nature. For this exception to apply, the item must be of a personal nature, used primarily by the spouse who was gifted, and the item must not be substantial taking into account the circumstances of the marriage.

Here, the necklace is an item of a personal nature because it is jewelry that is worn by a person. Furthermore, Wendy, the spouse who was gifted with the necklace, is presumably the one who primarily uses the necklace. The issue here would be whether the necklace was substantial in value taking into account the circumstances of Henry and Wendy's marriage. The facts do not tell us about Henry's employment but we do know that he has a job. Furthermore, we know that Wendy has a corporate job. Nevertheless, the spouses came into the marriage with no savings and Henry had a monthly child support payment. Considering that the necklace was $25,000, it was most likely substantial taking into account the circumstances of their marriage. Therefore, the necklace would most likely remain Henry's separate property and did not change into Wendy's separate property.

Distribution at Divorce

At divorce, a spouse's SP remains his or her SP.

If the necklace was substantial in value taking into account the circumstances of Henry and Wendy's marriage, then the necklace would remain Henry's SR If it was not substantial taking into account the circumstances of marriage, then the necklace was changed into Wendy's SP.

b.   The Car Accident Settlement Proceeds

Personal Injury Award

The character of a personal injury award is determined when the cause of action arose, not when the spouse receives a settlement or judgment. If the cause of action arose during marriage, then the personal injury award is CP. If the cause of action arose before marriage or after permanent physical separation, then it is SP.

Here, the car accident settlement arose out of Wendy getting injured in a car accident in 2012. Thus, the cause of action arose in 2012. Although there may be an issue as to whether the economic community ended in 2013 or 2015 (discussed below), the community was certainly continuing in 2012, and thus the personal injury award would be CP.

Division At Divorce

The general rule is that each CP asset is divided 50/50 in kind at divorce. One special rule that requires deviation from the equal division requirement is for personal injury awards. At divorce, a personal injury award will be awarded entirely to the injured spouse unless the interests of justice require otherwise.

Here, the personal injury award will be awarded to Wendy at divorce since she was the injured spouse. We would need more facts to determine whether the interests of justice would require that the community receive part of the award, such as where part of the settlement was reimbursement for medical expenses that were paid from community funds. As it is, the personal injury award of $30,000 will be awarded entirely to Wendy at divorce.

c. The Stock Option Profits

The rents, issues and profits of community property are community property. Stock options get special treatment under the rules when the stock options are granted during the marriage but are not exercisable until after the marital community ends. It first must be determined when the marital community ended.

End of The Marital Community

The marital community ends when there is permanent physical separation and an intention not to resume the marriage. Intention not to resume the marriage by one spouse only is effective so long as it is communicated to the other spouse.

Here, Henry and Wendy permanently separated and Henry moved away in 2013. Thus, we have permanent physical separation. The issue is whether the spouses intended to resume the marriage. Henry moving away permanently is indication of an intention not to resume the marriage, but we would need more facts about intent to make that determination. Wendy filing for dissolution in 2015 is certain evidence of an intention not to resume the marriage. Thus, it is certain that the economic community ended in 2015, but it most likely ended before that, in 2013 when Henry and Wendy permanently separated and Henry moved away.

Stock Options

The community interest in stock options depends on which formula is used. Which formula is used depends on what the intent of the employer was in granting the options. If the employer's intention was to reward the employee for past services, then the formula is: The numerator is the years that the employee was married until the economic community ended and the denominator is the years the employee was married until the options became exercisable. The community gets a larger percent under this formula because community labor is community property. If the employer's intention was to grant the options as an incentive to continue working for the company the formula is: The numerator is the date the option was granted until the economic community ends and the denominator is the date the option was granted until the date the options became exercisable. The fraction represents the community property interest.

Here, Henry would argue that the employer was granting the options as remuneration for past services because when Wendy was granted the options, it was in part because she has been a very effective employee. Wendy would argue that it was an incentive to keep working and doing a good job because she was told when she began working there that she would receive stock options in the near future if she performed well. Since it is a difficult determination on these facts, the stock options will be analyzed using both formulas.

Reward for Past Services

Here, when Wendy was hired in 2010, she was married to Henry. Henry and Wendy permanently separated in 2013, which is when the economic community ended. Thus the numerator is 3. The options became exercisable in 2014, so the denominator is 4 (2010–2014). Thus, the community interest in the stock option profits would be 3/4.

Incentive

Here, the options were granted in 2012 and the economic community ended in 2013. Thus, the numerator is 1. The options were granted in 2012 and became exercisable in 2014, making the denominator 2. Thus, the community interest in the stock option profits would be 1/2.

<u>Division at Divorce</u>

If the employer's primary intent in granting the options was to reward Wendy for past services, then the community interest in the $80,000 stock profits is 3/4, or $60,000. The $60,000 would be divided equally between Henry and Wendy; thus each would receive $30,000 of the profit. Wendy would end up with $50,000 ($30,000 (her half of the CP) and $20,000 (SP interest) and Henry would get $30,000.

If the employer's primary intent in granting the options was to incentivize Wendy to keep working, then the community interest in the $80,000 stock profits is 1/2, or $40,000. The $40,000 would be divided equally between Henry and Wendy; thus each would receive $20,000 of the profit. Wendy would end up with $60,000 ($20,000 (her half of the CP) plus $40,000 (SP interest)) and Henry would end up with $20,000.

Should Henry be required to reimburse the community for child support payments and if so, what amount?

Child Support Payments

Child support payments from a previous marriage are treated like a debt incurred before marriage. The CP is liable and the parent spouse's SP is liable. The other spouse's SP is not liable. The community is entitled to reimbursement for child support payments made with community funds to the extent that separate property was available and not used. A spouse's salary during marriage is community property.

Here, the child support payments were for Henry's child from a prior relationship so his SP is liable and the CP is liable. Henry paid $1000 a month for child support payments from his salary. Henry's salary is community property because it is from his labor during marriage. Since CP funds were used to pay the child support payments, the issue is whether there was Henry's separate property available that could have been used instead.

Reimbursement

Here, the spouses had no money saved coming into the marriage in 2008. Henry received an inheritance of $100,000 in 2011. Thus from 2008–2011, the community is not entitled to reimbursement because there was no separate property available. Henry tied up $75,000 of the $100,000 in a municipal bond and used the other $25,000 for Wendy's necklace. Since the bond had profits of $300 per month that went to Henry that is SP that was available (as stated above, rents issues and profits of SP are SP, and this was SP because it was inherited). Thus, the community is entitled to reimbursement for at least $300 of the $1000 paid in child support until the economic community ended in 2013.

At Divorce

$7200. At divorce, the $7,200 will be divided equally between Henry and Wendy. Wendy will get $3,600 and Henry will get $3,600.

§ 14.2 Law School Community Property Exams

This section contains five community property essay exams. These are my exams. Your professor may structure exam questions differently. Check with your professor. Following each question you will find an outline of the issues raised by the question. The outlines are not full "model answers." I'm too lazy to write full model answers.

Question 1

Henry Giramendi immigrated to Sacramento, California from Europe in 1950 and started a small jewelry store. Over the years, the store grew in prominence and became one of Sacramento's most successful jewelry stores. Henry's son Philip was born in 1980. Philip began working at the jewelry store while in high school, and worked there throughout college. Henry died in 2018, and Philip inherited the business. Philip works full time at the jewelry store, which continues to increase in value.

In 2011, Philip and Rachael married.

Philip has a defined contribution retirement pension at the store. Rachael is a school teacher, and has a defined benefit pension through her employment.

In 2012, Philip and Rachael purchased a home in Sacramento, taking title as joint tenants with right of survivorship. Philip provided the $40,000 down payment with money he inherited from his father. Monthly mortgage payments are made with funds from the joint bank account where Philip and Rachael deposit their paychecks.

In 2017, Rachael added a swimming pool to the home, paying for it with the proceeds of stock she sold. Rachael owned the stock before marriage.

In 2019, Rachael told Philip she was interested in learning to sail. Rachael said, "Is it okay with you if I buy a small sailboat?" Philip replied, "Great idea. Get a boat for yourself. I think it sounds like a relaxing hobby for you." Rachael made the $10,000 down payment on the boat with money she withdrew from the couple's joint bank account. She put title in her name alone. She financed the remainder of the $30,000 purchase price with a loan from a credit union.

Call of the Question: Rachael and Philip are divorcing. Discuss community property issues.

Issues Raised by Question 1

Philip has a defined contribution retirement plan, while Rachel has a defined benefit plan. Your answer should discuss such plans. You would say that the time rule is applied to determine the community interest.

The Sacramento home is in joint tenancy, so § 2581 applies, and there are no facts to suggest the § 2581 community property presumption is rebutted. The home is 100% community property. The down payment was with separate property, so discuss § 2640 and the right to reimbursement. The mortgage payments are with community property.

The addition of the swimming pool is an improvement. Rachel used her separate property to improve community property (*See* § 7.8(d)). Section 2640 applies to this, and Rachel is entitled to reimbursement.

As for the sailboat, it falls under the general community property presumption (§ 5.4). Putting title in Rachel's name alone does not help characterize the boat. The down payment was with community property. The loan from the credit union needs to be analyzed under the intent of the lender test (*See* § 7.6).

Question 2

Sue and Tim graduated from Columbia University Law School in 2006. They married in New York, right after taking the New York bar exam in July, 2006. Sue went to work for a large Wall Street corporate law firm, with a starting salary of $140,000 a year. Tim went to work for Manhattan Legal Aid, helping poor people. His salary was $50,000 a year. Sue and Tim had defined contribution retirement plans at work. In 2008, they purchased a condominium in Manhattan for $1,000,000, taking title in both their names. The

$200,000 down payment was made with a gift from Tim's parents. Monthly mortgage payments are from their income. In 2009, they had their first child. They decided that Tim would stop full-time work to stay at home with the baby. Tim worked part time from home doing contract appellate work for the Legal Aid Society.

In 2016, Sue was offered the position of managing partner at her law firm's Silicon Valley, California office, at a starting yearly salary of $400,000. Sue moved to San Jose to take up the position. Tim and the child remained in New York.

In 2016, Tim left law practice and started a small business renting motorized scooters to tourists in New York City. Tim started the business with money he inherited from his mother, who passed away in 2015. Tim works full time at the business, but has flexible hours so he can take care of the child.

Beginning in 2016, one week each month, Tim and the child fly to San Jose to spend time with Sue. They stay in the home Sue purchased in San Jose, taking title in her name. Sue's law firm gave Sue a no-interest loan to cover the entire $2,000,000 purchase price of the home. Every month, the firm deducts $6,000 from Sue's pay to repay the loan.

In 2020, Tim took out a $500,000 loan from a New York bank to purchase new scooters for his business. The monthly loan payment is $3,000.

In 2021, one of Tim's scooter customers got into an accident, and sued Tim, claiming the scooter's brakes were defective. Tim settled the case for $60,000, but the money has not been paid.

In 2022, Sue and Tim agreed they would divorce, and a divorce was filed in California.

Call of the Question: Sue and Tim are divorcing in California. Discuss community property issues.

Issues Raised by Question 2

Sue and Tim have defined contribution retirement plans, and you should discuss what such a plan is, and that it is community property (CP) to the extent earned during marriage and prior to separation.

The NY condo was taken in joint form, thus § 2581 applies (§ 5.15). There are no facts to indicate the § 2581 presumption is rebutted. Sue and Tim were living in NY when they acquired the condo. Thus, the condo is quasi-community property, not CP (§ 5.6). Section 2581 applies to quasi-CP. Sue moved to CA, but Tim didn't. However, beginning in 2013, Tim and the child spent one week each month in CA, and this will give CA personal jurisdiction over Tim, so the CA court can characterize the NY condo as quasi-CP. The down payment on the condo is from Tim's separate property (SP), and he is entitled to reimbursement pursuant to § 2640 (§ 5.16). Mortgage payments were with CP.

Tim's scooter business in NY was capitalized with SP, so the business is Tim's SP. If the question provided facts suggesting the business increased in value during marriage due to Tim's efforts, you would do a *Van Camp* and *Pereira* analysis (§ 7.2(a)). However, the facts don't indicate increased value.

The San Jose home is in Sue's name alone, but that does not help characterize the home. Sue purchased the home with a loan from her law firm. Under the intent of the lender test (§ 7.6), it seems pretty clear the law firm is relying on Sue's credit worthiness to repay the loan. Thus, the loan is CP. The loan payments are from Sue's pay, which is CP.

The loan for the scooter business will be addressed with the intent of the lender test, and the two approaches to the test (§ 7.6).

The accident involving the scooter customer gives us a debt to deal with. See Chapter 9. This debt lies in contract or tort, I don't know which (probably tort). This debt arose during marriage and prior to separation (§ 9.7(e)). Debts during this period can be community or separate, depending on whether the debtor was engaged in an activity for the benefit of the community at the time the debt arose. Tim's scooter business is an activity for the benefit of the community, so this debt should be a community debt.

Question 3

Sue and Bill met, fell in love, and married while attending the University of Pennsylvania Law School. They married in January, 2005. Upon graduation in 2007, both got jobs at law firms in Pittsburgh, PA. They settled into professional life in Pittsburgh, and in January, 2010 purchased a home in Pennsylvania, taking title as joint tenants. The purchase price of the home was $500,000. They made a down payment of $100,000 with money Sue inherited from an uncle. The balance of the purchase price was financed with a loan to Sue and Bill from a local bank. Mortgage payments have always been paid with income from employment.

Sue and Bill have 401(k) defined contribution retirement plans through their law firms.

In 2015, Sue and Bill paid cash for a vacation cabin at Stinson Beach, California, 30 miles north of San Francisco. Sue took title to the cabin in her name alone.

In January, 2021, Sue decided she wanted to separate from Bill. Sue was not sure the marriage was over, but she was leaning in that direction. Sue got a job at a San Francisco law firm. In April, 2021, Sue told Bill, "Bill, I don't think this marriage is working. I have an offer at a firm in San Francisco. I'm moving to California." True to her word, Sue moved to California and took up residence in the Stinson Beach cabin.

In February, 2022, Sue was in California, staying at the Stinson Beach cabin. On February 15, 2022, Sue was injured in a car accident on Highway 1, a few miles from the cabin.

In September, 2022, Bill took out a loan for $50,000, which he used to buy a sail boat, taking title in his name alone.

In January, 2023, Sue commenced divorce proceedings in California. Bill filed a response and a general appearance submitting to the jurisdiction of the California court.

A month after Sue filed for divorce, she received a check for $75,000 to settle a lawsuit against the driver of the car involved in the accident on Highway 1.

Call of the Question: Discuss all community property issues raised above.

Issues Raised by Question 3

The Pennsylvania home was acquired in joint tenancy. This raises the § 2581 community property (CP) presumption. There are no facts to rebut § 2581's CP presumption. Because Sue and Bill were living in PA when they bought the home, it is quasi-community property in their CA divorce. Section 2581 applies to quasi-CP. Discuss the fact that the down payment was with Sue's separate property (SP). The SP down payment triggers § 2640, and Sue is entitled to reimbursement. The balance of the purchase price was paid with a loan, so you need to discuss the intent of the lender test (§ 7.6). Mention that the monthly mortgage payments are with CP.

Sue and Bill have defined contribution retirement plans. Discuss that pensions are CP to the extent earned during marriage. You may, if you have time, discuss how a court could divide defined contribution plans, and the need for a QDRO. There is a lot you can discuss about pensions, but, often, you won't have time to go into everything you know.

The vacation cabin at Stinson Beach (if you haven't been to Stinson Beach, go), was purchased while they were living in PA, so it will be quasi-CP. Title in one spouse's name does not help characterize the property. Look to the source of the funds used to pay for the cabin. In this case, they paid cash, but we aren't told whether the cash was SP or CP. The cabin would fall under the general CP presumption of Family Code § 760.

The date of separation becomes important in this case. The date of separation is governed by Family Code § 70, discussed § 5.12. The facts tell us that in January, 2021, Sue decided she wanted to separate. The issue is whether January, 2021 is the date of separation. The answer is, probably, not. Sue was not sure the marriage was over. Sue told Bill she didn't think the marriage was working, and that she accepted a job in San Francisco. But still, she didn't say, "The marriage is over." Clearly, the parties are separated when they file for divorce, but that didn't happen until January, 2023. What happened between the two possible separation dates of January, 2021 and January, 2023? Sue was hurt in a car accident. Sue eventually received $75,000 for the injuries suffered in the accident. How should the $75,000 be characterized, SP or CP? The answer depends on whether Sue and Tim were separated when the accident happened on February 15, 2022. According to Family Code §§ 780–781, discussed at §§ 7.9(a) and 7.9(b), characterization of tort recoveries depends on whether the cause of action occurred before or after the couple separated.

Bill took out a loan in September, 2022 to purchase a sail boat. Title in his name does not characterize the boat. Discuss the intent of the lender test. It appears the debt for the boat remains unpaid. Thus, you need to characterize the debt on divorce. Here again, it is important to know whether Bill and Sue had separated on the date the debt was incurred. This is a contract debt. If they were still together, then this was a debt during marriage, which is governed by Family Code § 2622, discussed at § 9.7(e). Such a debt can be separate or community. If they were separated, then look at Family Code § 2623(a), discussed at § 9.7(d). A boat is clearly not a common necessary of life, therefore, this debt should be characterized as Bill's separate debt, and assigned to him, without offset, in the divorce.

Because Bill filed a general appearance in CA, he submitted himself to CA jurisdiction over his person. The CA Family Court can character property as quasi-CP.

The fact that Sue got the check for $75,000 after the divorce was filed makes no difference. What is important is when did the cause of action that led to the $75,000 arise?

Question 4

Kim and John met in 2005, while they were undergraduates at the University of the Pacific in Stockton, California. They fell in love and married in 2007. In May, 2008, they graduated from Pacific and, in August of that year Kim entered the evening division at McGeorge School of Law, in Sacramento, CA. John went to work for the Sacramento Fire Department as a firefighter. John has a defined benefit pension with the fire department. While in law school, Kim worked part time as a secretary for her dad, who owned a construction company. To pay for law school, Kim obtained student loans. Part of Kim's tuition was paid each semester from Kim and John's earnings from employment. Kim graduated from McGeorge in 2012, passed the bar on the first try, and took a job with the State Public Defender's Office. Kim has a defined benefit retirement plan with the Public Defender's Office. When they married, Kim and John opened a joint bank account. They deposit their paychecks in the joint account.

In 2014, Kim's father died and left the construction company to Kim. As a firefighter, John has quite a few days off, and he started managing the construction company on his off days. In addition to the construction company, Kim's father's will left Kim $1,000,000 in stock, which is in a portfolio held by Morgan Stanley, a brokerage firm. Kim was also the beneficiary of her father's life insurance, in the amount of $1,000,000. Kim placed the life insurance proceeds in the joint account, where it stayed until 2016, when Kim withdrew $500,000 as the down payment on the couple's home in Placerville, CA. The purchase price of the home was $2,000,000. Title to the home is "Kim and John as joint tenants."

In 2019, Kim withdrew $30,000 from her stock account at Morgan Stanley, and used the money to add a pool to the family home in Placerville.

Kim meets monthly with her Morgan Stanley stock broker to make investment decisions about her stock portfolio.

In 2021, John was injured fighting a fire. He could no longer serve as a firefighter, and he was retired from the fire department with a disability pension that he will receive for the rest of his life. Although his disability makes it impossible for John continue as a firefighter, John was able to continue managing the construction company, which he did.

In January 2022, Kim decided she no longer loved John, and asked for a divorce. John wanted to save the marriage, and the couple started seeing a marriage counselor. After a few months of counseling, Kim moved out of the family home in March, 2023. She withdrew $400,000 from the joint bank account to pay cash for a condominium in downtown Sacramento near, her office, taking title in her name alone. Kim started dating. John stayed in the Placerville home. From March, 2023 forward, John paid the mortgage payments on the Placerville home. In 2024, John finally agreed that the marriage was beyond saving, and filed for divorce.

Call of the Question: What community property issues arise in Kim and John's divorce? How should the issues be resolved?

Issues Raised by Question 4

There is a *lot* going on in this question!

Kim and John both have defined benefit pensions with their employment. Your answer should state that pension benefits earned during marriage, and prior to separation, are community property (CP). You can discuss the time rule as the devise used to determine how much of each pension belongs to the community (§ 6.5). They were married before they started working, so their pensions will be entirely CP, up to the time they separate.

Kim took out student loans to help pay for law school (sound familiar?). Hopefully, the student loans are paid off. If they are not paid off, student loan debts are assigned on divorce to the student (Family Code § 2627).

Part of Kim's tuition at McGeorge was paid with community property. Family Code § 2641 provides a reimbursement remedy when community property pays for education. However, after ten years, § 2641 presumes the community has benefitted sufficiently from the education that reimbursement of CP contributions is not warranted. In this case, it has been 10 years since Kim graduated law school, and it not likely that § 2641 requires reimbursement to the community.

The joint bank account contains Kim and John's paychecks, so the account contains CP.

Kim inherited the construction company. Thus, the company is her separate property (SP). John manages the construction company. The facts don't state whether the construction company increased in value during marriage. If it did, then you need to discuss *Van Camp* and *Pereira,* to apportion the increased value (§ 7.2(a)).

Kim inherited the stock portfolio, which is SP. Kim meets monthly with her stock broker to make investment decision about the stock. These meetings very likely amount to more than *de minimus* effort on Kim's part, and if the portfolio increased in value during marriage, you have another *Van Camp* and *Pereira* issue.

Kim inherited the $1 million in life insurance, which is SP. She put the SP life insurance into the joint bank account, which contains CP. You have a commingled bank account.

Kim and John purchased the Placerville family home as joint tenants, which means § 2581 applies. There are no facts to rebut the § 2581 presumption, so the Placerville home is 100% CP.

If Kim wants to claim that she used her SP for the down payment, she will need to trace the $500,000 down payment to SP. Since the money was in a commingled bank account, she can use direct or indirect tracing to try to uncommingle the account and prove she withdrew SP (§ 7.7). It is unlikely Kim will be able to trace the down payment to SP. Thus, it is unlikely Kim will be able to use § 2640 to claim reimbursement of the down payment.

Kim used $30,000 from her SP stock account to add a pool to the family home. This is an improvement. Kim's of SP to improve CP invokes § 2640, and allows Kim to be reimbursed the $30,000 (§ 7.8(d)).

John is retired on a disability pension. Disability is considered SP if the payments are to compensate for pain and suffering and lost future income (§ 6.14). John worked as a firefighter for 14 years before he was injured. John would not have been able to retire with a regular retirement pension after 14 years. It is likely that his disability pension will be awarded to John as his SP. Kim could argue John's pension is, at least in part, a regular retirement pension, based on number of years of service. It seems likely Kim will lose this argument.

What is the date of separation? Was it January, 2022, when Kim asked for a divorce? Probably not, since they continued to work on saving the marriage. Is the date of separation March, 2023, when Kim moved out? Likely, yes. (See Family Code § 70, and the text at § 5.12).

Following separation, Kim withdrew $400,000 from the commingled bank account to pay cash for a condo. Title in her name does not help characterize the condo. The general community property presumption applies. If Kim wants to claim the condo is her separate property, she needs to employ direct or indirect tracing to establish that she withdrew SP to buy the condo.

John staying in the family home raises the issue of *Watts* charges (§ 11.8). John paid the mortgage on the home following separation, which may give John the right to *Epstein* credits.

Question 5

Paula and Nick have always lived in California. They met and married in 2015, in San Diego. They have two kids. Paula and Nick separated in May, 2022. Today, they are getting divorced in San Diego. In 2012, Paula took out a loan from Wells Fargo Bank. The loan amount was $200,000, and was used to purchase Blackacre. Today, Paula still owes $75,000 to Wells Fargo on the loan. In September, 2020, Nick used his credit card to finance a trip to Ireland for the family. The trip cost $6,000, and Nick still owes $4,000 on the credit card for the trip. In 2021, Nick was driving to work, when he accidentally ran a red light and collided with another car, injuring the driver. Nick was sued, and owes the injured driver $40,000. In 2022, Paula took $25,000 from the couple's joint bank account and invested in a start-up company. Paula didn't tell Nick about the investment. The start-up company declared bankruptcy, and Paula lost the entire investment. In 2017, Paula and Nick purchased the family home, taking title as joint tenants with right of survivorship. All mortgage payments have been made with community property earnings from employment. The down payment was with an inheritance received by Paula from her father.

Call of the Question: In the divorce case, what community property issues must be addressed? Describe how all issues should be resolved.

Issues Raised by Question 5

Question 5 focuses primarily on characterization of debts on divorce. See § 9.7. Remember, there are four sets of rules governing debts (§ 9.1). One set deals with what property creditors can take to satisfy debts during marriage. Another set deals with characterization of debts on divorce. Question 5 requires you to work with the rules on characterization of debts on divorce.

Paula's $75,000 owed to Wells Fargo is easy: It is premarital debt, and § 2621 provides that premarital debt is separate debt. See Figure 2, in § 9.7(f).

When Nick used his credit card to finance the trip to Ireland, the couple was still together. Debts during marriage, and prior to separation, can be community or separate § 9.7(e). Contract debts for the benefit of the community create community debt. The vacation debt will be community debt.

Nick committed a tort. The debt from the tort arose during marriage, and prior to separation. Nick was driving to work when the tort happened, an activity for the benefit of the community, so this is a community debt.

Paula invested $25,000 of community property, and lost the money. Was her use of the money a breach of fiduciary duty? Spouses have equal management and control of community property (Family Code § 1100. Text § 10.1). According to Family Code § 1100(a), a married person can spend or invest community personal property without the consent of the other spouse. Doing so may not be a good idea from the stand point of marital harmony and good communication between spouses, but the law allows one spouse to unilaterally sell or invest community property. The fact that the investment turned out badly does not necessarily mean Paula breached her fiduciary duty to Nick. Mere negligence in handling community property is not a breach of fiduciary duty. Even if Paula's investment decision was negligent, it was probably not a violation of her fiduciary duty. On the other hand, when a married person's handling of community property is grossly negligent or reckless, a court is likely to find a breach of fiduciary duty. If Paula was grossly negligent or reckless in the investment decision, she might owe reimbursement pursuant to the remedy provisions of Family Code § 1101(h).

The family home was taken as joint tenants, so Family Code § 2581 applies, and the home is presumptively 100% community property (§ 5.15). There are no facts suggesting a writing sufficient to rebut the § 2581 presumption. The down payment was with Paula's separate property, and she is entitled to reimbursement via Family Code § 2640 (§ 5.16).

§ 14.3 Analysis of Chapter Questions and Examples

The book contains many questions and examples. Section 14.3 provides analysis of these questions and examples.

Chapter 1

§ 1.3 Are Mary and John married?

Texas recognizes common law marriage. I think these facts point to the conclusion they have a common law marriage.

Chapter 2

§ 2.3 Questions

1. It does not appear that Wesley and Judy have an express *Marvin* agreement. The Supreme Court ruled in *Marvin* that trial courts may recognize implied agreements and may employ equitable devices to do justice between the parties. If Wesley and Judy were married in CA, the community property system would apply and the results would be pretty clear: As you will see when you have finished this book and your community property course, there would be a lot of community property. In *Estate of McFarlin*, the court ruled in favor of the estate and against Judy's claim that she was entitled to a share of property based on her theory of unjust enrichment.

2. The thing to note here is that Abe and Beth never lived together. Can there be an implied *Marvin* agreement when parties didn't actually cohabit? The answer in California is unclear. The cited cases don't resolve the issue.

3. It seems the better policy is to require *Marvin* agreements to be in writing. In 1985, the California Legislature changed the law that allowed transmutations to be oral. It seems the same policies support requiring *Marvin* agreements to be in writing.

Chapter 3

§ 3.11 Is the Prenup Voluntary?

1. The advanced state of wedding planning is a factor.

2. The fact that Victor paid for the attorney should not defeat the argument that the agreement was voluntary.

3. Some attorneys video record the signing of prenups. It is a good idea to have both parties initial each page, or even each paragraph.

§ 3.14 Problems on Premarital Agreements

1. The Virginia appellate court ruled the prenup was not enforceable.

2. The Iowa court ruled the prenup was voluntary and enforceable.

3. The Vermont Supreme Court ruled the prenup was unconscionable because it was so one-sided. However, the court stated that unconscionable prenups are not necessarily invalid.

4. The South Dakota Supreme Court ruled the prenup was ambiguous and unenforceable.

5. It may surprise you to learn that the court upheld the prenup! Seems wrong to me.

Chapter 5

§ 5.7 Exercises on Characterization

These exercises give you the opportunity to get comfortable with Family Code §§ 125, 760, and 770. With each exercise, study carefully the language of the controlling statute.

1. Blackacre is community property under § 760.

2. Greenacre is community property. When characterizing property, note carefully where the couple lived when they acquired the property.

3. Quasi-community property. They were living in Montana so § 125 applies.

4. The car falls under the general community property presumption of § 760.

5. Rocket is Alice's separate property, § 770. Rocket Booster is "issue" of Rocket. Thus, Booster is Alice's separate property. As for the equine love affair, probably CP, don't you think?

6. Anything produced with the time, talent, energy, or skill of a married person is community property. Ruth and Sally were married during the time Sally completed the screen play. The $1 million is community property. What is important is not when the million is received, but when it was earned.

7. The surfboard is half community property and half separate property. Problem 7 introduces you to the concept of pro rata apportionment, discussed in §§ 5.10, 5.15, 5.17, and elsewhere in the book.

8. The portfolio is separate property pursuant to § 770. Problem 8 introduces you to the issue of increases in value of separate property, discussed in § 7.2.

9. Problem 9, like problem 8, is an example of increased value of a separate property business. The car dealership was acquired prior to marriage, so it is separate property (§ 770). Abe's paycheck for working at the dealership is community property (§ 760). You will learn how to deal with the increased value of the dealership in § 7.2.

§ 5.12 Beginning and End of the Community—Date of Separation

In *Marriage of Baragry*, the Court of Appeal felt as much sympathy for husband as you do. The date of separation was when the Petition for divorce was filed.

§ 5.20 Exercises with Family Code §§ 2581 and 2640

1. Section 2581 applies because they took title as joint tenants. The home is 100% community property. There are no facts indicating a writing sufficient to rebut the 2581 presumption. The down payment was separate property. Section § 2640 does not apply because § 2640 is not retroactive, and cannot be applied before January 1, 1984. The down payment is a gift to the community (*Lucas* gift presumption).

2. Gilbert owned the Lucerne home prior to marriage. His was the only name on the title. The home was Gilbert's separate property. By conveying the property to Gladys and himself as joint tenants, Gilbert transmuted the property. Section 2581 applied, and the property became community property. In *Marriage of Walrath*, the Supreme Court ruled that the § 2640 right to reimbursement of separate property contributions to community property can carry through to other property acquired with funds from the original property.

3. Greenacre falls under the community property presumption of § 2581. Mary should be entitled to reimbursement of her separate property down payment, pursuant to § 2640. Marley paid off the balance owing on Greenacre with a separate property inheritance. Section 2640 applies to Marley's payment.

If title to Greenacre was in Marley's name alone, §§ 2581 and 2640 would not apply. Greenacre would be characterized using pro rata apportionment, and would be part separate property and part community property.

Chapter 6

§ 6.5 Apply the Time Rule to the Following Cases

1. To apply the time rule, it is often useful to create a time line. Wendy worked and earned her pension for the ten years prior to marriage, so that portion of her pension is her separate property. All pension benefits earned after separation are separate property. The important date is the date of separation, not the date the divorce is final. The numerator of the time rule is 5, the number of years Wendy and Bill were married. The denominator is 20, the number of years Wendy worked. The community owns ¼ of the pension, and Bill get ½ of the community interest in the pension.

2. With Elenore and Mike, I get a numerator of 11, and a denominator of 23. Do you agree? Our numbers may differ depending on what years we include. It may be better to use months rather than years.

§ 6.19 Accrued Vacation and Sick Days

It looks as though the $100,000 in accrued sick-vacation days is community property. All the money was "earned" during marriage, and prior to separation.

Chapter 7

§ 7.2(a) Increased Value of Separate Property Business— *Van Camp* or *Pereira*

Hank registered a domain name in his name two weeks before he married Wendy. During marriage, Hank devoted many hours to the online business, and the business thrived. The domain name is separate property because it was acquired prior to marriage. The increased value appears to be due, at least partially, to Hank's efforts during marriage. Thus, the increased value needs to be apportioned under *Van Camp* or *Pereira*. If you represent Hank, and if Hank wants you to get as much in the divorce for him as possible, you urge the judge to apply *Van Camp*. You will provide evidence—probably expert testimony—that most of the increased value was caused by market forces rather than Hank's efforts. If you represent Wendy you will urge the judge to apply *Pereira* because *Pereira* usually yields more for the community.

In *Robertson v. Robertson,* the Florida Court of Appeals applied Florida law to the increased value issue.

§ 7.7(c) Simple Samples

1. For these problems, create a simple balance sheet, accounting for deposits and withdrawals. In this case, the fact that the account is in Mary's name alone does not make the money in the account hers.

January: Deposit of $50,000 is community property (CP). Entire balance is CP.

May: The withdrawal of $20,000 is obviously CP, since the account contains only CP. Balance now is $30,000, all CP.

June: Withdraw $20,000 to buy Apple stock. This is easy. The stock is purchased with CP because that is the only money in the account at the time of the withdrawal. Balance: $10,000, all CP.

July: Deposit $10,000 of CP. Balance: $20,000, all CP.

August: Deposit $30,000 of Mary's separate property (SP). Ah ha! Now we have a commingled account! Balance $50,000, of which $30k is Mary's SP, and $20k is CP.

September: Withdraw the entire balance of $50,000 to pay Richard's medical bill. Balance: Zero. Note that all of Mary's $30k in SP was used to pay Richard's medical bill. When SP is used to pay community expenses, the owner of the SP is not entitled to reimbursement unless the couple had an agreement the SP would be reimbursed.

October: Deposit $10,000 CP. Balance: $10k, all CP. Mary's SP is not entitled to be reimbursed for payment of the medical bill.

2. Rachel and Tom's accounting is more complicated, but is still much simpler than you find in real marriages that last years, and in which there are hundreds if not thousands of deposits and withdrawals.

Wedding day: Balance: $20,000, all Tom's SP.

January 1: Withdraw $1k for rent, a family expense. Obviously, the money is SP because the account contains only SP. Tom will not be entitled to reimbursement for the $1k expended on rent. Balance: $19,000, all Tom's SP.

January 20: Withdraw $2k to pay Rachel's medical bill, another family expense. Balance $17k, all Tom's SP.

Feb. 3: Deposit $2k CP. The account is now commingled. Balance: $19k: $17K Tom's SP; $2k CP.

Feb. 20: Deposit $1k CP. Balance: $20k. $17k SP. $3k CP.

March 3: Deposit $1k CP. Balance: $21k. $17k SP. $4k CP.

April 1: Withdraw $1,000 for a new suit for Tom. This is where things get complicated. The suit was acquired during marriage and prior to separation, while domiciled in CA. Thus, the suit falls under the general community property presumption of § 760. If we characterize the suit as CP, then the balance is $20k. $17K Tom's SP. $3k CP. But suppose Tom says, "I withdrew some of my SP to pay for the suit, so the suit is my SP." To make this claim, Tom needs to use direct or indirect tracing to prove he withdrew SP rather than CP (See § 7.7). Tom could not use indirect tracing since all of the community property in the account was *not* used up—exhausted—when he made the withdrawal on April 1. He could, however, try to use direct tracing. Tom argues that on April 1 there was sufficient SP in the account to cover the withdrawal. That's true. Tom argues that he intended to withdraw SP to buy the suit. If he carries the burden of proof with direct tracing, then the suit is his SP. Do you see that depending on whether the April 1st withdrawal was of CP or SP, *every subsequent calculation differs?* For argument's sake, let's assume Tom does not argue that he withdrew SP on April. Let's assume he withdrew CP. So, the balance is $20. $17k Tom's SP. $3k CP.

May 23: Tom withdraws $3k to buy Apple stock. We have the same dilemma we had with the suit. Did Tom withdraw SP to buy the stock or did he withdraw CP? There was enough CP in the account on May 23 to purchase the stock. The stock would fall under the general community property presumption. Tom might try to use direct tracing to prove that he used his SP to buy the stock. And again you see that depending on whether the $3k was SP or CP, everything that follows thereafter differs. Let's assume Tom withdrew CP to buy the stock. Balance: $17k, all Tom's SP. No CP in the account.

May 30: Deposit $2k CP. Balance: $19k. $17k Tom's SP. $2k CP.

June 5: Withdrawal of $1k for a trip. Let's assume the withdrawal was CP. Balance: $18k. $17k Tom's SP. $1k CP.

July 6: Deposit $2k CP. Balance: $20k. $17k Tom's SP. $3k CP.

July 25: Withdraw $6k to buy Xerox stock. In the divorce, unless Tom is feeling charitable, he is likely to try to prove the Xerox stock is his SP. He will use direct or indirect tracing. Direct tracing might work since there is enough SP in the commingled account to cover the $6k withdrawal. Tom can't prove that all of the CP was exhausted at the time of the purchase. There was enough CP in the account to cover half the cost of the stock.

These simple exercises give you some insight into the complexity of uncommingling commingled bank accounts. In practice, you will employ a forensic accountant to perform direct and/or indirect tracing.

§ 7.8(a) One Spouse Uses Her/His Separate Property to Improve the Other Spouse's Separate Property

If the improvement occurred after January 1, 2005, Husband can argue the community should be reimbursed.

§ 7.8(b) One Spouse Uses Community Property to Improve the Other Spouse's Separate Property

The barn and the orchard are improvements. The community should be reimbursed.

Chapter 8

§ 8.4 Uniform Voidable Transactions Act

Sue's proposal violates the Act.

Chapter 9

§ 9.2(c) Questions on Debts During Marriage

1. The creditor can take: (a) All the community property (CP) (§ 910(a)); (b) All the debtor spouse's separate property (SP) (§ 913(a)); (c) The creditor cannot take the non-debtor spouse's SP (§ 913(b)(1)).

2. In this problem, Beth and Tom are both liable for the debt. Thus, the creditor can take all the CP and all the SP of both debtor spouses.

3. The creditor can take: (a) All the CP (§ 910(a)); (b) All the debtor spouse's SP (§ 913(a)); (c) The creditor can't take the non-debtor's SP (§ 913(a)(1)).

§ 9.5 Necessaries—Mary and Abe, a Married Couple

1. The medical bill is for a common necessary of life, medical care. All the community property is liable for the debt (§ 910(a)). All the separate property of the debtor spouse (Abe) is liable for the debt (§ 913((a)). The separate property of the non-debtor spouse (Mary) is liable for the debt because it is a debt for common necessaries of life during marriage and prior to separation (§ 914(a)(1). See text § 9.5).

2. Is a fancy sports car a common necessary of life? Nope. Is it a necessary of life? This depends, of course, on how rich or poor the couple is. My guess is that even for rich folk, a fancy sports car is not a necessary of life. Title in Abe's name alone makes no difference. All community property is liable for the debt (§ 910(a)). All Abe's separate property is liable for the debt (§ 913(a)). Is Mary's separate property liable for the debt? Only if the sports car is a necessary of life, so probably, the answer is, no.

3. This is a premarital debt. All the community property is liable for the debt (§ 910(a)). All the debtor spouse's separate property is liable for the debt (§ 913(a)). The non-debtor spouse's separate property is not liable for the debt. Section 914(a) applies to

debts incurred during marriage. This debt, even though it is for common necessaries of life, does not fit within § 914. Therefore, § 913(b)(1) controls and Mary's separate property is not liable for the debt.

4. In today's world, maybe braces are a common necessary of life. I don't know. It seems pretty clear braces can be a necessary of life. Assuming that is so, what property is liable for the debt for the braces? All the community property (§ 910(a)). All Mary's separate property (§ 913(a)). All Todd's separate property is liable pursuant to § 914(a)(1).

5. Now you are dealing with a post-separation debt for necessaries of life of the child. All the community property is liable for the debt (§ 910(a)). All Mary's separate property is liable (§ 913(a)). Is Abe's separate property liable? Section 914(a)(2) refers to post-separation debts incurred for common necessaries of life of the person's spouse. If this language is interpreted to include debts incurred by a spouse to pay for a child's common necessaries of life, then Abe's separate property is liable for the debt.

Chapter 11

§ 11.8 *Epstein* Credits and *Watts* Charges

Husband remained in the family home during the year it took to get to trial. Wife may argue that *Watts* charges should apply. Husband will counter that the court is not required to impose *Watts* charges, and doing so in this case is not wise because Husband stayed in the home to take care of the kids. For his part, Husband paid the mortgage, for which he could seek *Epstein* credits. The rental value is $2,000 a month, and the monthly mortgage is $1,500. Wife will argue for *Watts* charges of $500 a month, of which she is owed $250 a month.

§ 11.11 Property Problems

1. In *Matter of Chamberlin*, the New Hampshire Supreme Court ruled the trust property was not marital property because it was in an irrevocable trust. The same result would apply in CA.

2. The Texas court ruled the property aspects of the divorce were res judicata. The result is the same in CA.

3. This is a shocking case, don't you agree? New York is an equitable distribution state. In New York, the court divides marital property equitably, not necessarily equally. The trial court analyzed the facts and, understandably, gave Husband less of the marital property.

California law requires equal division of community property (Family Code § 2550). Family Code § 2603.5 may provide justice. The section states: "The court may, if there is a judgment for civil damages for an act of domestic violence perpetrated by one spouse against the other spouse, enforce that judgment against the abusive spouse's share of community property, if a proceeding for dissolution of marriage or legal separation of the parties is pending prior to the entry of final judgment." In addition to Section 2603.5, Wife may argue Husband violated his fiduciary duties to Wife, and, for that reason, should forfeit any interest he would normally have in community property as a penalty.

4. This one is pretty easy. A contingent fee earned prior to separation is community property, regardless of when the fee is paid.

5. Sue wrote part of the book prior to separation, and part after. These facts probably call for apportionment of the royalties into community property and separate property portions.

Suppose Sue wrote a novel entirely during marriage and prior to separation. The royalties are community property. Suppose Sue always intended a trilogy—three books. Sue writes the second and third books after separation. Could Sam claim royalties paid for the second and third books? Sam argues that the second and third books are popular *because of* the first book, and the first book was created with community labor and time. I don't know the answer.

Or suppose, Sue is a law professor. During marriage, Sue writes a best selling community property book for students—a real page turner! The royalties are community property. After Sue and Sam divorce, Sue publishes a second edition of her popular community property book. Does Sam have a claim to share the royalties on the second edition? I don't know the answer to this one either. The one thing I know for sure is that no book on community property is a page turner!

6. The Maryland Court of Appeals ruled in *Aleem v. Aleem* that the Maryland state court would not extend comity to the Pakistan divorce. The result would be the same in CA.

7. Who gets the goat? If the parties can't agree, the judge is likely to order the goat sold, and the proceeds divided. When the parties realize the judge can order the goat sold, maybe they will find a way to keep it in the family.

Chapter 12
§ 12.6 Relation-Back Doctrine

1. It is very unlikely a court would employ the relation-back doctrine to reinstate Sue's support obligation. Bill waited a year before he started annulment proceedings. During that year, Sue had a right to rely on Bill's remarriage and to re-order her financial affairs. *See Sefton v. Sefton*, 45 Cal. 2d 872, 291 P.2d 439 (1955).

2. In the second scenario, the court will likely be more sympathetic to Pat's plea to reinstate spousal support.

§ 12.7 Questions on Annulment

1. The Missouri Court of Appeals affirmed the trial court's order granting wife an annulment based on fraud. I doubt wife would succeed in California.

2. The Kentucky Court of Appeals ruled that the Catholic tribunal's ruling had no impact on state law. The same would be true in CA.

3. Not surprisingly, the New York court ruled against Nidia. In California, the marriage could be annulled because Howard was not competent to enter the marital relationship—he could not consent to marry. However, this ground for divorce renders the marriage voidable rather than void. Once one of the spouses dies, a voidable marriage is no longer subject to attack. Nevertheless, this looks like a pretty straight forward case of elder financial abuse. I don't think Nidia will get anything in CA.

4. The Texas Court of Appeal ruled in favor of annulment. The result would probably be the same in California because it appears Betelehem lied—committed fraud—about the procreative aspects of the marital relationship.

Chapter 13

§ 13.4 Problems on Characterization

In the following problems, characterize the property (1) when the marriage ends in divorce, and (2) when the marriage ends in death.

1. Wife and Husband, living in Davis, California, buy Blackacre in Davis. Don't consider how title is held.

   (a) Characterize on divorce. CP, Family Code (FC) § 760.

   (b) Characterize on death. CP, Probate Code (PC) § 28(a).

2. Wife and Husband, living in Davis, buy Blackacre in Davis, taking title as joint tenants with right of survivorship.

   (a) Characterize on divorce. CP, FC § 2581 applies.

   (b) Characterize on death. On death, do not apply FC § 2581. When marriage ends in death, the right of survivorship of joint tenancy applies and the survivor owns the property.

3. Wife and Husband, living in San Luis Obispo, California, buy Orangeacre, in Utah. Don't consider how title is held.

   (a) Characterize on divorce. CP, FC § 760.

   (b) Characterize on death. CP, PC § 28(a).

4. Wife and Husband, living in San Luis Obispo, buy Orangeacre, in Utah. They take title as joint tenants.

   (a) Characterize on divorce. CP, FC § 2581 applies.

   (b) Characterize on death. On death, do not apply FC § 2581. Right of survivorship applies.

5. Wife and Husband, living in Los Angeles, California, buy Niceacre, in Texas. Don't consider how title is held.

   (a) Characterize on divorce. CP, FC § 760.

   (b) Characterize on death. CP, PC § 28(a).

6. Wife and Husband, living in Los Angeles, buy Niceacre, in Texas. They put title in Wife's name alone.

   (a) Characterize on divorce. Title in wife's name makes no difference, unless it was before January 1, 1975, in which case the married woman's separate property presumption would apply, FC § 803(a). Assuming it was after 1/1/75, CP, FC § 760.

(b) Characterize on death. CP, PC § 28(a).

7. Wife and Husband, living in Texas, buy Prettyacre, in Sacramento, California. Don't consider how title held.

(a) Characterize on divorce. If the parties divorce in CA, and both moved to CA, the property is quasi-CP, FC § 125.

(b) Characterize on death. PC § 28(a) does not apply because they were not living in CA when they acquired Prettyacre. PC § 28(b) applies. This is California real property. Texas is a community property state. Let's assume the property would be CP under Texas law.

8. Wife and Husband, living in Texas, buy Prettyacre in Sacramento, taking title as joint tenants.

(a) Characterize on divorce. Quasi-CP under FC § 125, provided the parties moved to CA, and divorce here. FC § 2581 applies.

(b) Characterize on death. PC § 28(a) does not apply because they were domiciled in Texas when they acquired the property. PC § 28(b) does apply, rendering the property CP in probate proceedings. The right of survivorship applies.

9. Wife and Husband, living in Utah, buy Greenacre in Utah. Later they move to California. Title to Greenacre is in Wife's name alone.

(a) Characterize on divorce. Title in Wife's name makes no difference. Since they moved to CA, Greenacre is quasi-CP, FC § 125.

(b) Characterize on death. PC § 28(a) does not apply because they were domiciled in Utah when they acquired the property. Does PC § 28(b) apply? No, because PC § 28(b) only applies to California real property. PC § 66 does not apply. The thing to do is start a probate proceeding in California, and an ancillary probate proceeding in Utah to take care of the Utah property.

10. Wife and Husband, living in Nevada, buy Redacre, in Nevada. Later, Wife moves to California, but Husband remains in

Nevada. Wife divorces Husband in a California court. Characterize on divorce. Redacre would be quasi-CP, FC § 125 if both spouses moved to CA and divorced here. That's not what happened. Husband remained in Nevada. Unless the California court can get personal jurisdiction over Husband or he voluntarily submits to the authority of the California family court the California court cannot adjudicate Redacre.

11. Wife and Husband, living in Nevada, buy Redacre, in Nevada. Later, Wife moves to California, but Husband remains in Nevada. Wife dies in California. Characterize on death. PC § 28 does not apply. PC § 66 does not apply. Start an ancillary probate proceeding in Nevada.

12. Wife and Husband living in New Mexico buy Purpleacre in New Mexico. Later, they move to California, and divorce here. Suppose the couple remains married until Wife passes away. Characterize on death. On divorce, Purpleacre is quasi-CP, FC § 125. On death, PC § 28 does not apply. Nor does PC § 66.

13. Wife and Husband, living in Egypt, buy a vacation home on the California side of Lake Tahoe. Later, they move to California, and divorce here. What if the marriage lasts until Husband passes away. Characterize on death. On divorce, the home is quasi-CP, FC § 125. On death, PC § 28(a) does not apply. PC § 28(b) could apply if Egypt's system of marital property is substantially equivalent to CA law. Interestingly, PC § 66(a) may also apply. If § 28(b) applies, the home is CP. If § 66 applies, the home is quasi-CP. When both §§ 28 and 66 apply, the tie breaker goes to § 28. We know this because PC § 66 states, "Quasi-community property" means the following property, other than community property as defined in Section 28."

14. Wife and Husband, living in San Diego, buy a car. Characterize the car, ignoring how title is held.

(a) Characterize on divorce. The car falls under the general CP presumption of FC § 760.

(b) Characterize on death. CP, PC § 28(a).

15. Wife and Husband, living in Montana, buy a car in Montana, taking title as joint tenants. Later they move to California.

(a) Characterize on divorce. Quasi-CP, FC § 125. FC § 2581 applies.

(b) Characterize on death. The right of survivorship applies.

Appendix

CALIFORNIA FAMILY CODE

§ 63. Community estate

"Community estate" includes both community property and quasi-community property.

§ 70. "Date of separation" defined

(a) "Date of separation" means the date that a complete and final break in the marital relationship has occurred, as evidenced by both of the following:

(1) The spouse has expressed to the other spouse his or her intent to end the marriage.

(2) The conduct of the spouse is consistent with his or her intent to end the marriage.

(b) In determining the date of separation, the court shall take into consideration all relevant evidence.

(c) It is the intent of the Legislature in enacting this section to abrogate the decisions in In re Marriage of Davis (2015) 61 Cal. 4th 846 and In re Marriage of Norviel (2002) 102 Cal. App. 4th 1152.

§ 80. Employee benefit plan

"Employee benefit plan" includes public and private retirement, pension, annuity, savings, profit sharing, stock bonus, stock option, thrift, vacation pay, and similar plans of deferred or fringe benefit compensation, whether of the defined contribution or defined benefit type whether or not such plan is qualified under the Employee Retirement Income Security Act of 1974 (P.L. 93–406) (ERISA), as amended . . . .

§ 125. Quasi-community property

"Quasi-community property" means all real or personal property, wherever situated, acquired before or after the operative date of this code in any of the following ways:

(a) By either spouse while domiciled elsewhere which would have been community property if the spouse who acquired the property had been domiciled in this state at the time of its acquisition.

(b) In exchange for real or personal property, wherever situated, which would have been community property if the spouse who acquired the property so exchanged had been domiciled in this state at the time of its acquisition.

§ 300. Consent; issuance of license and solemnization

(a) Marriage is a personal relation arising out of a civil contract between a man and a woman, to which the consent of the parties capable of making that contract is necessary. Consent alone does not constitute marriage. Consent must be followed by the issuance of a license and solemnization as authorized by this division. . . .

§ 306. Procedural requirements

. . . [A] marriage shall be licensed, solemnized, and authenticated, and the authenticated marriage license shall be returned to the county recorder of the county where the marriage license was issued . . . .

§ 308. Validity of foreign marriages

A marriage contracted outside this state that would be valid by the laws of the jurisdiction in which the marriage was contracted is valid in this state . . . .

§ 310. Methods of dissolution

Marriage is dissolved only by one of the following:

(a) The death of one of the parties.

(b) A judgment of dissolution of marriage.

(c) A judgment of nullity of marriage.

§ 420. Essential element of solemnization

(a) No particular form for the ceremony of marriage is required for solemnization of the marriage, but the parties shall declare, in the physical presence of the person solemnizing the marriage and necessary witnesses, that they take each other as husband and wife. . . .

§ 720. Mutual obligations

Husband and wife contract toward each other obligations of mutual respect, fidelity, and support.

§ 721. Transactions with each other and third parties; fiduciary relationship

(a) Subject to subdivision (b), either husband or wife may enter into any transaction with the other, or with any other person, respecting property, which either might if unmarried.

(b) . . . A husband and wife are subject to the general rules governing fiduciary relationships which control the actions of persons occupying confidential relations with each other. This confidential relationship imposes a duty of the highest good faith and fair dealing on each spouse, and neither shall take any unfair advantage of the other. This confidential relationship is a fiduciary relationship subject to the same rights and duties of nonmarital business partners, as provided in Sections 16403 [access to books and records], 16404 [transfers of partnership interest], and 16503 [fiduciary duties] of the Corporations Code, including, but not limited to, the following:

(1) Providing each spouse access at all times to any books kept regarding a transaction for the purposes of inspection and copying.

(2) Rendering upon request, true and full information of all things affecting any transaction which concerns the community property. Nothing in this section is intended to impose a duty for either spouse to keep detailed books and records of community property transactions.

(3) Accounting to the spouse, and holding as a trustee, any benefit or profit derived from any transaction by one spouse without the consent of the other spouse which concerns the community property.

§ 750. Methods of holding property

A husband and wife may hold property as joint tenants or tenants in common, or as community property, or as community property with a right of survivorship.

§ 751. Interests of spouses in community property

The respective interests of the husband and wife in community property during continuance of the marriage relation are present, existing, and equal interests.

§ 752. Interest of spouses in separate property

Except as otherwise provided by statute, neither husband nor wife has any interest in the separate property of the other.

§ 760. Community property

Except as otherwise provided by statute, all property, real or personal, wherever situated, acquired by a married person during the marriage while domiciled in this state is community property.

§ 770. Separate property of married person

(a) Separate property of a married person includes all of the following:

(1) All property owned by the person before marriage.

(2) All property acquired by the person after marriage by gift, bequest, devise, or descent.

(3) The rents, issues, and profits of the property described in this section.

(b) A married person may, without the consent of the person's spouse, convey the person's separate property.

§ 771. Earnings and accumulations while living separate and apart

(a) The earnings and accumulations of a spouse and the minor children living with, or in the custody of, the spouse, while living separate and apart from the other spouse, are the separate property of the spouse . . . .

§ 780. Personal injury damages; community property

Except as provided in Section 781 and subject to the rules of allocation set forth in Section 2603, money and other property received or to be received by a married person in satisfaction of a judgment for damages for personal injuries, or pursuant to an agreement for the settlement or compromise of a claim for such damages, is community property if the cause of action for the damages arose during the marriage.

§ 781. Personal injury damages; separate property

(a) Money or other property received or to be received by a married person in satisfaction of a judgment for damages for personal injuries, or pursuant to an agreement for the settlement or compromise of a claim for those damages, is the separate property of the injured person if the cause of action for the damages arose as follows:

(1) After the entry of a judgment of dissolution of a marriage or legal separation of the parties.

(2) While the injured spouse is living separate from the other spouse.

(b) Notwithstanding subdivision (a), if the spouse of the injured person has paid expenses by reason of the personal injuries from separate property or from the community property, the spouse is entitled to reimbursement of the separate property or the community property for those expenses from the separate property received by the injured person under subdivision (a).

§ 803. Property acquired by married woman before January 1, 1975

Notwithstanding any other provision of this part, whenever any real or personal property, or any interest therein or encumbrance thereon, was acquired before January 1, 1975, by a married woman by an instrument in writing, the following presumptions apply, and are conclusive in favor of any person dealing in good faith and for a valuable consideration with the married woman or her legal representatives or successors in interest, regardless of any change in her marital status after acquisition of the property:

(a) If acquired by the married woman, the presumption is that the property is the married woman's separate property.

(b) If acquired by the married woman and any other person, the presumption is that the married woman takes the part acquired by her as tenant in common, unless a different intention is expressed in the instrument.

(c) If acquired by husband and wife by an instrument in which they are described as husband and wife, the presumption is that the property is the community property of the husband and wife, unless a different intention is expressed in the instrument.

§ 850. Transmutation by agreement or transfer

Subject to Sections 851 to 853, inclusive, married persons may by agreement or transfer, with or without consideration, do any of the following:

(a) Transmute community property to separate property of either spouse.

(b) Transmute separate property of either spouse to community property.

(c) Transmute separate property of one spouse to separate property of the other spouse.

§ 851. Transmutation subject to fraudulent transfer laws

A transmutation is subject to the laws governing fraudulent transfers.

§ 852. Requirements for transmutation

(a) A transmutation of real or personal property is not valid unless made in writing by an express declaration that is made, joined in, consented to, or accepted by the spouse whose interest in the property is adversely affected.

(b) A transmutation of real property is not effective as to third parties without notice thereof unless recorded.

(c) This section does not apply to a gift between the spouses of clothing, wearing apparel, jewelry, or other tangible articles of a personal nature that is used solely or principally by the spouse to whom the gift is made and that is not substantial in value taking into account the circumstances of the marriage.

(d) Nothing in this section affects the law governing characterization of property in which separate property and community property are commingled or otherwise combined.

(e) This section does not apply to or affect a transmutation of property made before January 1, 1985, and the law that would otherwise be applicable to that transmutation shall continue to apply.

§ 902. Debt

"Debt" means an obligation incurred by a married person before or during marriage, whether based on contract, tort, or otherwise.

§ 903. Time debt is incurred

A debt is "incurred" at the following time:

(a) In the case of a contract, at the time the contract is made.

(b) In the case of a tort, at the time the tort occurs.

(c) In other cases, at the time the obligation arises.

§ 910. Community estate liable for debt of either spouse

(a) Except as otherwise expressly provided by statute, the community estate is liable for a debt incurred by either spouse before or during marriage, regardless of which spouse has the management and control of the property and regardless of whether one or both spouses are parties to the debt or to a judgment for the debt.

(b) "During marriage" for purposes of this section does not include the period during which the spouses are living separate and apart before a judgment of dissolution of marriage or legal separation of the parties.

§ 911. Earnings of married persons; liability for premarital debts; earnings held in deposit accounts

(a) The earnings of a married person during marriage are not liable for a debt incurred by the person's spouse before marriage. After the earnings of the married person are paid, they remain not liable so long as they are held in a deposit account in which the person's spouse has no right of withdrawal and are uncommingled with other property in the community estate, except property insignificant in amount.

§ 912. Liability of quasi-community property

For the purposes of this part, quasi-community property is liable to the same extent, and shall be treated the same in all other respects, as community property.

§ 913. Liability of separate property

(a) The separate property of a married person is liable for a debt incurred by the person before or during marriage.

(b) Except as otherwise provided by statute:

(1) The separate property of a married person is not liable for a debt incurred by the person's spouse before or during marriage.

(2) The joinder or consent of a married person to an encumbrance of community estate property to secure payment of a debt incurred by the person's spouse does not subject the person's separate property to liability for the debt unless the person also incurred the debt.

§ 914. Liability for necessaries; right of reimbursement

(a) Notwithstanding Section 913, a married person is personally liable for the following debts incurred by the person's spouse during marriage:

(1) A debt incurred for necessaries of life of the person's spouse while the spouses are living together.

(2) Except as provided in Section 4302, a debt incurred for common necessaries of life of the person's spouse while the spouses are living separately. [Section 4302 provides: "A person is not liable for support of the person's spouse when the person is living separate from the spouse by agreement unless support is stipulated in the agreement."]

(b) The separate property of a married person may be applied to the satisfaction of a debt for which the person is personally liable pursuant to this section. If separate property is so applied at a time when nonexempt property in the community estate or separate property of the person's spouse is available but is not applied to the satisfaction of the debt, the married person is entitled to reimbursement to the extent such property was available . . . .

§ 915. Liability for support obligation; right of reimbursement to community

(a) For the purpose of this part, a child or spousal support obligation of a married person that does not arise out of the marriage shall be treated as a debt incurred before marriage, regardless of whether a court order for support is made or modified before or during marriage and regardless of whether any installment payment on the obligation accrues before or during marriage.

(b) If property in the community estate is applied to the satisfaction of a child or spousal support obligation of a married person that does not arise out of the marriage, at a time when nonexempt separate income of the person is available but is not applied to the satisfaction of the obligation, the community estate is entitled to reimbursement from the person in the amount of the separate income, not exceeding the property in the community estate so applied.

(c) Nothing in this section limits the matters a court may take into consideration in determining or modifying the amount of a support order, including, but not limited to, the earnings of the spouses of the parties.

§ 916. Division of property; subsequent liability; right of reimbursement

(a) Notwithstanding any other provision of this chapter, after division of community and quasi-community property:

(1) The separate property owned by a married person at the time of the division and the property received by the person in the division is liable for a debt incurred by the person before or during marriage and the person is personally liable for the debt, whether or not the debt was assigned for payment by the person's spouse in the division.

(2) The separate property owned by a married person at the time of the division and the property received by the person in the

division is not liable for a debt incurred by the person's spouse before or during marriage, and the person is not personally liable for the debt, unless the debt was assigned for payment by the person in the division of the property. Nothing in this paragraph affects the liability of property for the satisfaction of a lien on the property.

(3) The separate property owned by a married person at the time of the division and the property received by the person in the division is liable for a debt incurred by the person's spouse before or during marriage, and the person is personally liable for the debt, if the debt was assigned for payment by the person in the division of the property. If a money judgment for the debt is entered after the division, the property is not subject to enforcement of the judgment and the judgment may not be enforced against the married person, unless the person is made a party to the judgment for the purpose of this paragraph.

(b) If property of a married person is applied to the satisfaction of a money judgment pursuant to subdivision (a) for a debt incurred by the person that is assigned for payment by the person's spouse, the person has a right of reimbursement from the person's spouse to the extent of the property applied, with interest at the legal rate, and may recover reasonable attorney's fees incurred in enforcing the right of reimbursement.

§ 1000. Liability for death or injury caused by spouse; property subject to satisfaction of liability

(a) A married person is not liable for any injury or damage caused by the other spouse except in cases where the married person would be liable therefor if the marriage did not exist.

(b) The liability of a married person for death or injury to person or property shall be satisfied as follows:

(1) If the liability of the married person is based upon an act or omission which occurred while the married person was performing an activity for the benefit of the community, the liability shall first be satisfied from the community estate and second from the separate property of the married person.

(2) If the liability of the married person is not based upon an act or omission which occurred while the married person was performing an activity for the benefit of the community, the liability shall first

be satisfied from the separate property of the married person and second from the community estate.

§ 1100. Management and control of community personal property; fiduciary duty

(a) Except as provided in subdivisions [not provided in this supplement], either spouse has the management and control of the community personal property, whether acquired prior to or on or after January 1, 1975, with like absolute power of disposition, other than testamentary, as the spouse has of the separate estate of the spouse.

(b) A spouse may not make a gift of community personal property, or dispose of community personal property for less than fair and reasonable value, without the written consent of the other spouse. This subdivision does not apply to gifts mutually given by both spouses to third parties and to gifts given by one spouse to the other spouse.

(c) A spouse may not sell, convey, or encumber community personal property used as the family dwelling, or the furniture, furnishings, or fittings of the home, or the clothing or wearing apparel of the other spouse or minor children which is community personal property, without the written consent of the other spouse.

(d) Except as provided in subdivisions (b) and (c), and in Section 1102, a spouse who is operating or managing a business or an interest in a business that is all or substantially all community personal property has the primary management and control of the business or interest. Primary management and control means that the managing spouse may act alone in all transactions but shall give prior written notice to the other spouse of any sale, lease, exchange, encumbrance, or other disposition of all or substantially all of the personal property used in the operation of the business (including personal property used for agricultural purposes), whether or not title to that property is held in the name of only one spouse. Written notice is not, however, required when prohibited by the law otherwise applicable to the transaction.

Remedies for the failure by a managing spouse to give prior written notice as required by this subdivision are only as specified in Section

1101. A failure to give prior written notice shall not adversely affect the validity of a transaction nor of any interest transferred.

(e) Each spouse shall act with respect to the other spouse in the management and control of the community assets and liabilities in accordance with the general rules governing fiduciary relationships which control the actions of persons having relationships of personal confidence as specified in Section 721, until such time as the assets and liabilities have been divided by the parties or by a court. This duty includes the obligation to make full disclosure to the other spouse of all material facts and information regarding the existence, characterization, and valuation of all assets in which the community has or may have an interest and debts for which the community is or may be liable, and to provide equal access to all information, records, and books that pertain to the value and character of those assets and debts, upon request. *affirmative duty*

§ 1101. Remedies for breach of fiduciary duty between spouses

(a) A spouse has a claim against the other spouse for any breach of the fiduciary duty that results in impairment to the claimant spouse's present undivided one-half interest in the community estate, including, but not limited to, a single transaction or a pattern or series of transactions, which transaction or transactions have caused or will cause a detrimental impact to the claimant spouse's undivided one-half interest in the community estate.

(b) A court may order an accounting of the property and obligations of the parties to a marriage and may determine the rights of ownership in, the beneficial enjoyment of, or access to, community property, and the classification of all property of the parties to a marriage.

(c) A court may order that the name of a spouse shall be added to community property held in the name of the other spouse alone or that the title of community property held in some other title form shall be reformed to reflect its community character, except with respect to any of the following . . . .

(g) Remedies for breach of the fiduciary duty by one spouse, including those set out in Sections 721 and 1100, shall include, but not be limited to, an award to the other spouse of 50 percent, or an amount equal to 50 percent, of any asset undisclosed or transferred in breach of the fiduciary duty plus attorney's fees and court costs. The value of the asset shall be determined to be its highest value at the date of the breach of the fiduciary duty, the date of the sale or disposition of the asset, or the date of the award by the court.

(h) Remedies for the breach of the fiduciary duty by one spouse, as set forth in Sections 721 and 1100, when the breach falls within the ambit of Section 3294 of the Civil Code [clear and convincing evidence of oppression, fraud, or malice] shall include, but not be limited to, an award to the other spouse of 100 percent, or an amount equal to 100 percent, of any asset undisclosed or transferred in breach of the fiduciary duty.

§ 1102. Management and control of community real property

(a) Except as provided in [sections not provided in this supplement], either spouse has the management and control of the community real property, whether acquired prior to or on or after January 1, 1975, but both spouses, either personally or by a duly authorized agent, must join in executing any instrument by which that community real property or any interest therein is leased for a longer period than one year, or is sold, conveyed, or encumbered.

(b) This section does not apply to a lease, mortgage, conveyance, or transfer of real property or of any interest in real property between husband and wife.

§ 1500. Effect of premarital agreements and other marital property agreements

The property rights of husband and wife prescribed by statute may be altered by a premarital agreement or other marital property agreement.

§ 1611. Formalities; consideration

A premarital agreement shall be in writing and signed by both parties. It is enforceable without consideration.

§ 1612. Subject matter of premarital agreement

(a) Parties to a premarital agreement may contract with respect to all of the following:

(1) The rights and obligations of each of the parties in any of the property of either or both of them whenever and wherever acquired or located.

(2) The right to buy, sell, use, transfer, exchange, abandon, lease, consume, expend, assign, create a security interest in, mortgage, encumber, dispose of, or otherwise manage and control property.

(3) The disposition of property upon separation, marital dissolution, death, or the occurrence or nonoccurrence of any other event.

(4) The making of a will, trust, or other arrangement to carry out the provisions of the agreement.

(5) The ownership rights in and disposition of the death benefit from a life insurance policy.

(6) The choice of law governing the construction of the agreement.

(7) Any other matter, including their personal rights and obligations, not in violation of public policy or a statute imposing a criminal penalty.

(b) The right of a child to support may not be adversely affected by a premarital agreement.

(c) Any provision in a premarital agreement regarding spousal support, including, but not limited to, a waiver of it, is not enforceable if the party against whom enforcement of the spousal support provision is sought was not represented by independent counsel at the time the agreement containing the provision was signed, or if the provision regarding spousal support is unconscionable at the time of enforcement. An otherwise unenforceable provision in a premarital agreement regarding spousal support may not become enforceable solely because the party against whom enforcement is sought was represented by independent counsel.

§ 1615. Enforcement of premarital agreement

(a) A premarital agreement is not enforceable if the party against whom enforcement is sought proves either of the following:

(1) That party did not execute the agreement voluntarily.

(2) The agreement was unconscionable when it was executed and, before execution of the agreement, all of the following applied to that party:

(A) That party was not provided a fair, reasonable, and full disclosure of the property or financial obligations of the other party.

(B) That party did not voluntarily and expressly waive, in writing, any right to disclosure of the property or financial obligations of the other party beyond the disclosure provided.

(C) That party did not have, or reasonably could not have had, an adequate knowledge of the property or financial obligations of the other party.

(b) An issue of unconscionability of a premarital agreement shall be decided by the court as a matter of law.

(c) For the purposes of subdivision (a), it shall be deemed that a premarital agreement was not executed voluntarily unless the court finds in writing or on the record all of the following:

(1) The party against whom enforcement is sought was represented by independent legal counsel at the time of signing the agreement or, after being advised to seek independent legal counsel, expressly waived, in a separate writing, representation by independent legal counsel. The advisement to seek independent legal counsel shall me made at least seven calendar days before the final agreement is signed.

(2) One of the following:

(A) For an agreement executed between January 1, 2002, and January 1, 2020, the party against whom enforcement is sought had not less than even calendar days between the time that party was first presented with the final agreement and advised to seek independent legal counsel and the time the agreement was signed.

(B) For an agreement executed on or after January 1, 2020, the party against whom enforcement is sought had not less than seven calendar days between the time that party was first presented with the final agreement and the time the agreement was signed, regardless of whether the party is represented by legal counsel. This requirement does not apply to nonsubstantive amendments that do not change the terms of the agreement.

(3) The party against whom enforcement is sought, if unrepresented by legal counsel, was fully informed of the terms and basic effect of the agreement as well as the rights and obligations he or she was giving up by signing the agreement, and was proficient in the language in which the explanation of the party's rights was conducted and in which the agreement was written. The explanation of the rights and obligations relinquished shall be memorialized in writing and delivered to the party prior to signing the agreement. The unrepresented party shall, on or before the signing of the premarital agreement, execute a document declaring that the party received the information required by this paragraph and indicating who provided that information.

(4) The agreement and the writings executed pursuant to paragraphs (1) and (3) were not executed under duress, fraud, or undue influence, and the parties did not lack capacity to enter into the agreement.

(5) Any other factors the court deems relevant.

§ 2033. Encumbrance to pay family law attorney's fees

(a) Either party may encumber his or her interest in community real property to pay reasonable attorney's fees in order to retain or maintain legal counsel in a proceeding for dissolution of marriage, for nullity of marriage, or for legal separation of the parties. This encumbrance shall be known as a "family law attorney's real property lien" and attaches only to the encumbering party's interest in the community real property.

(b) Notice of a family law attorney's real property lien shall be served either personally or on the other party's attorney of record at least 15 days before the encumbrance is recorded . . . .

§ 2040. Temporary restraining order in summons

(a) . . . [T]he summons shall contain a temporary restraining order:

(1) Restraining both parties from removing the minor child or children of the parties, if any, from the state without the prior written consent of the other party or an order of the court.

(2) Restraining both parties from transferring, encumbering, hypothecating, concealing, or in any way disposing of any property, real or personal, whether community, quasi-community, or

separate, without the written consent of the other party or an order of the court, except in the usual course of business or for the necessities of life, and requiring each party to notify the other party of any proposed extraordinary expenditures at least five business days before incurring those expenditures and to account to the court for all extraordinary expenditures made after service of the summons on that party.

Notwithstanding the foregoing, nothing in the restraining order shall preclude a party from using community property, quasi-community property, or the party's own separate property to pay reasonable attorney's fees and costs in order to retain legal counsel in the proceeding. A party who uses community property or quasi-community property to pay his or her attorney's retainer for fees and costs under this provision shall account to the community for the use of the property. A party who uses other property that is subsequently determined to be the separate property of the other party to pay his or her attorney's retainer for fees and costs under this provision shall account to the other party for the use of the property.

(3) Restraining both parties from cashing, borrowing against, canceling, transferring, disposing of, or changing the beneficiaries of any insurance or other coverage, including life, health, automobile, and disability, held for the benefit of the parties and their child or children for whom support may be ordered . . . .

§ 2102. Fiduciary relationship; length and scope of duty; termination

(a) From the date of separation to the date of the distribution of the community or quasi-community asset or liability in question, each party is subject to the standards provided in Section 721, as to all activities that affect the assets and liabilities of the other party, including, but not limited to, the following activities:

(1) The accurate and complete disclosure of all assets and liabilities in which the party has or may have an interest or obligation and all current earnings, accumulations, and expenses, including an immediate, full, and accurate update or augmentation to the extent there have been any material changes.

(2) The accurate and complete written disclosure of any investment opportunity, business opportunity, or other income-producing opportunity that presents itself after the date of separation, but that results from any investment, significant business activity outside the ordinary course of business, or other income-producing opportunity of either spouse from the date of marriage to the date of separation, inclusive. The written disclosure shall be made in sufficient time for the other spouse to make an informed decision as to whether he or she desires to participate in the investment opportunity, business, or other potential income-producing opportunity, and for the court to resolve any dispute regarding the right of the other spouse to participate in the opportunity. In the event of nondisclosure of an investment opportunity, the division of any gain resulting from that opportunity is governed by the standard provided in Section 2556.

(3) The operation or management of a business or an interest in a business in which the community may have an interest.

(b) From the date that a valid, enforceable, and binding resolution of the disposition of the asset or liability in question is reached, until the asset or liability has actually been distributed, each party is subject to the standards provided in Section 721 as to all activities that affect the assets or liabilities of the other party. Once a particular asset or liability has been distributed, the duties and standards set forth in Section 721 shall end as to that asset or liability.

(c) From the date of separation to the date of a valid, enforceable, and binding resolution of all issues relating to child or spousal support and professional fees, each party is subject to the standards provided in Section 721 as to all issues relating to the support and fees, including immediate, full, and accurate disclosure of all material facts and information regarding the income or expenses of the party.

§ 2251. Status of putative spouse; division of community or quasi-community property

(a) If a determination is made that a marriage is void or voidable and the court finds that either party or both parties believed in good faith that the marriage was valid, the court shall:

(1) Declare the party or parties to have the status of a putative spouse.

(2) If the division of property is in issue, divide, in accordance with Division 7 (commencing with Section 2500), that property acquired during the union which would have been community property or quasi-community property if the union had not been void or voidable. This property is known as "quasi-marital property".

(b) If the court expressly reserves jurisdiction, it may make the property division at a time after the judgment.

§ 2252. Liability of quasi-marital property for debts of parties

The property divided pursuant to Section 2251 is liable for debts of the parties to the same extent as if the property had been community property or quasi-community property.

§ 2310. Grounds for dissolution or legal separation

Dissolution of the marriage or legal separation of the parties may be based on either of the following grounds, which shall be pleaded generally:

(a) Irreconcilable differences, which have caused the irremediable breakdown of the marriage.

(b) Incurable insanity.

§ 2311. Irreconcilable differences defined

Irreconcilable differences are those grounds which are determined by the court to be substantial reasons for not continuing the marriage and which make it appear that the marriage should be dissolved.

§ 2335. Evidence of specific acts of misconduct

Except as otherwise provided by statute, in a pleading or proceeding for dissolution of marriage or legal separation of the parties, including depositions and discovery proceedings, evidence of specific acts of misconduct is improper and inadmissible.

§ 2337. Motion to bifurcate

(a) In a proceeding for dissolution of marriage, the court, upon noticed motion, may sever and grant an early and separate trial on the issue of the dissolution of the status of the marriage apart from other issues. . . .

§ 2550. Equal division of community estate

Except upon the written agreement of the parties, or on oral stipulation of the parties in open court, or as otherwise provided in this division, in a proceeding for dissolution of marriage or for legal separation of the parties, the court shall, either in its judgment of dissolution of the marriage, in its judgment of legal separation of the parties, or at a later time if it expressly reserves jurisdiction to make such a property division, divide the community estate of the parties equally.

§ 2551. Characterization of liabilities; confirmation or assignment

For the purposes of division and in confirming or assigning the liabilities of the parties for which the community estate is liable, the court shall characterize liabilities as separate or community and confirm or assign them to the parties in accordance with Part 6 (commencing with Section 2620).

§ 2552. Valuation of assets and liabilities

(a) For the purpose of division of the community estate upon dissolution of marriage or legal separation of the parties, except as provided in subdivision (b), the court shall value the assets and liabilities as near as practicable to the time of trial.

(b) Upon 30 days' notice by the moving party to the other party, the court for good cause shown may value all or any portion of the assets and liabilities at a date after separation and before trial to accomplish an equal division of the community estate of the parties in an equitable manner.

§ 2556. Continuing jurisdiction to award community estate assets or liabilities

In a proceeding for dissolution of marriage, for nullity of marriage, or for legal separation of the parties, the court has continuing jurisdiction to award community estate assets or community estate liabilities to the parties that have not been previously adjudicated by a judgment in the proceeding. A party may file a postjudgment motion or order to show cause in the proceeding in order to obtain adjudication of any community estate asset or liability omitted or not adjudicated by the judgment. In these cases, the court shall equally divide the omitted or unadjudicated community estate asset or liability, unless the court finds upon good cause shown that the interests of justice require an unequal division of the asset or liability.

§ 2581. Community property presumption for property held in joint form

For the purpose of division of property on dissolution of marriage or legal separation of the parties, property acquired by the parties during marriage in joint form, including property held in tenancy in common, joint tenancy, or tenancy by the entirety, or as community property, is presumed to be community property. This presumption is a presumption affecting the burden of proof and may be rebutted by either of the following:

(a) A clear statement in the deed or other documentary evidence of title by which the property is acquired that the property is separate property and not community property.

(b) Proof that the parties have made a written agreement that the property is separate property.

§ 2601. Conditional award of an asset of the community estate to one party

Where economic circumstances warrant, the court may award an asset of the community estate to one party on such conditions as the court deems proper to effect a substantially equal division of the community estate.

§ 2602. Award or offset of amount deliberately misappropriated by party

As an additional award or offset against existing property, the court may award, from a party's share, the amount the court determines to have been deliberately misappropriated by the party to the exclusion of the interest of the other party in the community estate.

§ 2603. Community estate personal injury damages

(a) "Community estate personal injury damages" as used in this section means all money or other property received or to be received by a person in satisfaction of a judgment for damages for the person's personal injuries or pursuant to an agreement for the settlement or compromise of a claim for the damages, if the cause of action for the damages arose during the marriage but is not separate property as described in Section 781, unless the money or other property has been commingled with other assets of the community estate.

(b) Community estate personal injury damages shall be assigned to the party who suffered the injuries unless the court, after taking into account the economic condition and needs of each party, the time that has elapsed since the recovery of the damages or the accrual of the cause of action, and all other facts of the case, determines that the interests of justice require another disposition. In such a case, the community estate personal injury damages shall be assigned to the respective parties in such proportions as the court determines to be just, except that at least one-half of the damages shall be assigned to the party who suffered the injuries.

§ 2610. Retirement plans; orders to ensure benefits

(a) Except as provided in subdivision (b), the court shall make whatever orders are necessary or appropriate to ensure that each party receives the party's full community property share in any retirement plan, whether public or private, including all survivor and death benefits, including, but not limited to, any of the following . . . .

§ 2620. Confirmation or division of community estate debts

The debts for which the community estate is liable which are unpaid at the time of trial, or for which the community estate becomes liable after trial, shall be confirmed or divided as provided in this part.

§ 2621. Premarital debts; confirmation

Debts incurred by either spouse before the date of marriage shall be confirmed without offset to the spouse who incurred the debt.

§ 2622. Marital debts after marriage but before separation; division

(a) Except as provided in subdivision (b), debts incurred by either spouse after the date of marriage but before the date of separation shall be divided as set forth in Sections 2550 to 2552, inclusive, and

Sections 2601 to 2604 to, inclusive [Section 2604 deals with community estates valued at less than $5,000].

(b) To the extent that community debts exceed total community and quasi-community assets, the excess of debt shall be assigned as the court deems just and equitable, taking into account factors such as the parties' relative ability to pay.

§ 2623. Marital debts incurred after separation; confirmation

Debts incurred by either spouse after the date of separation but before entry of a judgment of dissolution of marriage or legal separation of the parties shall be confirmed as follows:

(a) Debts incurred by either spouse for the common necessaries of life of either spouse or the necessaries of life of the children of the marriage for whom support may be ordered, in the absence of a court order or written agreement for support or for the payment of these debts, shall be confirmed to either spouse according to the parties' respective needs and abilities to pay at the time the debt was incurred.

(b) Debts incurred by either spouse for nonnecessaries of that spouse or children of the marriage for whom support may be ordered shall be confirmed without offset to the spouse who incurred the debt.

§ 2624. Marital debts incurred after entry of judgment of dissolution or after entry of judgment of legal separation; confirmation

Debts incurred by either spouse after entry of a judgment of dissolution of marriage but before termination of the parties' marital status or after entry of a judgment of legal separation of the parties shall be confirmed without offset to the spouse who incurred the debt.

§ 2625. Separate debts incurred before separation; confirmation

Notwithstanding Sections 2620 to 2624, inclusive, all separate debts, including those debts incurred by a spouse during marriage and before the date of separation that were not incurred for the benefit of the community, shall be confirmed without offset to the spouse who incurred the debt.

§ 2626. Reimbursement for debts paid after separation but before trial

The court has jurisdiction to order reimbursement in cases it deems appropriate for debts paid after separation but before trial.

§ 2640. Separate property contributions to community estate property acquisition

(a) "Contributions to the acquisition of property," as used in this section, include downpayments, payments for improvements, and payments that reduce the principal of a loan used to finance the purchase or improvement of the property but do not include payments of interest on the loan or payments made for maintenance, insurance, or taxation of the property.

(b) In the division of the community estate under this division, unless a party has made a written waiver of the right to reimbursement or has signed a writing that has the effect of a waiver, the party shall be reimbursed for the party's contributions to the acquisition of property of the community property estate to the extent the party traces the contributions to a separate property source. The amount reimbursed shall be without interest or adjustment for change in monetary values and may not exceed the net value of the property at the time of the division.

(c) A party shall be reimbursed for the party's separate property contributions to the acquisition of property of the other spouse's separate property estate during the marriage, unless there has been a transmutation in writing pursuant to Chapter 5 of Part 2 of Division 4, or a written waiver of the right to reimbursement. The amount reimbursed shall be without interest or adjustment for change in monetary values and may not exceed the net value of the property at the time of the division.

§ 2641. Community contributions to education or training

(a) "Community contributions to education or training" as used in this section means payments made with community or quasi-community property for education or training or for the repayment of a loan incurred for education or training, whether the payments were made while the parties were resident in this state or resident outside this state.

(b) Subject to the limitations provided in this section, upon dissolution of marriage or legal separation of the parties:

(1) The community shall be reimbursed for community contributions to education or training of a party that substantially enhances the earning capacity of the party. The amount reimbursed shall be with interest at the legal rate, accruing from the end of the calendar year in which the contributions were made.

(2) A loan incurred during marriage for the education or training of a party shall not be included among the liabilities of the community for the purpose of division pursuant to this division but shall be assigned for payment by the party.

(c) The reimbursement and assignment required by this section shall be reduced or modified to the extent circumstances render such a disposition unjust, including, but not limited to, any of the following:

(1) The community has substantially benefited from the education, training, or loan incurred for the education or training of the party. There is a rebuttable presumption, affecting the burden of proof, that the community has not substantially benefited from community contributions to the education or training made less than 10 years before the commencement of the proceeding, and that the community has substantially benefited from community contributions to the education or training made more than 10 years before the commencement of the proceeding.

(2) The education or training received by the party is offset by the education or training received by the other party for which community contributions have been made.

(3) The education or training enables the party receiving the education or training to engage in gainful employment that substantially reduces the need of the party for support that would otherwise be required.

(d) Reimbursement for community contributions and assignment of loans pursuant to this section is the exclusive remedy of the community or a party for the education or training and any resulting enhancement of the earning capacity of a party. However, nothing in this subdivision limits consideration of the effect of the education, training, or enhancement, or the amount reimbursed pursuant to this section, on the circumstances of the parties for the purpose of an order for support pursuant to Section 4320. [Section 4320 deals with setting the amount of support].

(e) This section is subject to an express written agreement of the parties to the contrary.

§ 2650. Jurisdiction; division of jointly held separate property

In a proceeding for division of the community estate, the court has jurisdiction, at the request of either party, to divide the separate property interests of the parties in real and personal property, wherever situated and whenever acquired, held by the parties as joint tenants or tenants in common. The property shall be divided together with, and in accordance with the same procedure for and limitations on, division of community estate.

§ 4300. Duty to support spouse

Subject to this division, a person shall support the person's spouse.

§ 4301. Use of separate property for support

Subject to Section 914, a person shall support the person's spouse while they are living together out of the separate property of the person when there is no community property or quasi-community property.

§ 4320. Determination of amount due for support; considerations

In ordering spousal support under this part, the court shall consider all of the following circumstances:

(a) The extent to which the earning capacity of each party is sufficient to maintain the standard of living established during the marriage, taking into account all of the following:

(1) The marketable skills of the supported party; the job market for those skills; the time and expenses required for the supported party to acquire the appropriate education or training to develop

those skills; and the possible need for retraining or education to acquire other, more marketable skills or employment.

(2) The extent to which the supported party's present or future earning capacity is impaired by periods of unemployment that were incurred during the marriage to permit the supported party to devote time to domestic duties.

(b) The extent to which the supported party contributed to the attainment of an education, training, a career position, or a license by the supporting party.

(c) The ability of the supporting party to pay spousal support, taking into account the supporting party's earning capacity, earned and unearned income, assets, and standard of living.

(d) The needs of each party based on the standard of living established during the marriage.

(e) The obligations and assets, including the separate property, of each party.

(f) The duration of the marriage.

(g) The ability of the supported party to engage in gainful employment without unduly interfering with the interests of dependent children in the custody of the party.

(h) The age and health of the parties.

(i) Documented evidence of any history of domestic violence, as defined in Section 6211, between the parties, including, but not limited to, consideration of emotional distress resulting from domestic violence perpetrated against the supported party by the supporting party, and consideration of any history of violence against the supporting party by the supported party.

(j) The immediate and specific tax consequences to each party.

(k) The balance of the hardships to each party.

(*l*) The goal that the supported party shall be self-supporting within a reasonable period of time. Except in the case of a marriage of long duration as described in Section 4336, a "reasonable period of time" for purposes of this section generally shall be one-half the length of the marriage. However, nothing in this section is intended to limit the court's discretion to order support for a greater or lesser length of time, based on any of the other factors listed in this section, Section 4336, and the circumstances of the parties.

(m) The criminal conviction of an abusive spouse shall be considered in making a reduction or elimination of a spousal support award in accordance with Section 4325.

(n) Any other factors the court determines are just and equitable.

CALIFORNIA EVIDENCE CODE

§ 662. Owner of legal title to property is owner of beneficial title

The owner of the legal title to property is presumed to be the owner of the full beneficial title. This presumption may be rebutted only by clear and convincing proof.

CALIFORNIA PROBATE CODE

§ 28. Community property

"Community property" means:

(a) Community property heretofore or hereafter acquired during marriage by a married person while domiciled in this state.

(b) All personal property wherever situated, and all real property situated in this state, heretofore or hereafter acquired during the marriage by a married person while domiciled elsewhere, that is community property, or a substantially equivalent type of marital property, under the laws of the place where the acquiring spouse was domiciled at the time of its acquisition.

§ 66. Quasi-community property

"Quasi-community property" means the following property, other than community property as defined in Section 28:

(a) All personal property wherever situated, and all real property situated in this state, heretofore or hereafter acquired by a decedent while domiciled elsewhere that would have been the community property of the decedent and the surviving spouse if the decedent had been domiciled in this state at the time of its acquisition.

§ 100. Community property

(a) Upon the death of a married person, one-half of the community property belongs to the surviving spouse and the other half belongs to the decedent.

§ 101. Quasi-community property

(a) Upon the death of a married person domiciled in this state, one-half of the decedent's quasi-community property belongs to the surviving spouse and the other half belongs to the decedent.

§ 6401. Surviving spouse or surviving domestic partner; intestate share

(a) As to community property, the intestate share of the surviving spouse is the one-half of the community property that belongs to the decedent under Section 100.

(b) As to quasi-community property, the intestate share of the surviving spouse is the one-half of the quasi-community property that belongs to the decedent under Section 101.

(c) As to separate property, the intestate share of the surviving spouse or surviving domestic partner . . . is as follows:

(1) The entire intestate share if the decedent did not leave any surviving issue, parent, brother, sister, or issue of a deceased brother or sister.

(2) One-half of the intestate share in the following cases:

(A) Where the decedent leaves only one child or the issue of one deceased child.

(B) Where the decedent leaves no issue but leaves a parent or parents or their issue or the issue of either of them.

(3) One-third of the intestate estate in the following cases:

(A) Where the decedent leaves more than one child.

(B) Where the decedent leaves one child and the issue of one or more deceased children.

(C) Where the decedent leaves issue of two or more deceased children.

Table of Cases

Ablamis v. Rober, 104
Age v. Age, 191
Aghaian v. Minassian, 142
Ahern v. Ahern, 123
Aleem v. Aleem, 183
Aljabban v. Fontana Indoor Swap Meet, Inc., 132
Allen, Marriage of, 133
Antoniadis, Marriage of, 128
Baragry, Marriage of, 73
Barneson, Marriage of, 140
Barocas v. Barocas, 32
Bergen v. Wood, 18, 19
Bibb, Estate of, 141
Bonds, Marriage of, 22, 23, 31, 34
Bonvino, Marriage of, 67, 126, 128
Brace, In re, 54, 74, 75, 76, 141, 146
Brandes, Marriage of, 120
Brooks, Marriage of, 120
Brown, Marriage of, 94
Buie and Neighbors, Marriage of, 165
Burts v. Burts, 113
Campbell v. Thomas, 192
Ceja v. Rudolph & Sletten, Inc., 189
Chamberlin, Matter of, 180
Chaplain v. Chaplain, 37
Clarke and Akel, Marriage of, 32
CMRE Financial Services, Inc. v. Parton, 174
Cochran v. Cochran, 19
Coppola v. Farina, 136
Craig v. Craig, 102
Crimes and Mou, Marriage of, 160
Davis, Marriage of, 71
Dawes v. Rich, 199

Dekker, Marriage of, 119
Della Zoppa v. Della Zoppa, 18
Desouza, Marriage of, 8, 167
Desta v. Anyaoha, 192
Direct Capital Corp. v. Brooks, 147, 151
Duffy, Marriage of, 167
Edwards v. Edwards, 32
Elfmont, Marriage of, 110
Elkus v. Elkus, 125
Elli, Marriage of, 113
Epstein, Marriage of, 176
Evans v. Evans, 107
Facter, Marriage of, 23, 29, 30, 33
Friezo v. Friezo, 34
Garcia, Marriage of, 186
Garrity & Bishton, Marriage of, 28
Gillmore, Marriage of, 109
Gonzalez, Marriage of, 114
Grinius, Marriage of, 127
Grunfeld v. Grunfeld, 178
Gudelj v. Gudelj, 127
Hall v. Hall, 28
Harper v. Harper, 69
Havell v. Islam, 182
Hehman, Marriage of, 112
Hill and Dittmer, Marriage of, 22, 23
Honer, Marriage of, 172
Hood v. Hood, 41
Howell v. Howell, 111
Howell, Marriage of, 30
Hug, Marriage of, 114
Huntley, Marriage of, 173
Joaquin, Marriage of, 70
Johnson v. Estate of McFarlin, 19
Kilbourne, Marriage of, 182
Krafick v. Krafick, 50

TABLE OF CASES

Kulko v. Superior Court, 6
Lee v. Lee, 95
Lorenz, Marriage of, 114
Lucas, Marriage of, 55, 85
Lucero, People v., 4
Lyons, In re, 121
MacDonald, Estate of, 140, 141
Marsden, Marriage of, 88
Marshall, Marriage of, 110
Marsocci v. Marsocci, 38
Marvin v. Marvin, 17
May v. May, 123
McCarty v. McCarty, 107
McLaren v. McLaren, 50
McReath v. McReath, 122, 179
McSparron v. McSparron, 178
McTiernan and Dubrow, Marriage of, 124
Meadows v. Meadows, 191
Mejia v. Reed, 143
Melissa, Marriage of, 29
Minkin, Marriage of, 169
Mohler, Marriage of, 176
Moore v. Knower, 135
Moore, Marriage of, 87
Morris, Marriage of, 102, 103
Mullonkal and Kodiyamplakkil, Marriage of, 177
Nagel v. Westen, 142
Nevai, Marriage of, 87
Nicholson and Sparks, Marriage of, 85
Nuveen v. Nuveen, 118
Obergefell v. Hodges, 3
Olski v. Olski, 179
Pearson v. Fillingim, 181
Pendleton and Fireman, Marriage of, 29
Pereira v. Pereira, 120
Perez v. Sharp, 2
Peterson, Marriage of, 108
Piscopo v. Piscopo, 125
Price v. Price, 49
Priebe v. Sinclair, 137
Quijano v. Quijano, 105
Ramirez, Marriage of, 187
Randall v. Randall, 137
Rapheal, Estate of, 139
Robertson v. Robertson, 120
Sailer v. Sailer, 33

Sampson v. Sampson, 178
Saslow, Marriage of, 110
Schleich, Marriage of, 166
Seaton, Marriage of, 186, 189
See v. See, 129
Sefton v. Sefton, 189, 245
Shanks, Marriage of, 35, 38
Sheldon, Estate of, 28
Shelton, Marriage of, 125
Sink v. Sink, 49
Smetana v. Smetana, 40
Stall v. Fulton, 46
State Board of Equalization v. Woo, 143
Steinberger, Marriage of, 114, 165
Steiner, Marriage of, 115
Strum v. Moyer, 142, 150
Suastez v. Plastic Dress-Up Co., 113
Taylor v. Fields, 19
Thomson v. Thomson, 102
Thorne and Raccina, Marriage of, 174
Thornton, Estate of, 63
Trenk v. Soheili, 60, 74
Valli, Marriage of, 66, 139, 140
Van Camp v. Van Camp, 120
Vasquez v. LBS Financial Credit Union, 92
Von Hohn v. Von Hohn, 123
Wall, Marriage of, 125
Walrath, Marriage of, 82, 87
Ware v. Ware, 41
Watts, Marriage of, 176
White, Marriage of, 179
Williams v. Massa, 50
Williams v. North Carolina, 5
Wirth v. Wirth, 47
Wisnom v. McCarthy, 151
Wolfe, Marriage of, 133
Worth, Marriage of, 182
Wozniak, Marriage of, 69, 141
Yeh v. Li-Cheng Tai, 168
Zharkova v. Gaudreau, 4

Table of Statutes

10 U.S.C. § 1408 110
11 U.S.C. § 523(a)(5) 13
26 U.S.C. § 414(p)(1)(B) 105
28 U.S.C. § 1738A..................... 6
29 U.S.C. § 1056(d)................ 108
29 U.S.C. § 1056(d)(1) 106
29 U.S.C. § 1056(d)(2) 106
29 U.S.C. § 1056(d)(3)(A) 107
29 U.S.C. § 1056(d)(3)(B)
 (ii) 105
Cal. Bus. & Prof. Code
 § 14100 123
Cal. Civil Code § 683.2 75
Cal. Civil Code § 1114............. 52
Cal. Civil Code § 2224............. 18
Cal. Civil Code § 3439.04(a)
 (1) 145
Cal. Civil Code § 3439.04(a)
 (2) 145
Cal. Code of Civil Proc.
 § 1008................................... 16
Cal. Evid. Code § 500 59
Cal. Evid. Code § 550 59
Cal. Evid. Code § 600 57
Cal. Evid. Code § 601 56
Cal. Evid. Code §§ 603–606..... 56
Cal. Evid. Code § 641 58
Cal. Evid. Code § 662 .... 74, 77
Cal. Family Code § 4(c) 30
Cal. Family Code § 63 82
Cal. Family Code § 70 .... 71, 72
Cal. Family Code § 80 115
Cal. Family Code § 125 .... 62, 63,
 64, 198
Cal. Family Code §§ 297
 et seq. 3
Cal. Family Code § 297(a)......... 3
Cal. Family Code § 300(a)..... 2, 3
Cal. Family Code § 300(b)........ 3
Cal. Family Code § 301 3
Cal. Family Code §§ 302–323 ... 3

Cal. Family Code § 306 3
Cal. Family Code § 308 4
Cal. Family Code § 310 2
Cal. Family Code § 310(a)..... 195
Cal. Family Code §§ 350–360.... 3
Cal. Family Code § 356 3
Cal. Family Code §§ 400–402.... 3
Cal. Family Code § 420(a).......... 3
Cal. Family Code § 420(b).......... 3
Cal. Family Code § 420(c) 4
Cal. Family Code §§ 422–423.... 3
Cal. Family Code § 721 22
Cal. Family Code § 721(a)..... 165
Cal. Family Code § 721(b).... 144,
 168, 169
Cal. Family Code § 721(b)
 (1).. 169
Cal. Family Code § 721(b)
 (2).. 169
Cal. Family Code § 721(b)
 (3).. 169
Cal. Family Code § 750 76
Cal. Family Code § 751 61
Cal. Family Code § 752 62
Cal. Family Code § 760 ....54, 55,
 60, 64, 66, 76, 77, 128, 130,
 197, 198
Cal. Family Code § 761 182
Cal. Family Code § 770 ....61, 64,
 121
Cal. Family Code § 771(a)........ 71
Cal. Family Code § 780 136
Cal. Family Code § 781 136
Cal. Family Code § 781(c) 136
Cal. Family Code § 803 .....56, 91
Cal. Family Code § 803(b)....... 92
Cal. Family Code § 803(c) 92
Cal. Family Code § 851 170
Cal. Family Code § 852(a)....142,
 143
Cal. Family Code § 852(b).....135

Cal. Family Code § 852(c) 167
Cal. Family Code § 852(e) 142
Cal. Family Code § 853(a) 144
Cal. Family Code § 902 .... 137, 147
Cal. Family Code § 903 147
Cal. Family Code § 910 .... 145, 148, 150, 152, 157
Cal. Family Code §§ 910–914 147
Cal. Family Code § 911 152
Cal. Family Code § 913 .... 77, 149, 153
Cal. Family Code § 913(a) 150, 157
Cal. Family Code § 913(b) (1) 145, 150
Cal. Family Code § 913(b) (2) 149
Cal. Family Code § 914 .... 148, 153, 155, 156, 176
Cal. Family Code § 914(a) 154, 156
Cal. Family Code § 915 156
Cal. Family Code § 915(b) 179
Cal. Family Code § 916 .... 147, 176
Cal. Family Code § 916(a) (2) 176
Cal. Family Code § 920 179
Cal. Family Code § 1000 ...... 150, 179
Cal. Family Code § 1000 (a) 151
Cal. Family Code § 1100 22
Cal. Family Code § 1100 (a) 165
Cal. Family Code § 1100 (c) 167
Cal. Family Code § 1100 (d) 168
Cal. Family Code § 1100 (e) 169
Cal. Family Code § 1101 ...... 169, 170
Cal. Family Code § 1101 (a) 169
Cal. Family Code § 1101 (b) 169

Cal. Family Code § 1101 (c) 169
Cal. Family Code § 1101 (g) 170
Cal. Family Code § 1101 (h) 170
Cal. Family Code § 1102 (a) 165, 168
Cal. Family Code § 1102(d) ... 168
Cal. Family Code § 1500 21
Cal. Family Code § 1610(a) 22
Cal. Family Code § 1611 28
Cal. Family Code § 1612(c) 29, 30
Cal. Family Code § 1615(a) (2) 33, 34
Cal. Family Code § 1615(c) 31
Cal. Family Code § 1615(c)(2) (B) 32
Cal. Family Code § 2010 7
Cal. Family Code § 2021(b) ... 109
Cal. Family Code § 2200 188
Cal. Family Code § 2201(a) ... 188
Cal. Family Code § 2210 189
Cal. Family Code § 2251 190
Cal. Family Code § 2251(a) (1) 63
Cal. Family Code § 2251(a) (2) 191
Cal. Family Code § 2320 6
Cal. Family Code § 2320(a) 5
Cal. Family Code § 2321 6
Cal. Family Code § 2330 7
Cal. Family Code § 2331 8
Cal. Family Code § 2339 160
Cal. Family Code § 2340 160
Cal. Family Code § 2550 ...... 110, 136, 172
Cal. Family Code § 2551 158
Cal. Family Code § 2552 172
Cal. Family Code § 2581 .... 55, 56, 70, 76, 78, 79, 80, 81, 83, 84, 85, 86, 87, 128, 129, 130, 177
Cal. Family Code § 2581(a) 55, 79, 85
Cal. Family Code § 2581(b) 55, 79, 85
Cal. Family Code § 2601 173
Cal. Family Code § 2602 172

TABLE OF STATUTES 285

Cal. Family Code § 2603 172
Cal. Family Code § 2603
   (b) 137
Cal. Family Code § 2604 172
Cal. Family Code § 2605 137
Cal. Family Code §§ 2620
   et seq. 147, 201
Cal. Family Code § 2621 160
Cal. Family Code §§ 2621–
   2625 .... 158, 159
Cal. Family Code § 2623
   (a) 161
Cal. Family Code § 2623
   (b) 160
Cal. Family Code § 2624 160
Cal. Family Code § 2625 162
Cal. Family Code § 2627 162
Cal. Family Code § 2640 .... 55, 68, 80, 82, 83, 84, 85, 86, 87, 179
Cal. Family Code § 2640(a) 82
Cal. Family Code § 2640(b) 82
Cal. Family Code § 2640
   (c) 135, 180
Cal. Family Code § 2641 127
Cal. Family Code § 2641(b)
   (1) 127
Cal. Family Code § 2650 177
Cal. Family Code § 2660
   (a) 177
Cal. Family Code §§ 3003–
   3007 11
Cal. Family Code § 3006 11
Cal. Family Code § 3011 12
Cal. Family Code § 3011(e)
   (2) 11
Cal. Family Code § 3020(b) 11
Cal. Family Code § 3022 11
Cal. Family Code § 3040(a)
   (1) 12
Cal. Family Code § 3041.5 12
Cal. Family Code § 3044(a) 12
Cal. Family Code § 3044(b)
   (1) 12
Cal. Family Code § 3085 11
Cal. Family Code § 3100 11
Cal. Family Code §§ 3400
   et seq. 6
Cal. Family Code § 3587 29
Cal. Family Code § 3753 13

Cal. Family Code § 3901(a) 12, 29
Cal. Family Code § 3910(a) 12
Cal. Family Code § 4053(a) 12
Cal. Family Code § 4055 13
Cal. Family Code § 4057(a) 13
Cal. Family Code § 4058(a) 13
Cal. Family Code § 4058(a)
   (1) 13
Cal. Family Code § 4058(b) 13
Cal. Family Code § 4059 13
Cal. Family Code § 4059(e) 13
Cal. Family Code § 4059(g) 13
Cal. Family Code §§ 4070–
   4073 13
Cal. Family Code § 4250 14
Cal. Family Code § 4302 154
Cal. Family Code § 4320 14
Cal. Family Code § 4330(a) 14
Cal. Family Code §§ 5700.101
   et seq. 13
Cal. Penal Code § 270 153
Cal. Penal Code § 270a 153
Cal. Probate Code § 28 .... 195, 198
Cal. Probate Code § 28(a) 196
Cal. Probate Code § 28(b) 196, 197, 198
Cal. Probate Code § 66 .... 197, 198
Cal. Probate Code § 100(a) 195
Cal. Probate Code § 101(a) 195
Cal. Probate Code §§ 5100 et
   seq. 129
Cal. Probate Code § 5130 129
Cal. Probate Code § 5305(a) ... 55, 129
Cal. Probate Code § 6401
   (a) 195
Cal. Probate Code § 6401
   (b) 195
Cal. Probate Code § 6401
   (c) 195
Cal. Probate Code §§ 8000 et
   seq. 200
Cal. Probate Code § 9052 200
Cal. Probate Code §§ 11440 et
   seq. 201
Cal. Probate Code § 11444 ... 147, 201

Cal. Probate Code § 11444
  (b) 201
Cal. Probate Code § 11446.... 201
Cal. Probate Code § 13550... 147,
  200
Cal. Probate Code § 13551.... 201
Conn. Gen. Stat. Ann. § 46b–
  81(a) 50
Ind. Code Ann. § 31–15–7–4
  (a) 50
Mass. Gen. Laws. Ann. Ch. 208,
  § 34 50
N.J. Stat. Ann. § 25:1–5(h) 20

Index

References are to Section

§ 2581 Presumption, §§ 5.15–5.20, 11.7
§ 2640 Reimbursement, §§ 5.16–5.20
Activity for the Benefit of the Community, §§ 9.3, 9.7, 9.7(e)
Alimony, §§ 1.10, 3.5, 3.8, 6.9, 11.5, 11.10
Annulment. Chapter 12.
Apportionment, §§ 5.10, 5.17
Bank Accounts, §§ 7.7, 10.9
Bankruptcy, §§ 1.9, 5.16
Business as Property, § 7.1
Cash out Method of Dividing Pension, § 6.7(b)
Characterization. Chapters 5–7.
Child Custody, §§ 1.8, 11.5
Child Support, §§ 1.9, 3.5, 3.7, 6.9, 11.5
Cohabitation Agreement. Chapter 2.
Commingled Bank Account, § 7.7
Common Law Marriage, § 1.3
Death Ends Marriage. Chapter 13.
Debts, Chapter 9, §§ 7.9(b), 8.4, 11.4, 13.5
Deed of Trust, § 4.6
Defined Benefit Plan, § 6.4
Defined Contribution Plan, § 6.4
Direct Tracing, § 7.7
Disability, §§ 6.14, 6.15
Division of Community Property on Divorce. Chapter 11.
Divorce, Steps, § 1.7
Educational Degree, § 7.4
Encumbrance, § 4.6
End of the community, § 5.12
Epstein Credits, § 11.8
Equal Division of Community Property, § 11.2(a)
ERISA, § 6.3
Family Expense Presumption, §§ 5.2, 7.7(b)

Fiduciary Duty, §§ 8.3, 10.7
Fixtures, § 7.8
Form of Title Presumption, § 5.18
  Joint form, §§ 5.2, 5.15–5.20, 7.6, 11.7
  Married Woman's Separate Property Presumption, § 5.22
Gambling, § 7.5
General Community Property Presumption, §§ 5.3(d), 5.4, 5.9, 7.6, 7.7
Gifts, §§ 10.2, 10.3
Gilmore Election, § 6.13
Goodwill, § 7.3
Improvements, § 7.8
Inception of Title, § 5.11
Indirect Tracing, § 7.7
Joint Bank Account, §§ 5.2, 7.7
Jurisdiction, § 1.4
Life Insurance, § 6.21
Long Marriage Presumption, §§ 5.2, 5.8
Lucas Gift Presumption, §§ 5.2, 5.19
Management and Control. Chapter 10.
Marriage, §§ 1.1, 1.2, 1.3
Marriage Agreement. Chapter 2.
Married Woman's Separate Property Presumption, § 5.22
Military, §§ 6.2, 6.11, 6.15
Moore/Marsden Apportionment, § 5.21
Mortgage, §§ 4.6, 5.18
Necessaries, §§ 9.5, 9.7
Nullity. Chapter 12.
Pensions. Chapter 6.
Pereira, § 7.2
Personal Injury Damage, §§ 7.9, 9.3, 11.2(a)
Pets, § 7.10
Premarital Agreement. Chapter 3.

Spousal support, § 3.8
Unconscionable agreements, § 3.11
Voluntariness, §§ 3.9, 3.10, 3.11
Writing requirement, § 3.6
Presumptions, §§ 5.2, 5.3
Family expense presumption, §§ 5.2, 7.7(b)
General community property presumption, §§ 5.2, 5.4
Joint bank accounts, §§ 5.2, 7.7
Long marriage presumption, §§ 5.2, 5.8
Lucas gift presumption, §§ 5.2, 5.19
Married woman's separate property presumption, §§ 5.2, 5.22
Separate property presumption, §§ 5.4, 5.5
Pro Rata Apportionment, §§ 5.10, 5.17
Prudent Investor Rule, § 10.7
Putative Spouse, § 12.5
QDRO, §§ 6.8, 6.9
Quasi-Community Property, §§ 5.6, 13.1, 13.3
Quasi-Marital Property, § 12.5
Reimbursement, §§ 5.19, 11.9
Retroactivity, §§ 3.8, 5.17–5.19
Separate Property Presumption, §§ 5.1, 5.4, 5.5
Separation, §§ 5.12, 7.9
Severance Pay, § 6.18
Sick Days, § 6.19
Social Security, § 6.12
Source of Funds, § 5.11
Spousal Support, §§ 1.10, 3.5, 3.8, 6.9, 11.10, 11.11
Stock Options, § 6.20
Time Rule, §§ 6.5, 6.20
Title in One Spouse's Name, § 5.14
Tracing, §§ 5.2, 5.9, 5.18, 7.5–7.7
Transmutations, Chapter 8, § 10.3
Trusts, § 2.2
Undue Influence, § 8.3
Uniform Fraudulent Transfer Act, § 8.4
Vacation Days, § 6.19
Van Camp, § 7.2
Void Marriage, § 12.3
Voidable Marriage, § 12.4

Wait and See Method of Dividing Pension, § 6.7(b)
Watts Charges, § 11.8